Laborers in the Vineyard of the Lord

The History of African-American Religions

Copyright 2001 by Larry E. Rivers and Canter Brown, Jr. This work is licensed under a modified Creative Commons Attribution-Noncommercial-No Derivative Works 3.0 Unported License. To view a copy of this license, visit *http://creativecommons.org/licenses/by-nc-nd/3.0/*. You are free to electronically copy, distribute, and transmit this work if you attribute authorship. *However, all printing rights are reserved by the University Press of Florida (http://www.upf.com). Please contact UPF for information about how to obtain copies of the work for print distribution.* You must attribute the work in the manner specified by the author or licensor (but not in any way that suggests that they endorse you or your use of the work). For any reuse or distribution, you must make clear to others the license terms of this work. Any of the above conditions can be waived if you get permission from the University Press of Florida. Nothing in this license impairs or restricts the author's moral rights.

Florida A&M University, Tallahassee
Florida Atlantic University, Boca Raton
Florida Gulf Coast University, Ft. Myers
Florida International University, Miami
Florida State University, Tallahassee
University of Central Florida, Orlando
University of Florida, Gainesville
University of North Florida, Jacksonville
University of South Florida, Tampa
University of West Florida, Pensacola

The History of African-American Religions

Edited by Stephen W. Angell and Anthony Pinn

This series will further historical investigations into African religions in the Americas, encourage the development of new paradigms and methodologies, and explore cultural influences upon African-American religious institutions, including the roles of gender, race, leadership, regionalism, and folkways.

Laborers in the Vineyard of the Lord

The Beginnings of the AME Church in Florida, 1865–1895

Larry Eugene Rivers and Canter Brown, Jr.

University Press of Florida
Gainesville · Tallahassee · Tampa · Boca Raton
Pensacola · Orlando · Miami · Jacksonville · Ft. Myers

Copyright 2001 by Larry E. Rivers and Canter Brown, Jr.

06 05 04 03 02 01   6 5 4 3 2 1

Library of Congress Cataloging-in-Publication Data
Rivers, Larry E., 1950-
Laborers in the vineyard of the Lord: the beginnings of the AME
Church in Florida, 1865-1895 / Larry E. Rivers and Canter Brown, Jr.
p. cm.—(The history of African-American religions)
Includes bibliographical references and index.
ISBN 0-8130-1890-0 (alk. paper)
1. African Methodist Episcopal Church—Florida—History—19th
century. 2. Florida—Church history—19th century. I. Brown, Canter.
II. Title. III. Series.
BX8444.F6 R58 2001
287'.8759—dc21   00-053658

The University Press of Florida is the scholarly publishing agency
for the State University System of Florida, comprising Florida A&M
University, Florida Atlantic University, Florida Gulf Coast University,
Florida International University, Florida State University, University of
Central Florida, University of Florida, University of North Florida,
University of South Florida, and University of West Florida.

University Press of Florida
15 Northwest 15th Street
Gainesville, FL 32611–2079
http://www.upf.com

For Betty Jean, Larry Omar, and Linje Eugene—my lilies of the valley
L.R.

With much love always, to Barbara
C.B.

CONTENTS

List of Figures ix

Foreword xi

Abbreviations xiii

Introduction xv

1. Before Freedom 1

2. A Tumultuous Peace, 1865–1867 23

3. The Florida Annual Conference and Republican Rule, 1867–1869 43

4. Connections at Live Oak, 1869–1872 62

5. Acts of God and Man, 1872–1876 82

6. Redemption and the East Florida Conference, 1876–1880 101

7. Bishop Wayman's Return, 1880–1884 122

8. Bishop Payne and the Democrats in Power, 1884–1888 142

9. A Healer Creates a College, 1888–1892 160

10. Tumult and Tragedy, 1892–1895 180

Notes 199

Bibliography 217

Index 229

FIGURES

1. Map of Florida, showing principal towns and cities served by the AME Church in the period 1865 to 1895   5
2. Ossian Bingley Hart, governor of Florida 1873 to 1874   7
3. Pioneer Baptist minister James Page   9
4. Robert Meacham, founder of Tallahassee's Bethel AME Church   14
5. Stella Meacham, wife of the Reverend Robert Meacham   15
6. Known as "Mother Midway," the Midway AME Church located just west of Jacksonville   18
7. Bishop and Mrs. Daniel A. Payne   20
8. The Reverend William G. Stewart   25
9. The heartland of African Methodism in post–Civil War Florida   29
10. The Reverend Charles H. Pearce   31
11. Minister and shoemaker Joseph J. Sawyer   33
12. As illustrated by this early drawing, Apalachicola's St. Paul's AME Church   38
13. Drawing of the Monticello AME Church   40
14. The Reverend John R. Scott Sr.   44
15. Jacksonville's Mount Zion AME Church   47
16. Bishop and Mrs. Alexander W. Wayman   49
17. One-time Florida slave Thomas Warren Long   53
18. Bishop and Mrs. John Mifflin Brown   60
19. Future AME bishop Josiah Haynes Armstrong   61
20. Presiding elder Charles H. Pearce   63
21. Poet, newspaper editor, legislator, and AME layman John Willis Menard   64
22. Jacksonville's William W. Sampson   69
23. Tampa's St. Paul AME Church   73
24. Carpenter and minister Francis B. Carolina   74
25. St. Paul AME Church, LaVilla, as it appeared in 1889   78
26. Bishop and Mrs. Thomas M. D. Ward   84
27. The Florida Senate in 1875   85
28. The Reverend Singleton H. Coleman   90

x · Figures

29. Wilberforce University graduate Benjamin W. Roberts 94
30. Governor Marcellus Stearns greets *Uncle Tom's Cabin* author, Harriet Beecher Stowe 97
31. AME minister, state official, federal official, and attorney Joseph E. Lee 105
32. Bishop Daniel A. Payne 107
33. Albert Julius Kershaw 111
34. William A. Bird 112
35. Bishop and Mrs. Jabez P. Campbell 114
36. Tallahassee's Bethel AME Church 115
37. Tallahassee drawn in 1885 124
38. Robert Burns Brookins 127
39. The Reverend Reuben B. Brooks 129
40. The Reverend Bulley William Wiley 131
41. Key West's Bethel AME Church during the 1880s 133
42. Pensacola's tall-steepled Allen Chapel AME Church as it appeared in 1885 135
43. John R. Scott Jr. 139
44. Pensacola minister Morris Marcellus Moore 147
45. The Florida Normal and Divinity High School 151
46. Fernandina's Macedonia AME Church 153
47. Palatka's Bethel AME Church 157
48. St. Augustine's newly constructed New St. Paul AME Church 158
49. Bishop and Mrs. Benjamin W. Arnett Sr. 161
50. The Reverend S. Timothy Tice 165
51. John H. Welch 169
52. Annie L. Welch 170
53. Benjamin W. Arnett Jr. 175
54. Edward Waters College's board of trustees in 1892 176
55. Ocala's brick Mt. Zion AME Church, erected in 1891 178
56. The Reverend John Walter Dukes 183
57. Bishop and Mrs. Abram Grant 186
58. The Reverend Caesar A. A. Taylor 188
59. The Edward Waters College faculty in 1892 191
60. Mary Alice LaRoche Certain 194
61. The Reverend W. D. Certain 195

FOREWORD

The History of African-American Religions series seeks to further historical investigations into the varieties of African-American religions and to encourage the development of new and expanded paradigms, methodologies, and themes for the study thereof. The editors of the series see this as an opportunity to expand our knowledge of African-American religious expression and institutional developments to include underappreciated regions and forms. The work done by Larry Eugene Rivers and Canter Brown Jr. provides an appropriate starting point.

There is scarcely any period more important to African-American religious history than the years examined in this book, the three decades after emancipation. One might well call it the period of Christian Reconstruction; when considering African-American religion, historians do well to extend the endpoint of this Reconstruction well past the premature demise of its political cousin in 1877. The AME bishops, writing in 1891 after a severe attack leveled on their southern ministers by Booker T. Washington, labeled this a heroic period. As one reads this fine new work by Larry Eugene Rivers and Canter Brown Jr., it is easy to see why. African Americans faced enormous problems in what was often called racial uplift: setting up viable congregations and functional church government, opposing white violence and discrimination, founding educational institutions, including women in all aspects of church life, figuring out how to maximize their political influence in rapidly changing times. Any one of these tasks would have been an enormous challenge in itself, but the AME churches in Florida, as well as Rivers and Brown as their historians, were obliged to tackle all these issues. Rivers and Brown provide invaluable insight into these important dimensions of African-American church life in their work. All the church's experiences of close cooperation and inner conflict, advances and setbacks, successes and failures are candidly yet sensitively discussed within these pages.

This work exemplifies a noteworthy trend in studies of American religious history to place an increasingly close focus on events at the state and local level. As Rivers and Brown point out, there are some scholarly studies that have examined African-American religious development during Reconstruction throughout the South. But, until now, the state of Florida has escaped close scrutiny in this regard. Thus Rivers and Brown provide future historians of this period with a crucial building block. Students of this era of African-American religious history stand to gain substantially by knowing in detail what went on in states like Florida, and it is this illuminating detail that Rivers and Brown deliver.

This book should help to bring Florida and African-American religious history from the margins to the center of the American consciousness. Figures of national, even worldwide, renown such as AME bishops Daniel Alexander Payne and Henry McNeal Turner demonstrated Florida's great importance with their frequent visits to the Sunshine State, visits that are noted in this book. Rivers and Brown take their narrative to 1895, virtually the threshold of the twentieth century, a year that saw both the death of Frederick Douglass and the emergence of Booker T. Washington into national leadership with a widely noticed speech at the Cotton States Exposition in Atlanta. Thanks to the self-sacrificing work of the ministers and laity in the state, the AME Church by 1895 was securely established in Florida.

Careful readers of this book will find a narrative crowded with vivid and unforgettable characters. The authors have deftly brought to life dramatic and all-but-forgotten events. With their thorough research and superb mastery of both Florida and African-American history, Rivers and Brown have created a lively work of history that persons of all ages and all walks of life will be able to read with both benefit and enjoyment. We are pleased to offer it as the first volume in this series.

Stephen W. Angell and Anthony Pinn
Series Editors

ABBREVIATIONS

AME	African Methodist Episcopal
Census	Manuscript returns, United States Decennial Census or Florida State Census, as appropriate
CH-RECs	Church Records. Questionnaires of the Historical Records Survey of the Florida Writers' Program, WPA
FSA	Florida State Archives, Tallahassee
JDFU	*Jacksonville Daily Florida Union*
JET	*Jacksonville Evening Telegram*
JFT-U	*Jacksonville Florida Times-Union*
JFU	*Jacksonville Florida Union*
JT-WFU	*Jacksonville Tri-Weekly Florida Union*
NA	National Archives, Washington, D.C.
NYA	*New York Age*
NYG	*New York Globe*
NYF	*New York Freeman*
PCR	*Philadelphia Christian Recorder*
PKY	P. K. Yonge Library of Florida History, University of Florida, Gainesville
RG	Record Group
SMN	*Savannah Morning News*
TFP	*Tampa Florida Peninsular*
TS	*Tallahassee Sentinel*
TWF	*Tallahassee Weekly Floridian*
WPA	Work Projects Administration

INTRODUCTION

Future realities lay far out of sight to church fathers as they prepared to dedicate Bartow's St. James AME Church on February 1–2, 1895. Led by Bishop Abram Grant, the ministers and laymen intended merely to set the new sanctuary's cornerstone and to perform associated functions. They completed most of their duties on Saturday, February 1, but not all. "On Sunday afternoon the dedication sermon was preached to a large congregation by the Rt Rev. Bishop A. Grant, D. D.," notes the occasion's only surviving account. It adds, "Quite a number of the white friends were present at these exercises thus showing their interest in the good work of our colored friends."[1]

Hindsight reveals that those simple ceremonies in early February 1895 constituted a major turning point for Florida's AME Church, at least in a symbolic sense—and contrary to anyone's expectations at the time. Given the institution's position in the African American community, not to mention in the state as a whole, the date marked the end of a remarkable age and the commencement of a distinctly different era. In the thirty years leading up to 1895, the AME Church had proved itself the single most effective organizational force for Florida's black residents. Having brought comfort and inspiration to thousands of its members, the church also had demonstrated its capability to rock Florida's political balance of power. In the early years, it nearly had succeeded in seizing control of the state's government. Now, on top of influences already at play, forces of nature were about to alter arbitrarily and dramatically Florida's economy, social fabric, and AME Church. The Bartow ceremonies would come to represent the church's last official acts before calamity struck.

From a late-twentieth-century perspective, the symbolism of the Bartow dedication stands out as varied and deep, offering glimpses of the church's past and future. Bishop Grant's presence, for instance, represented the AME's great success story. Emerging from slavery with little but the clothes on his back, this Floridian had determined to help make a better world. He answered the ministry's call, and, beginning as a rough young preacher, he matured within the church. In the late 1870s Grant and various colleagues had transported Florida AME's dynamism to Texas, where his achievements earned Grant elevation to the episcopacy. Back in Florida by 1894, the bishop enjoyed a heartwarming popularity. He represented all the eager hopes so integral to the church's formative years, as well as its pioneering churchmen.[2]

That whites attended the St. James AME Church dedication and showed "interest in the good work" touches upon another important point. From the AME Church's earliest days in Florida, some whites had helped its religious endeavors along, even as they opposed its political agenda. The color line had begun to harden in the 1880s, though, as racial violence left bloody stains in many areas of the state. By the 1890s, laws had both blunted black political power and begun to mandate racial discrimination. Florida had become one of the most lynch-prone states in the union, at least on a per capita basis. The year following the Bartow ceremonies, the U.S. Supreme Court would legitimize Jim Crow discrimination with its famous "separate but equal" decision in the case of *Plessy* v. *Ferguson*. Subsequently, as the church faced greater and greater problems, white friends would be hard to find.[3]

While the published reports of St. James's dedication do not say so, almost certainly Baptists—that is to say, African American adherents of various Baptist churches—attended and perhaps participated in the ceremony. By 1895 the Baptist Church had gained so much strength in Florida that it could afford to extend a hand to a struggling AME church, even though the previous three decades had seen the two sects contending for power and membership. The divisions, now hazy, once had involved conflict, with the more conservative Baptists backing particular Republican factions against the AME Church's demands for a radical Reconstruction, social and political equality, and black empowerment. But times had changed.[4]

The dedication's site held meaning, as well. Bartow, the Polk County seat, lay at the juncture of the peninsula's central and southwestern portions. Through the region in the 1880s and early 1890s, railroad magnate Henry B. Plant had woven steel rails and a virtually inexhaustible supply of capital into a tightly knit fabric of easy transportation, alluring luxury resorts, and community development. Immigration, new towns, agricultural and mining enterprises, and chronic labor shortages then had served as magnets to attract black laborers and their families.[5]

In turn, the AME Church had blossomed in Central and Southwest Florida, its growth acknowledged in 1892–1893 by the creation of the South Florida Conference. Here lay the church's hopes for further increase and rejuvenation, aspirations justified by the progress of the Bartow church. Just as Plant's rails reached Polk County's seat, Charles Henry Macon Sr., a recent arrival from Attapulgus, Georgia, sparked the founding of a new church, St. James. Congregation members could not afford a church building, so they met in private homes for four years. Little by little, they saved toward the day when good fortune would permit them to erect a small frame building as their first sanctuary. That day came in 1889. As a result of somewhat better times and enlarged membership rolls, by 1894 St. James's adherents believed that they could make a greater statement of their commitment. They constructed a second and grander church. St. James now boasted a spacious rectangular building, complete with bell tower, bell, and pipe organ, a far cry from the church's humble origins.[6]

Hope for growth and rejuvenation through expansion in Central and Southwest Florida burned bright in church leaders' minds by 1895. That rejuvenation had become a necessity was a fact not yet well appreciated. The old AME heartland of Middle Florida—the one-time cotton plantation counties that centered on the state capital at Tallahassee—suffered from racial violence, poor economic conditions, and population stagnation or decline. The Florida Conference had been buffeted and battered as a consequence. The East Florida Conference fared better, but its prospects were not glowing. Jacksonville, its headquarters, had emerged as Florida's largest city, with twenty-five thousand residents. Yet nearby St. Augustine, Fernandina, and Palatka all lost residents from 1890 to 1895. With the century's turn, much of Jacksonville's heart, along with the church's Edward Waters College, would burn in the Great Fire of 1901.[7]

The church's Florida leadership itself was undergoing change. The giants of its early years were slipping quickly from the scene. Charles H. Pearce, who as presiding elder had dominated AME affairs in the late 1860s and 1870s, had passed away in 1887. His principal lieutenants—John R. Scott Sr., William Bradwell, and George W. Witherspoon—were gone. Of the seven bishops who had overseen the state from 1865 to 1895, only three survived, including Grant. Jabez Pitt Campbell had succumbed in 1891, with John Mifflin Brown, Daniel A. Payne, and Thomas M. D. Ward following within a few years. Alexander W. Wayman would die later in 1895.

As the giants fell, the men who picked up the reins of church power were college educated and relatively affluent. They stood on the other side of a wide and hard-to-bridge chasm from the average church member. Intra-church relations increasingly fractured.[8]

Then nature imposed its own will on Florida and the AME Church. On February 7, 1895—five days after Bishop Grant consecrated St. James Church—a hard freeze struck Florida. Deep into the peninsula, temperatures plunged below freezing. The frigid conditions persisted for days. This disaster, coming on the heels of the national economic depression after the Panic of 1893, brought with it economic and personal ruin. Corn, cotton, potato, citrus, and other crops lay blackened by frost. Many farmers were wiped out. With these farms' demise, the economic underpinnings of African American life in Florida's towns and cities were shaken and rent, as were those of the AME Church.[9]

A myriad of reverberations ensued, as new stresses appeared within the AME Church and old ones intensified. As the church's focus for the future shifted from stricken Central and Southwest Florida to the lower Atlantic coast, financial hardship quickly emerged as a pressing and persistent concern for Florida's AME community. The village of Miami had survived the freeze without damage, confirming railroad builder Henry Flagler's plans to extend his lines down the shore to that remote and sparsely inhabited area. Resorts, tourists, immigrants, and workers followed. So, too, did AME clergymen. Thus, Miami's Greater Bethel Church traces its origins to 1896, and AME lay leaders such as Alexander C. Lightbourn Sr. can be counted among the city's founding fathers.[10]

The Florida church would never be the same again. Even its memory of its own past would not survive unscathed. To some extent, pre-1895 AME history came to be colored by later divisions, stresses, and other problems. Almost forgotten were the magnificent story of the building up of the church from virtually nothing amidst the ruins of slavery and the epic saga of its subsequent attempt to remake Florida. Only one work, Charles Sumner Long's *History of the A. M. E. Church in Florida*, even attempted the task. Compiled with the best intentions, the 1939 book consisted primarily of material reprinted from Bishop Benjamin W. Arnett's *Proceedings of the Quarto-Centennial Conference of the African M. E. Church, of South Carolina, at Charleston, S. C., May 15, 16 and 17, 1889*. A hard-to-obtain book thus succeeded a very rare one.

Given that African American Christianity long has been at the core of the black experience in America, we offer this history of one of its movements in Florida—the AME Church from 1865 to 1895. By focusing on the early AME Church, we are able to examine the continued development of one dimension of African American culture in Florida. We intend, in so doing, to underscore and illustrate the critical role played by AME ministers and laypeople in state and local affairs, as well as dynamics within the church and society that either assisted or undermined church initiatives.

Standing high among issues neglected until now are questions of ministerial involvement in politics; the effects of the temperance movement on the church and its members; the impact of personal affinities and dislikes of church leaders; the traits and facets of episcopal leadership that aided or hindered church development; and rivalries between local church authorities and bishops. We also consider the formation of the AME Church as a demonstration of independence and as an expression of social and cultural solidarity that linked various segments of the black community.

We further desire to encourage recent interest in the post–Civil War role and contributions of African American churches in the United States and particularly in the South. Among works that speak to these issues are *Masters and Slaves in the House of the Lord: Race and Religion in the American South, 1740–1870*, edited by John Boles; *"Ain't Gonna Lay My Ligion Down": African American Religion in the South*, edited by Alonzo Johnson and Paul Jersild; and William E. Montgomery's *Under Their Own Vine and Fig Tree: The African American Church in the South, 1865–1900*. On the AME Church itself, Clarence E. Walker's *A Rock in a Weary Land: The African Methodist Episcopal Church During the Civil War and Reconstruction* and Stephen Ward Angell's *Bishop Henry McNeal Turner and African American Religion in the South* are significant contributions. On the black church in Florida, the studies of Robert L. Hall stand out, especially his dissertation, "'Do Lord, Remember Me': Religion and Cultural Change Among Blacks in Florida, 1565–1906."

We are indebted to many individuals and institutions for their assistance in compiling, and encouragement in our pursuing, this work. Our thanks go to James H. Ammons, provost and vice president for academic affairs, Aubrey M. Perry, former dean of the College of Arts and Sciences, and James N. Eaton, curator of the Black Archives Research Center and Museum, Florida A&M University; Bob Hall, associate professor of history and director of the African American Studies Program, Northeastern University; David M. Fahey, Miami University of Ohio; David J. Coles, formerly of the Florida Archives and now at Longwood College; Jody Norman, Florida Archives; Cynthia C. Wise, Dorothy L. Williams, and Judy Holesmier, Florida Collection, State Library of Florida; William W. Rogers, Professor Emeritus, Florida State University; Tom Muir, Historic Pensacola Preservation Board; Nathan Woolsey, Milton; Barbara G. Brown, Tallahassee; Robert W. Saunders Sr. and the late Rowena Ferrell Brady, Tampa; Leland M. Hawes, *Tampa Tribune;* Donald J. Ivey, Pinellas County Historical Museum and Heritage Village, Largo; Clifton P. Lewis, Neighborhood Improvement Corporation, Bartow; Ernest and Fredi Brown, Family Heritage House, Bradenton; Marsha Dean Phelts, Jacksonville; Willie Mae Ashley, Fernandina Beach; Willie Speed, Apalachicola; the late Joe Lang Kershaw, Miami; Ed Norwood, Tallahassee; Vernon Peeples, Punta Gorda; Joe Knetsch, Florida Department of Environmental Protection, Tallahassee; Michael Woodward, Miami; David Jackson Jr. and Daryhill D. Brown, Tallahassee; Charles Wessels, Savannah, Georgia; and Kenneth Harris, Chicago. Special words of thanks also are due to Joan Morris, Florida Photographic Collection at the Florida Archives, who for years has cooperated with us in collecting rare photographs and other images of the African American presence in Florida; our series editors, Professors Stephen Ward Angell and Anthony Pinn, for their always generous encouragement and support; Peter A. Krafft, director of cartography for the Florida Resources and Environmental Analysis Center at Florida State University; and the director and staff of the University Press of Florida.

Incorrect spellings and usage in direct quotations have been left as they appear in the original, and the use of [*sic*] has been avoided. Responsibility for the interpretation of events and for errors of fact rests with us alone.

1

BEFORE FREEDOM

*Oh! that every soul would
love and serve their God.*

When the African Methodist Episcopal Church commenced its mission to Florida in 1865, black Methodists already had worshipped in the state for almost a half century. During that time Methodism had reached out first to slaves and free blacks. Then its policies and the actions of many of its ministers turned the church in a far different direction. Desire began to grow in the hearts and minds of black Methodists for racially separate forums for worship and fellowship. As this process evolved, African Americans stamped Methodism in the South and in Florida with their special influences and traditions, some of which derived directly from African roots. Thus, when African Methodist Episcopal (AME) ministers eventually set out to win Florida for their church, they discovered the seeds of a church waiting to be nurtured.

Florida Methodism's initial interest in African Americans had arisen from a curious legacy of the new territory's religious heritage. Acquired from Spain in 1821, Florida had only two towns of consequence, St. Augustine and Pensacola. Both communities were steeped in the Roman Catholic faith and its traditions. Accordingly, when Methodist missionary Joshua Nichols Glenn received an assignment to St. Augustine in 1823, his mind, he recorded, "recoiled at the very thoughts of it." Subsequently rebuffed by white citizens as he attempted to establish a Methodist society in the town, the pioneer preacher turned to free blacks and slaves in the area. By year's end his mission membership numbered fifty-two, forty of whom were black. Of the minister's service at hostile St. Augustine, a church historian wrote, "Glenn's only solace lay in prayer, visitation and sermons; but little ray of joy shines forth [from his] diary except in the deep gratitude he must have felt toward the Negro members of his flock, who ministered to him when he was ill and came regularly to hear him preach." The historian added, "Their eagerness to become members of the church became characteristic of Territorial Florida."[1]

It should be noted in passing that the Methodists' problems at St. Augustine and in other Catholic locales persisted, to the chagrin of white preachers and, later, AME clergymen. In 1845, to cite one example, Simon Peter Richardson arrived at St. Augustine to serve as its new pastor. He discovered that the Methodist Church had been closed and sold. It was being used as a workshop. "All the churches discouraged my continuance," he recorded. Only one bright spot lightened Richardson's experience. "On my arrival, no one greeted me, except one negro, named Jack," the minister recalled. Richardson continued, "He thanked the Lord that the missionary had come."[2]

In the years following the Reverend Glenn's 1823 sojourn at St. Augustine, Florida developed rapidly and somewhat at odds with previous patterns. Most Spanish settlement had occurred in Northeast Florida (East Florida) and around Pensacola (West Florida). By the time of the transfer of Florida to the United States from Spain in 1821, though, King Cotton had taken hold elsewhere in the lower South. Accordingly, speculators and planters prized and quickly gobbled up lands suitable for cotton culture. It turned out that much of the soil that lay between the Apalachicola and the Suwannee Rivers was ideal for the purpose. Within a few years, the broad stretch of fertile land would be divided into the counties of Gadsden, Leon, Jefferson, Madison, and Hamilton, along with Jackson, which was actually west of the Apalachicola. Into this region, which came to be known as Middle Florida, poured a modest flood of immigrants intent upon making their fortunes or enhancing pre-existing ones. Many of them hailed from the most prominent planter families of the Old South. They brought with them gangs of slaves to work their new plantations or else purchased new bond servants after arriving in the territory.[3]

Methodism arrived for Middle Florida slaves in the very early stages of the region's organization. The legislative council by 1823 had recognized the future by creating a new town, Tallahassee, as the territorial capital. It stood at the heart of what would become the plantation belt. Within months a Methodist preacher had arrived on site, and the Methodist mission became the capital's first organized congregation. Already, though, Methodist circuit riders had reached into the Middle Florida countryside. James Tabor and Isaac Sewell preached in 1823 at the Centerville neighborhood, located eleven miles northeast of Tallahassee. They reported organizing a church there consisting of six white and four black members.[4]

With the passage of years and the growth of the Middle Florida slave population, the Methodist Church extended its reach through the region. In 1829, for example, the Holmes Valley Mission came into being in Jackson County; it included congregations at Marianna, Webbville, and Campbellton. Marianna Station commenced services in 1834 with fifty-one white and thirteen black members. A log cabin sufficed as a church there for several years, but in 1838 members erected a suitable frame building. A side entrance offered slaves access to a segregated seating area.[5]

Generally speaking, Methodist missionaries sought out slave converts throughout the antebellum period. "We are now enabled to get round in four weeks, preaching three times every Sabbath save one," reported the Reverend William Edwards of the Spring Creek Mission in 1851. "There are 18 plantations from which the blacks assemble," he continued. "We have arranged it so as to meet as many as we could at one place, although the patrons prefer to have preaching at the plantations." A few months earlier, Samuel Woodbury had conveyed word of similar efforts from the South Madison Mission. "On Madison C[ourt] H[ouse], on the 29th [of July 1850]," he observed, "we commenced a meeting which continued for twelve successive days." Woodbury added, "There were a number of conversions, 7 whites and 6 colored were added to the Church."[6]

Eventually, the Methodists refined their approach to slave recruitment in several ways. For one thing, they identified white ministers with special qualities that would appeal to slave listeners. In Jefferson County, for instance, Anderson Peeler preached often to black audiences and enjoyed considerable success. Individuals with such talents were being assigned by the 1850s to a number of "colored missions." The Aucilla Mission in Jefferson County constituted an important example. Alachua County and the Long Pond area of northern Marion County, toward which the Middle Florida plantation belt had stretched by the 1850s, also experienced this approach.[7]

The church enjoyed enthusiastic support from many planters in its outreach program for slaves. A post–Civil War visitor to the state explained the situation this way. "Before the war it was for the interest of the master that the slave should be under the control of a religious sentiment," he commented. "It was one means of subjection, of obtaining obedience." Slaves understood this dynamic. "The slaves went to the 'white folks' church on Sundays," one woman recalled long after emancipation. She continued: "They were seated in the rear of the church. The white minister would arise and exhort the slaves 'to mind your masters, you owe them respect.' An old Christian slave who perceived things differently was heard to mumble, 'Yeah, wese jest as good as deys is only deys white and we's black, huh." Former slave Bolden Hall concurred. He insisted that religious teachings meant for slaves simply to "obey their master and mistress at all times."[8]

Such awareness of the Methodist Church's accommodation with slavery and the needs of slaveholders caused many bond servants to resist Methodism. Pastor Edwards, in his 1851 report from Spring Creek Mission, acknowledged as much. "As yet there is but little interest manifest among the blacks; they are very ignorant of the principles of Christianity and seem not to understand the design we have in view," he reported. "At some places they would not come out to meeting were it not for their master's influence." Indeed, slaves knew more about their masters' brand of Christianity than many whites realized, and they sought to defend themselves from its one-sided teachings.[9]

Yet the church's early work had held out a very different view of Methodism and its relationship with slavery. Out of the spirit of freedom sparked by the American Revolution, some members of the church at its 1780 conference had insisted that the peculiar institution of slavery was both morally wrong and contrary to religious principles. Three years later, the Methodist general conference debated whether to suspend local clergy who held slaves. In the final analysis, only preachers who owned slaves in states where it became illegal to do so were suspended from the church. A potentially more explosive question—whether to suspend the relatively large number of clergy slave masters in Virginia—would be postponed for a year.[10]

The issue of slave ownership among the Methodist clergy continued to pull the membership asunder. At the 1784 Methodist general conference, outspoken minister Thomas Coke added fuel to the fire when he noted that slavery ran contrary to the laws of God, of men, and of nature and should be abolished. The gathering enacted rules encouraging all members of the society to emancipate their bond servants within a twelve-month period. With the large numbers of bondspeople held by the clergy in Virginia, the measure encouraged those ministers to lead by example in manumitting their enslaved blacks within two years, under the threat of expulsion from the church.[11]

1. Map of Florida, showing principal towns and cities served by the AME Church in the period 1865 to 1895. Collection of the authors.

In 1785, another highly regarded Methodist minister joined Coke in denouncing American slavery; John Wesley declared it "that execrable sum of all villainies." Again during that year Coke tried to bring the issue of slave ownership among Methodism's clergy and members to a head. He circulated emancipation petitions, but the Virginia Methodists met him head on to insist on repeal of the church's slave rules. Under extreme pressure, the slave rules concerning emancipation were suspended for six months. Some church members believed that the rules were "offensive to most of our southern friends" and "were so much opposed by many of our private members, local preachers and some of the travelling preachers" that a hands-off policy seemed best.[12]

At the height of the slave crisis in Saint-Domingue (Haiti) in 1795, some twenty-three Methodist ministers convened in Charleston, South Carolina, to continue their fight to abolish slavery. They condemned clergymen who held bond servants "to the scandal of the ministry and the strengthening of the hands of oppression." Again, all members of the clergy were encouraged to manumit their enslaved blacks where the law permitted it. A year afterward the Methodist general conference held firm on its antislavery position. "We declare that we are more than ever convinced of the great evil of slavery, which still exists in these United States," its resolution read. Given that antislavery preaching did not fill the pews and disturbed the ecclesiastical tranquility of the church's members, the antislavery preachments of Coke, Wesley, and other clergymen fell largely on deaf ears during the later part of the eighteenth century.[13]

In 1804 a gradual trend away from the first statement of slavery's immorality made at the 1780 general conference continued. This fact became more evident when North and South Carolina, Georgia, and Tennessee were released from any conference slave rules that either encouraged or sought to force its slaveholding clergy and members to emancipate their bond servants. In later years, Methodism's antislavery commitment waned, although the slave rules concerning emancipation remained on the books. "The rule in our church, became a dead letter, and ceased to operate," explained one Florida minister.[14]

With the rise of abolitionist sentiment in the North during the 1830s and 1840s, tensions over the slavery issue mounted again within the church to such an extent that it broke apart. The reasons for the separation of southern from northern Methodists differed from the divisive stances of the 1780s and 1790s. The main issue did not boil down to whether the clergy or members should possess slaves. Rather, it concerned whether a clergyman seeking the highest church position—that of bishop—should own slaves.[15]

According to historian C. C. Goen, southerners' insistence that Georgia slaveholder James Osgood Andrew retain his bishopric split the Methodist Church apart. Andrew had been elected in 1832 as bishop largely because he did not own slaves. Within several years of his election, the prelate's deceased wife's will conveyed him two bond servants. After her death, he married a woman who owned slaves, as well. This made Andrew, in appearance at least, a slaveholder two times over. The bishop had clearly articulated his position that he had become an "unwilling trustee" of several enslaved blacks and could not emancipate them because of state law. He offered to

2. Ossian Bingley Hart, governor of Florida 1873 to 1874. Courtesy Photographic Collection, Florida State Archives.

resign his episcopal office, but "his fellow Southerners would not hear of it." Southern members, viewing this assault on Andrew as an attempt by abolitionists in the church to end slavery throughout the country, fought against the bishop's ouster. Although clergy and members had since the 1820s entertained constitutional questions that concerned slaveholding, the "slavery issue," as Donald G. Mathews has argued perceptively, became the overriding issue that led to the division of Methodism.[16]

Many of the 500,000 southern Methodists viewed the attack on the slave issue by northerners and abolitionists as an attack from within and from without. The Methodist debates as to the morality or immorality of clergymen and members holding slaves paralleled the national dispute over slavery. Many members saw the assault on Andrew as an assault on slavery throughout the South. The bishop emerged as a symbol of resistance to members who did not believe that slavery was a moral evil. Historian Goen noted that northerners' willingness to stand firm on this limited issue and southerners' steadfast insistence that Andrew be retained as a bishop brought about the ultimate confrontation and split between northern and southern Methodists. On June 7, 1844—the same day that a bill conferring statehood on Florida was reported to the U.S. House of Representatives—the Methodist general conference adopted a plan of separation. Florida achieved statehood March 3, 1845, and the Methodist Episcopal Church South came into being at Louisville, Kentucky, two months later.[17]

The formation and significance of the southern Methodist Church could not have escaped the attention of black church members any more than it did that of whites. This particularly was the case in Florida, where many whites, some of them slaveholders, prized attachment to the United States over regional pride. One of them, future governor Ossian B. Hart, expressed their reactions when writing of a young minister, Oscar A. Myers of Tallahassee. "He was one of those preachers who in 1844 encouraged the example of Secession for slavery by seceding from the church and establishing a sectional church with the Sectional word *South* engrafted into its name," Hart declared, "and who from that time used all their great influence all over the South to bring about secession and dissolution of the Union."[18]

The new church's proslavery overtones enhanced the challenge faced by Methodist ministers in luring African Americans into the church, but those were not the only problems the clergymen encountered. Some whites grew anxious in the late 1840s and 1850s at the influence preachers could exert on slaves during those increasingly tumultuous times. Simon Peter Richardson knew this situation firsthand. Assigned to Key West, which rapidly was becoming the state's largest town, he received troubling news early on. "When I first went out on the island the brother I was boarding with told me the council and citizens generally had decided that I should not preach to the negroes, and to so inform me," he related. "They had some trouble with the negroes and abolition preachers from the North who came to the island for their health," Richardson continued. "I was indignant that they should send me such a prohibition, when I had made no arrangements to preach to the negroes at all." He concluded: "I replied that if they wanted their negroes to go to the devil it was their lookout, and if they chose to go with them it was their own concern, not mine. I was astonished, a few days after, to receive from the council and a long list of the slaveholders a request for me to take the negroes under my pastoral charge and preach to them."[19]

The Methodists also contended with stiff competition from the Baptists, whose church in some respects attempted to address more sensitively the needs and desires of blacks. Where the Methodists proved unwilling to license African Americans as ministers in Florida and declined to permit creation of all-black churches, the Baptists took steps forward. By the early 1850s, they had ordained James Page, a slave of Leon County's Parkhill

3. Pioneer Baptist minister James Page. Courtesy Photographic Collection, Florida State Archives.

family. They did so upon the recommendation of prominent whites, including governor-elect James E. Broome. They also accepted as a regular church Page's Bethlehem Baptist Church at Bel Air, six miles south of Tallahassee. Bethlehem Baptist is believed to be Florida's first regularly organized all-black church.[20]

Not too much credit should be handed in this regard to the Florida Baptists, for they failed during the antebellum period to ordain additional African American ministers and to accept additional all-black churches. When confronted with the issue in 1854 by a request from Apalachicola, the West Florida Association temporized. "We do not regard the colored portion of the church formally a branch, but only as constituting a part of the Apalachicola church," it responded, "yet owing to their great disproportion of members and means, and in view of the intelligence and piety they manifest, we approve of their holding separate conferences and transacting such business as belongs peculiarly to themselves, yet always under the supervision of the white brethren, one of whom should act as moderator."

The authority accorded individual Baptist churches and their associations permitted a flexibility from place to place in a manner that the hierarchical Methodist Church did not. Confusion reigned among Baptist congregations on occasion when it came to racial matters. Thus, in some of them, a church historian insisted, slaves were "treated just as were other members, and the quality of their contribution to the life of the church was not only recognized, but praised." Most black Baptists, though, "were generally relegated to a status in the church which could not be described as equal, despite the fact that in many Florida Baptist churches Negroes were in the majority."[21]

A historian of black Baptists illustrated the point more bluntly. "We have been reliably informed by some of the ex-slaves who had such membership that while they were received into the churches on their experience of grace, and were baptized and fellowshipped," reported George P. McKinney, "that this was about as far as their membership privileges extended." McKinney added: "As slaves, of course, they were not allowed to vote, and therefore they had no voice in the business of the churches. There were believers without real church membership."[22]

Resistance from within the slave community understandably greeted many Baptist and Methodist overtures. Slaves aplenty abhorred forced attendance at church meetings and deeply resented preachers' insistence that they obey their "earthly masters." Even James Page sometimes felt the resentments, suffering many rejections and failing to bring numerous slaves to "accept Christ." One-time bondsman Douglas Dorsey recalled the attitudes and actions of one fellow slave. "[She could] read and write a little," he told an interviewer, "[and] would tell the slaves that what the minister had just said was all lies." The more the minister bore down on obedience and the less he shared the gospels, the more the alienation. "Dey never tole us nothing 'bout Jesus," complained Margrett Nickerson.[23]

In the circumstances, many slaves created their own "invisible churches." They might be convened under specific trees, in slave cabins, or in any number of other places. Amanda McCray, for instance, recollected one "praying ground." There, she declared, "the grass never had a chancet ter grow fer the troubled knees that kept it crushed down." These "brush meetings" permitted a fellowship and an opportunity for religious expression and leadership unavailable in white-supervised churches. One prayer commonly found voice. It was the prayer of freedom.[24]

Given the drawbacks of slave membership in the Methodist and Baptist Churches, it is not too surprising that relatively few men and women stepped forth, despite masters' attempts to commit them. In 1845, the year of Florida's admission to the Union, the state boasted a population of 66,500. Of that number, 47 percent (roughly 31,000) were black. At the same time, the Methodist conference contained 6,874 souls, of whom 2,653 (39 percent) were black. Fifteen years later, as the nation teetered on the brink of civil war, 61,745 slaves and 932 free blacks made up about 45 percent of the state's total of 140,424. The 1860 membership numbers for black Methodists were 8,110, which equaled 42 percent of all Florida Methodists.[25]

African Americans who chose to join and maintain membership in the Methodist Church attempted to make it their own. Ira Berlin, who studied this phenomenon in the South, has recognized that its impact was so profound as to create a "new faith." African Americans especially introduced an even higher level of emotionalism into services. When allowed, they clapped their hands, beat drums, prayed loudly, shouted, and sang. "Their singing is peculiar & very hearty," commented future Union general Oliver O. Howard after attending Methodist services at Tampa in 1857. "Some of them shout & some look very happy." Clapping of hands and "amens" and "hallelujahs" resounded. In these activities, an African heritage shone through, with a special debt to the traditional "ring shout." Water also held great importance in West African culture. So baptism carried tremendous significance and was celebrated elaborately.[26]

The exuberance of black Methodist worship practices scared some whites, but it provoked a touch of envy in others, as Simon Peter Richardson noted in his memoirs when discussing his Key West pastorate. "It was the best negro congregation I ever had," he began. "Among them there was a negro singing master, who taught the negroes to sing. He led the music." Richardson continued: "Over a hundred negroes singing with well-trained voices is something seldom heard. Many of the better classes came to the services of the negroes to hear them sing." The minister concluded: "I remarked to Dr. M. on one occasion how well my negroes sang. He replied: 'Yes, and how well you preach when you preach to them! Why not preach that way to the whites?'"[27]

What had typified Florida Methodism prior to the Civil War shifted dramatically after 1860 as the nation, the state, and the church were torn apart. When it came to the Methodists, actions of ministers and white laymen fueled fires that ultimately resulted in a flood of slaves and freedmen from the halls of Methodism to their own houses of worship. Tensions that previously had simmered now burst out in the open. The church bled itself into a state of weakness from which it has yet to recover fully.

As black Floridians watched the parade of events, Florida lurched toward secession in late 1860 and early 1861. They could see or hear of white preachers, a good number of them slaveholders, who pleaded the cause of disunion. Oscar A. Myers was such a man. "[He was] one of the eloquent ones in 1860 [who] came out of the pulpit to the political arena and made public speeches to the people in favor of secession and most bitterly denouncing and even ridiculing the Union," one correspondent noted of the minister in words that could have applied to many of his colleagues. Myers's contemporary John C. Ley recalled that "the church in all its operations sympathized with the excitement." When wartime arrived, not fewer than seven Methodist clergyman entered Confederate service, including Ley.[28]

At least early on, Methodist ministers who remained in Florida during the Civil War tended to exhibit just as much enthusiasm for the Confederacy as did those who departed with the troops. In early 1861, Key West's Robert J. McCook "invoked Heaven against the Federal Government." Union authorities promptly arrested him. W. L. Murphy evidenced the same intransigence from Tampa in 1862. "Every preacher has remained at his post, and God has blessed their labors to some extent, and the country with abundance of the necessaries of life," he reported. Murphy then added, "Whilst we all want peace on *honorable* terms, I, for one, believe if the war continues a while it will be productive of great good to the nation."[29]

Although the great good of emancipation came to the nation as a result of the war, the great good anticipated by the Reverend Murphy turned into disaster for his church. African Americans, already skeptical of the Methodist Episcopal Church South, now commenced to turn away from it. As historian William E. Montgomery has noted, such an evolution should have been expected. A separate church, he explained, permitted slaves a genuine and obtainable expression of freedom in troubled times. The movement was apparent by 1861. The following year a trickle of departures became a steady stream. A total of 987 African Americans—more than 10 percent of all black members—withdrew from churches of the Florida Conference. John C. Ley called it a year of "general discouragement." Once the artery had opened, the ME Church South bled throughout the war. When peace finally arrived in 1865, half the church's black members were gone. The remainder were prepared to make the same journey.[30]

Surviving records offer only hints as to when and where the first black Methodist congregations began forming after withdrawal from the ME Church South. One Marion County church traced its origins to about the time of secession. According to an early account, local preacher D. Watson organized Mt. Moriah in a log cabin at Daisy in 1860. Jackson County, somewhat isolated from the rest of the state, also saw congregations formed. Bethlehem, situated at Cottondale (ten miles or so west of Marianna), coalesced in 1861. Mt. Olive followed in 1862. It lay ten miles north of Marianna. Both Jackson County churches also used log cabins as "meeting houses." Under wartime regulations, they and similar groups often were restricted to meeting only when a white man could be present.[31]

Numerous other churches also were born during the war, although the names of only a few are known with certainty. Two miles south of Miccosukee in Leon County, Concord detached itself from a white-dominated church. In Madison County, Jeslam appeared in 1864 at a spot four miles northeast of Madison on the Old Valdosta Road. Hope Henry, located in Columbia County five miles southwest of Lake City, likely began holding meetings in early 1865. By then, meetings also were taking place at Quincy in Gadsden County, Tallahassee in Leon County, and Midway in Duval County.[32]

These and other churches usually organized thanks to the leadership of one or more individuals, all of them important to the later history of the AME Church in Florida. Jackson County was blessed with the labors of at least two such outstanding local preachers. One of these men, Henry Call, will be considered shortly. The other, Jacob Livingston, was born about 1835 in Florida. He is credited as a founder of Bethlehem and Mt. Olive Churches. Little personal information remains available concerning him, except brief comments from two of his later AME peers. A. J. Kershaw described Livingston as "meek." To J. J. Sawyer, Livingston was "energetic," "self-sacrificing," and "strongly attached to the Church." Livingston himself enthused after one particularly successful revival, "In the fields, in the highways, and in the valleys, shouts of the new born souls were heard in every direction." He added, "Oh! that every soul would love and serve their God in purity and in truth." He would die as presiding elder of the AME Marianna District, likely in 1877.[33]

Gadsden County served as home to a number of Civil War–era local preachers. The foremost among them, Allen Jones Sr., hailed from Queen Anne's County, Maryland, where he was born about 1813. "Sold South long before the war," according to Bishop Alexander W. Wayman, Jones lived in or near Quincy. Lauded for his style of preaching, he would draw praise as a minister throughout his long career. "He preaches 'Christ and him crucified,' as though he was upon Mount Calvary, when the spear pierced His side and the metallic spikes his hands," observed one colleague. In 1865, Jones joined with Dennis Wood to erect a brush arbor church near Quincy's Tan Yard Branch. It later would carry the name Arnett Chapel. After his death at Quincy on February 28, 1888, an admirer would describe him as "probably the greatest minister Florida ever had."[34]

Allen Jones's friend Dennis Wood apparently arrived in Gadsden County during the Civil War. Born in North Carolina in 1830, he ended up in

4. Robert Meacham, founder of Tallahassee's Bethel AME Church and Reconstruction-era political power in Florida. Courtesy Photographic Collection, Florida State Archives.

5. Stella Meacham, wife of the Reverend Robert Meacham. Courtesy Photographic Collection, Florida State Archives.

Florida as the slave of Henry L. Hart of Palatka. Perhaps as a result of Union incursions during the war, Hart sent Wood to Quincy. In addition to aiding the organization of Arnett Chapel, Wood operated what a fellow townsman described as "a fine blacksmith shop." The man added that Wood was considered "an honest, hard-working, and reliable man." Following decades of service to the AME Church, Wood would die at Palatka on April 18, 1893.[35]

At about the same time in early 1865 that Allen Jones and Dennis Wood were erecting their brush arbor church, Robert Meacham was organizing the future Bethel AME Church of Tallahassee. He too claimed roots in Quincy. The son of a slave woman and a Gadsden County physician and planter, Meacham was born in 1835. He learned at a young age to read and write. He even briefly attended the Quincy Academy. Then, in the early 1850s, he was relocated to Tallahassee as a house servant. Family tradition suggests that Meacham "carried [his] education to the other slaves secretly and by night, using the dim glare of a candle for light." By the Civil War years he also was preaching. As the war wound down, he led 116 individuals out of the Tallahassee Methodist Episcopal Church South and into a congregation of their own. After a stellar career in the church and in public service, Meacham would pass away at Tampa on February 27, 1902.³⁶

One hundred fifty miles to the east of Tallahassee, a young man named John Thomas yearned for an opportunity to preach openly to his fellow bondsmen. He had been born in South Carolina in 1839 but was living in early 1865 at Midway, a village located a few miles west of Jacksonville. With a friend, G. B. Hill, he began holding services there with a few others. Within only a short time he would enter the AME clergy, where he earned an unusual nickname, as the Reverend Andrew Jackson Ferrell Sr. later explained. "He was called 'Rabbit,'" Ferrell wrote, "because, during his preaching, he usually turned a 'hand spring' and jumped up like a jack rabbit." Thomas's death at Enterprise on June 20, 1892, terminated a distinguished career of service.³⁷

Henry W. Call stands out from John Thomas and the other wartime preachers mentioned for one simple reason. While they apparently held services during the war within the general context of Methodist tradition, Call intended to found an AME Church. His decision came about this way. Born in Florida in 1834, Call was raised in the Jackson County neighborhood of Cottondale. He had preached to slaves under the auspices of the ME Church South and, in 1861, acted with Jacob Livingston to found Bethlehem Church. Thanks to his owner, Call had learned to read and write. In 1863 he was ordered to accompany the master, who had joined the Confederate army, in the capacity of body servant. Near Chattanooga, Tennessee, in late November, a series of events occurred that changed Call's life and the history of African Methodism in Florida.³⁸

The Reverend Charles Sumner Long told Henry Call's story from that point with fascinating detail. First mentioning that General Braxton Bragg's Confederate forces had clashed with those of Union general William S. Rosecrans, Long explained:

> Under the command of General Rosecrans was a large contingent of black troops. The Battle above the clouds was fought November 23, 24, and 25, 1863. After the battle, Henry Call went among the dead in search of his master who was killed in the engagement. While searching among the dead men that lay like stones, Henry Call came across a dead black soldier with a paper sticking out of his pocket. He took

the paper and saw that it was the "Herald," afterwards the Christian Recorder. President Lincoln had thousands of copies printed for the black soldiers through Rev. Elisha Weaver, Business Manager of the Book Concern of the AME Church. Young Call saw the picture of Richard Allen in the left corner and Sarah Allen in the right corner. It was the first time brother Call had ever seen the pictures of Negroes in a paper.

This paper told of the movement of the AME Church in following up the Union lines in the South, planting the church and housing the people. In it [were references to] the appointment of Rev. James Lynch, and Rev. James D. S. Hall of the Baltimore Conference, as missionaries to South Carolina in 1863. This paper also stated that the AME Church had black Bishops and would cover the whole South as soon as the union armies occupied it. This was *multum in parvo* to the young mind of Brother Call. The Herald was a four page paper, 7 x 18. Brother Call folded it carefully, put it in his bosom and continued his search for his master. After he had found him and buried him, he was sent back to Cottondale, Florida.

It took him a month to read through the Herald, this he did in the hammock in a secluded place, where on his stomach at such times as he could get away from his owners he poured over the Herald that interested him more than anything he had ever come in contact with. He couldn't keep this news, so he called three other men, among them Brother Jackson, who has since been a class leader in Bethlehem for more than fifty years, and read to them what he had found. Henry Call told them, that he was going to lead prayer meeting on Thursday night, and when they got through they were to have a general hand shaking, which meant that they had joined the AME Church. When he made the announcement, Brother Jackson was to shake his hand first, then the other two, but they were not to let any of the other slaves know about it; for if it became known they would all be hung or sold to New Orleans slave traders. This was carried out, in that, on every prayer meeting night, a patrol was present to examine all passes, for no meeting could be held among black people unless a white man was present. However, Henry Call and his three companions organized the AME Church, while the white overseer looked on unaware of anything more than a prayer meeting or a hand shaking was going on.[39]

6. Known as "Mother Midway," the Midway AME Church located just west of Jacksonville traces its origins to the Civil War–era initiative of minister John Thomas. Courtesy Photographic Collection, Florida State Archives.

Call's desire to create Florida's first AME Church fell short of accomplishment because he could not yet obtain official sanction from proper authorities, but the preacher would not give up. He would go on to an extraordinary vocation as an AME minister, presiding elder, and public official. As his son the Reverend C. F. Call would recollect, "He proceeded to spread the Church all over the State." Henry Call would remain in service to the church until after 1910.[40]

Although the Jackson County slave preacher experienced frustration in his efforts to found an AME congregation in late 1863 and early 1864, his understanding that such a church was on the way eventually proved correct. The route had been a tortuous one, though, and had taken generations to negotiate. But Call could derive inspiration from tales of the difficulties that had beset Richard Allen and others in creating the first African Methodist Episcopal Church in America.

Indeed, the creation of the first all-black Methodist church in Philadelphia slowly had begun to take shape in 1787. During that year Richard Allen and other blacks had sought comfort and security in the Free African Society of Philadelphia. Blacks could control the religious and secular activities of this organization. The society originally did not stress any particular denomination. But by 1792 denominational strains were starting to show. The association's decision to build an Episcopalian, rather than a Methodist, church caused Allen great difficulty. Ultimately, he parted ways with the society. Still, a small group of blacks oriented toward Quakerism who wanted neither an Episcopalian nor a Methodist church kept the Free African Society alive after blacks of the other denominations concerned withdrew their memberships.[41]

Prior to the schism that divided the Free African Society into various denominational factions, Allen and other blacks had joined Philadelphia's St. George Methodist Church. Somewhat similar to the decision that faced blacks regarding the Free African Society, a decision ultimately had to be made about whether to withdraw their membership or remain in the church. That saga began in 1792, when the St. George Church compelled black members to abandon seats they had taken in the sanctuary's gallery. The incident proved too much for most blacks to accept.[42]

With Richard Allen's leadership, most black Methodists left St. George. Allen subsequently pressed for a church that would be controlled largely by blacks, believing that it should be a Methodist one. "I was confident that

7. Bishop and Mrs. Daniel A. Payne. Courtesy Photographic Collection, Florida State Archives.

there was no religious sect or denomination which would suit the capacity of the colored people as well as the Methodist," he explained, "for this plain and simple gospel suits best for any people; for the unlearned can understand, and the learned are sure to understand; and the reason that the Methodists [are] so successful [in] the awakening and conversion of the colored people, [is their] plain doctrine and . . . good discipline."[43]

Allen's dream began to come true in 1794. That year, he collected a group of fellow believers at his home in Philadelphia. The purpose, he declared, was "to provide for ourselves a house to meet in for religious worship agreeable to our desires, according to the light God through grace has given us—separate from our white brethren." Bethel African Methodist Episcopal Church resulted. For more than two decades Allen and his followers struggled for independence from the white Methodist Church, achieving it only after a Pennsylvania Supreme Court decision in 1816. Meanwhile, additional all-black congregations had begun to coalesce at New York, Baltimore, and several other places. Allen convened delegates representing all but those from New York on April 9, 1816. That "general conference" opted for unification as the African Methodist Episcopal Church. Six years later, black New Yorkers created their own "African Methodist Episcopal Church." Because its first church, dating to 1796, became known as Zion, that branch of African Methodism subsequently would be known as the African Methodist Episcopal Zion Church.⁴⁴

In its formative years the AME Church embraced a southern ministry, even though the largest part of its membership resided in the North. The border state of Maryland offered fertile grounds for church recruitment. Also, Morris Brown was leading efforts for an all-black congregation at Charleston, South Carolina, prior to the 1816 AME organizational conference. The South Carolina church officially formed during 1817 and 1818 and prospered for several years. Its rolls soon carried the names of fourteen hundred individuals. With the discovery by whites of Denmark Vesey's incipient slave revolt in 1822, though, the growth abruptly halted. Bishop Daniel A. Payne, himself a Charleston native, explained why. "The slaveholders of South Carolina were not satisfied with punishing with death the conspiracy against slavery in that State," he wrote; "they did not stop their proceedings till our Church in that State was entirely suppressed."⁴⁵

From that point until the Civil War was under way, the church concentrated its efforts in the North and in border states such as Maryland. Morris Brown, who had escaped Charleston thanks to the intercession of white friends, achieved episcopal status in 1828, second only to Bishop Allen. He survived for twenty-two years, nineteen of them as senior bishop after Bishop Allen's death in 1831. Edward Waters, born a slave at West River, Maryland, came third in 1836 and gained fame as Bishop Brown's closely trusted assistant. Waters died as the result of an 1847 accident. William Paul Quinn followed as fourth bishop in 1844, with Willis Nazrey obtaining the honor in 1852. The sixth and final pre–Civil War bishop was Daniel Alexander Payne, about whom a great deal more will be said here.⁴⁶

Since most African Americans lived elsewhere than in the North and border states, membership for the AME Church grew slowly. An 1822 count showed 7,257. Seventeen years later, the figure had risen to only 9,018. The rise of antislavery sentiment in the 1840s helped push the number to 17,375, organized in six conferences. It was thought that the 1848 approval of an official newspaper, the *Christian Herald*, would boost church outreach. The investment did not pay off as expected. African Methodism was dealt a blow in Louisiana that also affected its declining membership profoundly. The New Orleans AME congregation, founded about 1843 by John Mifflin Brown, had witnessed steadily increasing membership until city authorities forced it to close in 1858. Within only a few years of the

Civil War's onset, membership of the national AME church had stagnated at around twenty thousand.⁴⁷

The direction of church affairs changed markedly in 1863. Shortly after President Abraham Lincoln's Emancipation Proclamation became effective on January 1, Henry McNeal Turner issued "A Call to Action" to his fellow AME adherents. The liberation of thousands of slaves had opened up new "obligations" to which the church must respond. In April, a southerner, Daniel A. Payne, chaired the Baltimore Annual Conference. At the session, white Methodist Episcopal Church minister C. C. Leigh requested assistance for missionary work in the coastal areas of South Carolina. Payne grasped the chance to return the church to his home state, blessing James Lynch and J. D. S. Hall who volunteered to pioneer the way. The Twelfth General Conference, held in May 1864 at Philadelphia, ratified the move by creating a South Carolina Conference and encouraging its expansion. When Bishop Payne organized that assembly at Charleston in early May 1865—one month following Confederate general Robert E. Lee's surrender—he quickly turned his sights to nearby fields in need of sowing. An ex-slave from Jacksonville helped him to decide that Florida was just the place he had in mind. It was at that point that Henry W. Call's hopes for an AME Church in Florida began to blossom.⁴⁸

2

A TUMULTUOUS PEACE, 1865–1867

*We are in the world,
as well as other people.*

The burden of bringing African Methodism to Florida rested first on the shoulders of a humble man, a former slave himself new to the ministry. Dispatched in the spring of 1865, as the guns of the Civil War yet resounded in parts of the dying Confederacy, William G. Stewart brought to the work a dedication born of simple faith. Nine months later, a second great leader, Charles H. Pearce—this one possessing education, long experience, and church position—relieved the first and pushed his uncompleted work toward enduring success. Between the two men, what W. E. B. Du Bois called "the greatest social institution of American negroes" found itself planted firmly in the State of Florida. Their achievement thereafter would mature to touch the nation. As one of its children would recall of the Florida AME Church, "We grew up under it and in it." Nothing, A. Philip Randolph would add, affected him "as deeply as the church relationship."[1]

The events leading directly to the AME Church's advent in Florida took place in Charleston, South Carolina, beginning on May 16, 1865. Confederate forces in the East were surrendering following the capitulation of Generals Robert E. Lee and Joseph E. Johnston in April. Florida-born general Edmund Kirby Smith would not stand down his western army for another ten days. Confusion reigned amid chaos in many places, and the meaning of the peace and of emancipation remained uncertain. On the other hand, newly freed slaves gleefully embraced the Day of Jubilee. "There was joy in the South," W. E. B. Du Bois declared. "It rose like perfume—like a prayer," he continued. "Men stood quivering. Slim dark girls, wild and beautiful with wrinkled hair, wept silently; young women, black, tawny, white and golden, lifted shivering hands; and old and broken mothers, black and gray, raised great voices and shouted to God across the fields, and up to the rocks and the mountains."[2]

Anxious to establish itself in the South now that slaveholder power could not keep it out, the AME Church moved quickly to set up an organizational beachhead. At the May 16 Charleston gathering, Bishop Daniel A. Payne and a handful of associates took the first step by organizing the South Carolina Conference. Its jurisdiction, they agreed, stretched northward to North Carolina, westward into Georgia, and southward toward Florida. "Thus organized," Payne would note, "the South Carolina Conference was like a ship sent to conquer other lands in the South—farther South."[3]

A stroke of luck and not much more permitted Payne to include Florida in the conference's early mission. Obviously still in its infancy in the region, the church could call upon few ministers to cover its huge potential missionary field. Then, as chance would have it, Payne's friend Elder James A. Handy brought to the conference a young man whom he had just met. The encounter had taken place on May 15 when Handy first attempted to hold AME services at nearby Hilton Head. "I opened the doors of the church for any one who would connect himself or herself with the African Methodist Episcopal Church," Handy recounted. "William G. Steward came forward as the first person and joined the church," he continued. "I received him that night with others." The future bishop added: "I examined him on that night and licensed him to preach. I took him to Charleston and had him ordained a deacon the next day."[4]

The man who appeared to Handy as a godsend had arisen from origins of the most humble sort. William G. Stewart had been born a slave in Decatur County, Georgia, on December 15, 1833. Within three years, his owner had sold him, his mother, and five brothers and sisters to a planter at Jacksonville, Florida, in Duval County. Raised in that North Florida county, the young slave eventually married Susan E. Raney and began a family. In 1862, Civil War disruptions in Northeast Florida afforded him the chance to escape bondage. Apparently taking his family with him, Stewart made his way to Beaufort, South Carolina, then held by Union forces. He entered school there and was likely taught by missionaries of the Methodist Episcopal Church. Stewart studied until war's end, when he stepped forward to join the AME ministry. It was said that the one-time slave possessed "a modest lamb like nature." All agreed that he was "of unusual high moral character."[5]

The task that Stewart and other AME emissaries agreed to undertake in

8. The Reverend William G. Stewart, Florida's first ordained AME minister. Courtesy Photographic Collection, Florida State Archives.

the wake of the May 1865 Charleston sessions stood before them as no small challenge. Bishop Payne, even more than some other AME leaders, conceived an aggressive, activist role for the church in the new South. "Society among the Colored people at that time needed as much reconstruction as did the Political Machinery of the whole South," explained the Reverend James H. A. Johnson. "The movement was made under the illustrious Bishop D. A. Payne . . . for the purpose of carrying on this reconstruction," he wrote further. "It was designed to bring up South Carolina, Georgia, Florida, and all, like phenixes from the smoldering ruins of slavery." Johnson concluded, "The founders therefore, went to work immediately after the adjournment of the first South Carolina Conference."[6]

In only three weeks, Payne, Handy, Johnson, and others had schooled Stewart in the ways of the AME Church and dispatched him southward. His official appointment as pastor of Florida came on May 22, 1865. The missionary arrived in the state alone on June 9. Stewart recorded some of the details of his journey. "Bishop Payne and Rev. J. A. Handy got permission from General Saxton, Provost Marshal under General Gilmore at Beaufort, to send me to Beaufort on the steamer Planter, Captain Robert Small in command," he wrote. "There I boarded a small Government boat for Jacksonville."[7]

Having been absent from the state for three years, Stewart found himself in June 1865 returning to a changed Florida, one where wartime devastation could be seen at every hand. The northeast and the settled areas of the peninsula, together with West Florida, had suffered tremendously as the tides of war had swept back and forth over the landscape. Although only rarely occurring on anything but a small scale, the fighting often had reflected the state's split loyalties and was all the more bitter for it. Refugees, black and white, struggled to survive, having lost most of their possessions to arson and flight. Those who sympathized with the Union naturally had gathered in the towns that were under U.S. control, mushrooming what had amounted before the war to little more than villages into small cities. Disease and hunger stalked in desperation's wake.[8]

The great exception to this picture of wartime disruption and destruction lay in the Middle Florida plantation belt that centered on the state capital at Tallahassee. Shielded by Confederate policy from much of the fighting, the area had survived the conflict virtually unscathed. In 1860 this region—including Jackson, Gadsden, Leon, Jefferson, Madison, and Hamilton Counties—had contained 38 percent of the state's population of 140,424, while its 31,412 slaves had constituted 51 percent of all persons held in bondage in Florida. Although unrest and fears of slave rebellion had stirred Middle Florida during the conflict, most freedmen and freedwomen still lived on the plantations when William G. Stewart landed at the Jacksonville wharf in June. Some, reportedly, had not yet been informed of their freedom.[9]

The picture that greeted Stewart when he stepped ashore at Jacksonville must have astounded him. "[It] presented a melancholy sight," observed one resident. "The old ruins of the burned buildings, the few rude shanties on the north side of Bay street, the neglected yards, the stumps of the once handsome shade trees, the broken fences, the dingy appearance of the former neat, painted dwellings, all were depressing to those who sought their old homes." A New York City reporter added more detail. "A few brick warehouses and stores make up the street fronting on the water, and a huge billiard saloon seems as much of an institution as the stores," he informed his readers. "Everywhere the sand was almost bottomless, and walking, for even a square or two, was exceedingly uncomfortable," the reporter continued. "A negro guard paced along the wharf; negroes in uniform were scattered about the streets, interspersed with a few Rebel soldiers, and a very neatly-policed negro camp occupied one of the vacant squares."[10]

Jacksonville had been a sleepy village when Stewart lived there before the war; now he discovered a small but teeming city imposing itself upon its own ruins. In 1860, the town had contained a population of 2,118, of whom 898 were slaves. The total had ranked it third in Florida behind Pensacola and Key West. Now, refugees had so swelled Jacksonville's citizenry that the city had become, temporarily, the state's largest urban center. "Jacksonville has been crowded to overflowing, for months past, with refugees, both white and colored," a northern teacher explained on June 23. "Of late . . . ," she added, "both classes have been flocking in, in great numbers, the colored people, a short time since, at the rate of one hundred per day." It was said that the freedmen were living in the "most wretched manner" and that everything in "the shape of a house, hut or hovel" was filled beyond capacity.[11]

These conditions might have seemed ideally suited for AME missionary work, but appearances in that regard deceived. For one thing, Florida's Methodist Episcopal Church South—already strong at Jacksonville—had decided in December 1864 to attempt to stem the tide of deserting black members that had been flowing since early in the war. It did so by implementing, within the limits of its modest resources, a program of "colored charges." Minister John C. Ley explained:

> The new relation to the freemen involved very delicate responsibilities. Previously our Church had spent large amounts for "missions to people of color." In addition to this, each minister was required to give one service each Sunday to them. We had also made special arrangements, for all who desired to do so, to worship with the whites in all our churches. Hence we had a large colored membership all over the South.
>
> But now with a change of circumstances there must be a change of operations. It was utterly impossible for us to keep up our missions; still we tried to render them all the service possible, and could we have served them with the whites, until they could have ministers of their own color, at least partially educated, it would have been better for them.[12]

The ME South initiative placed a serious stumbling block in the path of the AME church, but the northern Methodist Church imposed a far greater one. Since early in the war, its missionaries and ministers had offered assistance and relief to black refugees inside the Union lines, including those at Jacksonville and its neighbor to the north, Fernandina. With inspiration from Timothy Willard Lewis, presiding elder of the district that encompassed the coastal islands of South Carolina and Georgia where William G. Stewart had attended school, the Reverend John Swaim had planned for the ME North Church to seize control of Florida and remold it into a state "founded on the eternal principles of freedom and equal rights." The plan depended, in good part, on support from black church members. In return, they would benefit from church policy that avoided paternalism and accorded them respect. Whites would assist the freedmen, not direct them. In the circumstances, the church already had won many adherents at Jacksonville.[13]

Thus, without instructions and distant from the advice of church authorities, William G. Stewart faced a complex problem at Jacksonville in June 1865. How and where do you begin church work when other churches already are established as competitors and you are without apparent resources? He chose to leave town. Instead of remaining at Jacksonville, Stewart ventured a few miles to the west to the community called Midway. This may have been the neighborhood in which Stewart grew up, or he may have received word that a young local preacher, John Thomas, had begun assembling a black Methodist congregation there. In any event, on June 10 Stewart gathered the small group into the arms of the AME Church. "This was the first church to be organized in the State under an authorized pastor," Stewart later confirmed. "Mother Midway" thus took pride of place in Florida AME history. Reverend Stewart left it in John Thomas's charge.[14]

Having made a concrete start by introducing the church officially into Florida, Reverend Stewart returned to Jacksonville to contemplate his next move. As he did so, word passed into the state about his arrival and soon reached, deep in Middle Florida, the eager ears of former slave Henry W. Call. Call, as discussed earlier, already had assembled an unsanctioned AME congregation at Jackson County's Cottondale. With the peace, Call seems to have relocated to the county seat and continued his religious endeavors there. For the onetime slave preacher, the news from the east came as a command from God. "As soon as William Steward landed in Jacksonville and Brother Call heard of it," Charles Sumner Long observed, "he walked from Marianna to Jacksonville to get Rev. Steward, and took him to Marianna where he and all the members were taken into our Church."[15]

The exact timing of Henry Call's appearance in Jacksonville and his subsequent departure with William G. Stewart for Middle Florida is not known

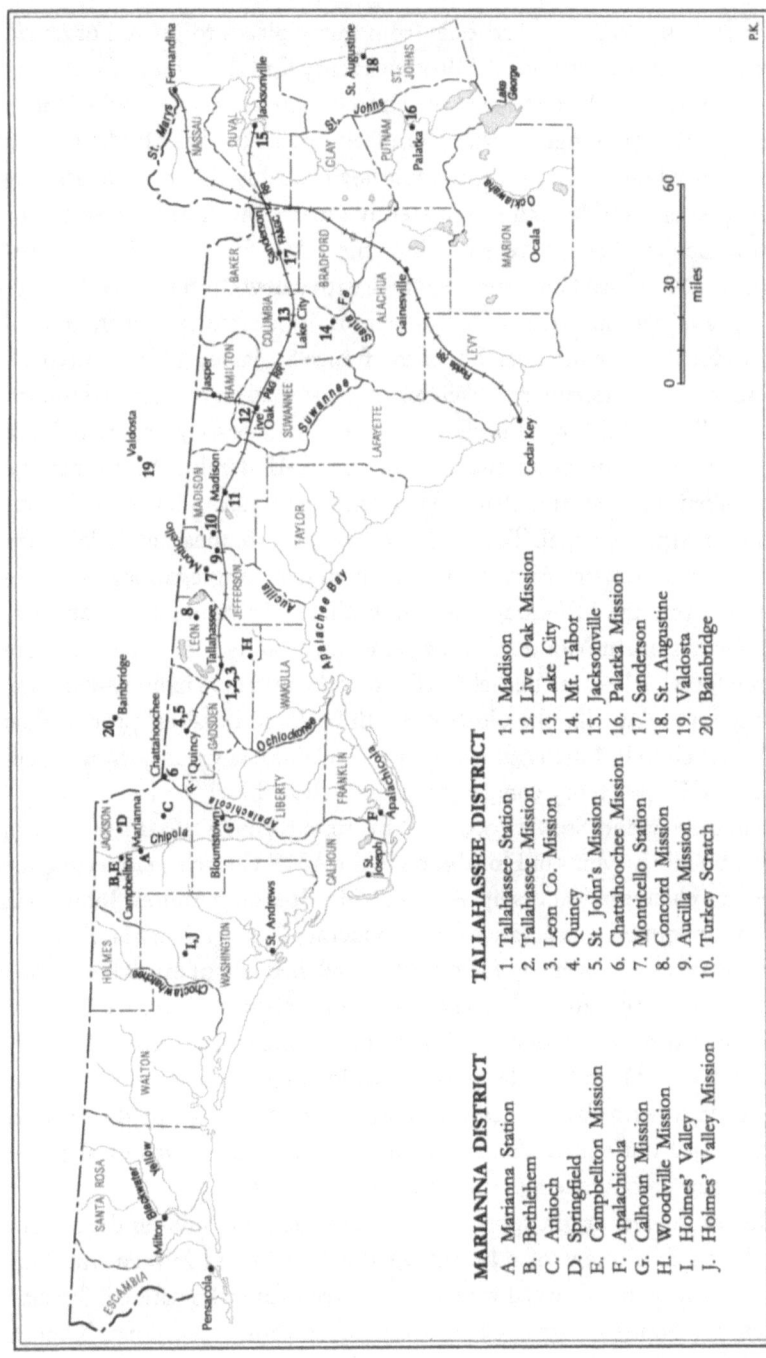

9. The heartland of African Methodism in post–Civil War Florida. Collection of the authors.

with certainty. "We soon had calls from many places to go and organize churches," Stewart chronicled. "Brother Henry Call came for us from Marianna," he added. "We organized the church there as best we could." Since regular railroad passenger service from Jacksonville toward Middle Florida recommenced only on July 20, the journey probably occurred in late July and August or soon thereafter. Apparently the two men headed directly for Jackson County. Stewart received into the AME fold the existing Bethlehem and Mt. Olive Churches, together with a new church called Springfield, located ten miles east of Campbellton. In Marianna proper, he held services for the core membership of the future St. James AME Church.[16]

The reverend thereafter worked his way eastward on the railroad toward Jacksonville, establishing churches where he found existing groups of black Methodists desirous of admission into the AME family. At Quincy, he joined Allen Jones Sr. and Dennis Wood in laying the organizational foundation for Arnett Chapel. Twenty-five or so miles southeast at Tallahassee, he discovered Robert Meacham's 116-member congregation, not long separated from the ME Church South. Bethel AME resulted. Twenty-five miles farther on, at Monticello, the Jefferson County seat, the seeds were planted for what became Bethel AME. Near the Jefferson County–Madison County line at Aucilla, the old ME South "colored mission" produced an additional church. Finally, at Lake City in Columbia County, Stewart accepted the Hope Henry congregation into fellowship.[17]

While Reverend Stewart occupied his time through the fall of 1865 in church building, events in Florida and in the AME Church were setting the stage for a change in leadership. As to Florida, President Andrew Johnson in July had appointed conservative former federal judge William Marvin as the state's provisional governor. He quickly squelched talk of extending voting rights to freedmen. Instead, Marvin oversaw elections in October that essentially returned control of the state to the same conservative white elements who had taken Florida out of the Union in 1861. The new legislature proceeded to write laws called the "black code" that attempted to restore slavery in all but name. Violence against African Americans escalated as whites grew emboldened, particularly in rural areas.[18]

One of the few bright spots on the Florida scene in mid- and late 1865 was the establishment of a branch of the Freedmen's Bureau, the U.S. government agency charged with assisting freed slaves. Its national director, Oliver O. Howard, designated his onetime Union army subordinate Thomas W. Osborn to head up the Florida office. Howard himself visited the state

10. The Reverend Charles H. Pearce as he appeared during his first years as Florida's AME presiding elder. Courtesy Photographic Collection, Florida State Archives.

in October and November, pausing at Tallahassee to address freedmen at Bethel AME Church. His words did not necessarily provide all the reassurance that his listeners might have desired. "He told them that they had now received their freedom, which could never be taken from them, and that it rested with them whether it would prove a blessing to them or otherwise," the *New York Herald* reported. He insisted that freedmen should stay on the plantations, avoid the cities, work hard, and refrain from "insolence to the white people." As the account concluded, "His speech was listened to with much attention and interest."[19]

Such lackluster encouragement, when viewed against alarming events occurring in the state, compelled many AME members to seek support and protection directly from the federal government. They gathered with others of like mind—including, at this early date, many Baptists—at Tallahassee's Bethel AME in January 1866. Perhaps under the chairmanship of minister Robert Meacham, they elected Joseph Oats, a former slave of then governor David Walker, to represent them in Congress and with the president. Oats did join Frederick Douglass and others in meeting with President Andrew Johnson at the White House on February 7. Frustrated at the results, Douglass announced that blacks now would have to depend on the "people." By the time Oats returned to Tallahassee in May, an increase in racial tensions had sparked fears for his safety. Rather than hearing his report at Bethel, his supporters, "armed with old cavalry swords and pistols," secretly gathered outside of town.[20]

As these events unfolded, Bishop Daniel A. Payne found time to reconsider the merits of William G. Stewart's appointment as pastor to Florida. One factor was the Florida-born preacher's limited schooling. As a church historian has put it, "The principal advocate of ministerial education at this time was Daniel Alexander Payne." A second factor related to Stewart's limited authority within the church. As a deacon, he could not ordain other ministers, giving him little option but to leave untrained and unordained local preachers in charge of the congregations he accepted. As an emergency compromise, this situation was tolerable to the church. For the long term, a minister of at least elder rank would be required to properly ordain AME clergymen and to regularize Florida affairs in general.[21]

In this situation Bishop Payne turned to an old and trusted friend, Elder Charles H. Pearce. An 1868 letter of Pearce's preserves the story of his early role in church affairs:

> I have been since 1849 a minister of the African Methodist Episcopal Church of America: was born and brought up in the State of Maryland, a free man: moved from there in 1852 at the age of 35 to Connecticut: in the year 1855 was appointed by Bishop D. A. Payne, then presiding over the New England Conference, to a missionary field in Canada connected with that conference; and on arriving in Canada in the same year took an oath of allegiance to the Government there, as required by special act of Parliament of all ministers of the gospel of Foreign birth, before entering upon the duties of my mission. I remained there till the close of the war in 1865....
>
> In 1865 I was recalled by the same Bishop, the Right Reverend D. A. Payne, and ordered to report to the Baltimore Conference where I received my appointment to Florida. I arrived here on the [16th] of February 1866.[22]

Those who knew Pearce were struck by the force of both his personality and his preaching. Although only an elder, out of respect he would be addressed as "Bishop" Pearce within the Florida church. The Reverend J. J. Sawyer recalled him in these words:

> He was a man of medium height, heavy built, well formed, gentlemanly bearing, and he showed the capacity of much endurance. As a preacher he seemed to have perfect control of his voice and an education ample for all intents and purposes; he addressed his subject to the brain of his hearers only so far as it would enable him to reach the heart through the sympathy, which he seldom failed to do. Among his brethren he was lively, friendly, and instructive. He was generally successful both as Pastor and Presiding Elder. As a debater he stood firmly by his cause and succeeded wonderfully in showing the best features of it, while he turned the argument of his opponent into ridicule, and few were they who engaged in conflict with him and came off victoriously. Elder Pearce was a sincere lover of the African M. E. Church and a faithful advocate of its doctrines and claims.[23]

11. Minister and shoemaker Joseph J. Sawyer helped to preserve the AME Church's early history while also holding office as an elected public official at Palatka. Courtesy Photographic Collection, Florida State Archives.

Sawyer struck an important chord in catching the gist of Pearce's persona when he described the elder as a "faithful advocate" of AME "doctrines and claims." He might have added a qualification, though. Pearce's commitment to those doctrines and claims came as they were interpreted by his distinguished and activist mentor, Bishop Payne. And the bishop desired radical change. Another of his protégés, Henry McNeal Turner, would illustrate the flavor of Payne's teachings in his famous 1868 speech to the Georgia legislature. "I shall neither fawn nor cringe before any party nor stoop to beg them for my rights," he declared. "I am here to demand my rights, and to hurl thunderbolts at the men who would dare to cross the threshold of my manhood."[24]

Accordingly, Pearce arrived in Florida during February 1866 intent upon working a revolution in matters religious, educational, and political. First, he would build and expand churches, open and operate Sunday schools, and spur development of public schools. "We are hunting for education, that will give us a name and position in the nation," he explained. "We have a right to aspire to and claim position with education." An 1882 church report summarized his views of Sunday schools. "Sunday Schools are, beyond doubt, the nurseries of the Church," it read. "Without them, we have no assurance of permanent stability in our work; but with them, we can realize a confident hope of success in establishing happy homes and an improved state of society."[25]

Once a proper foundation of church and school had been laid, Pearce determined to plunge the church deeply into state and local politics. Eventually, he would emerge as one of Florida's premier political powers. "A man in this State cannot do his whole duty as a minister except he looks out for the political interests of his people," Pearce declared on one occasion. "They are like a ship out at sea, and they must have somebody to guide them; and it is natural that they should get their best informed men to lead them."[26]

In early 1866 a political role for the church remained in the future, but Elder Pearce quickly set to work on more fundamental chores. In so doing, he gained assistance from some surprising friends. "I left Beaufort, S. C., on the 13th of February, 1866, *en route* for my new missionary field of labor and arrived in Jacksonville on the 16th of the same month," he later recalled. "I found no church nor congregation of ours there," he added. "The people were all strangers to me, but very kind and bade me God-speed." With Deacon Stewart apparently absent from the town, Pearce passed three days there without making progress.[27]

Pearce's luck took a turn for the better on February 19. While out walking he chanced to encounter two ministers of the ME Church South, Franklin A. Branch and Robert L. Wiggins. Branch held office as conference secretary, and Wiggins worked as presiding elder of the Jacksonville District. Both men had come to the conclusion that the almost bankrupt southern Methodist Church could not meet the needs of freedmen. As a result, they had begun encouraging local blacks to form their own churches. Branch and Wiggins agreed to open up the Jacksonville ME South church to Pearce on February 25.[28]

The elder's first AME services at Jacksonville went well. Former ME South members who had formed a society for religious worship attended. Sixty-four persons cast their lot with the new church. By July 28, Mount Zion AME would achieve formal organization. From the first, it followed Pearce's program of stressing education. Its ability to do so resulted from another chance encounter. A young freedwoman from Warren County, Georgia, approached Pearce soon after his arrival. She confessed that, although a Methodist, she was teaching at "the Baptist Sabbath school." She informed him further that she had received a basic education after taking refuge at Jacksonville. Pearce gladly welcomed Mary E. Miller (some sources say Waller) to the Mount Zion Church. She quickly established a Sunday school, even though the church then consisted only of a "brush arbor" rather than a regular sanctuary. It was said that she "labored early and late, in season and out of season, during the darkest age of our Church in this State." Pearce clearly was impressed. This example left him wondering where else he might obtain such dedicated and talented women for the church.[29]

By the end of his first month in Florida, Elder Pearce had achieved a permanent AME presence at Jacksonville, but, having assessed the situation around him, he realized that he needed to look elsewhere than Northeast Florida for a place to concentrate his early work. To the south at St. Augustine, Roman Catholicism remained a formidable barrier to African Methodism and other Protestant churches. As one local missionary put it, "This is a Catholic city." In the region generally, including places such as Fernandina and Gainesville, the northern Methodist Church presented stiff competition. At Jacksonville, that church's labors already were manifesting tangible evidence of major success. On February 18, two days after Pearce's appearance in the city, the Reverends John Swaim and Timothy Willard Lewis had organized an all-black ME congregation. Construction of a sanctuary began in late May, and the church's Sunday school soon flourished.

Pearce could not yet match that example, and so he turned elsewhere for the time being.[30]

Pearce's decision-making process convinced him that William G. Stewart had been right all along. The deacon's emphasis on church development in Middle Florida and nearby areas did offer the greatest promise for quick progress. Accordingly, with Stewart as his guide, the elder headed for the plantation belt to the west. The first stop came at Tallahassee, where he and Stewart arrived on March 1. What they found delighted them. Local pastor Robert Meacham had managed to raise sufficient funds to build a fine new sanctuary. Cornerstone-laying ceremonies at the Duval Street site had occurred on February 20 and had drawn a large crowd, including the region's most popular black preacher, the Baptist James Page. "[I] found the AME church in course of erection, but not properly organized," Pearce recorded of his visit. "I appointed the officers and organized the church properly with 116 members."[31]

From Tallahassee, Pearce and Stewart toured the nearby congregations already accepted by the deacon. In Gadsden County, Pearce met Allen Jones, Dennis Wood, and their followers. The elder described the occasion as he saw it. "On the 9th of March I arrived in Quincy; had an interview with the former members of the M. E. Church South and they readily agreed to join the AME Church," he wrote, "and on the 15th I received 453 members and appointed the proper officers." The party then ventured to Jackson County, before turning eastward again. Of his subsequent rounds, Pearce added:

> On the 25th of March, 1866, I arrived in Monticello, preached in the AME church, receiving 343. On the 27th of March I organized the Church in Wau-keenah with 163 members. On the 30th of March I arrived at Madison and organized the AME Church with 81 members. On the 2d day of April, 1866, I arrived in Lake City, organized the AME Church and received 154 members.[32]

Stewart described the journey simply. "He ... inspected what I had done at Marianna, Tallahassee, and elsewhere," the deacon wrote, "and whatever I lacked he was able to furnish it."[33]

Some evidence suggests that Pearce also determined to reach out to Pensacola's freedmen at the earliest possible moment. It appears that the elder, having encountered Henry Call in Jackson County, directed the local preacher to visit West Florida's old capital at the earliest possible time. Call's son C. F. Call remembered that on May 16, 1866, his father organized what became Allen Chapel. "Father called the people whom he had been meeting from house to house and perfected a legal organization of the AME Church in Pensacola," C. F. Call recorded. "The Church was organized in a rented hall," he continued, "and I do not know where they met until they had purchased a church home."[34]

The tour allowed Pearce to assess his needs in anticipation of the second session of the AME South Carolina Conference, which was to be held at Savannah beginning May 14. With Bishop Payne presiding, Pearce pressed the Florida church's needs at that meeting. The conference responded positively. Among other things, Pearce had decided to assume the pastorate of the Tallahassee church and to supervise the state from a headquarters there. Deacon Stewart would return to South Carolina. Tallahassee's displaced preacher, Robert Meacham, would receive ordination and take up the church at Monticello. Pearce and Meacham would come face-to-face on church and political matters in future years, but in 1866 Pearce likely saw himself as offering Meacham a boon, a place in the regular ministry. Quincy's Dennis Wood also would be ordained and would oversee church affairs in Gadsden and Jackson Counties ("the Chattahoochee Mission"). The two men would work under Pearce's watchful eye. With Middle Florida thus taken care of, Pearce's plans called for filling two other key pastorates with ordained ministers. One would serve the Gulf of Mexico port town of Apalachicola, giving the church a toehold in West Florida. The other would take up residence in East Florida at Jacksonville. Pearce's dilemma was this: Who could be relied upon to carry the church's cause in areas far distant from the sight of the presiding elder?[35]

Doubtless, Bishop Payne guided Pearce in making his selections. For West Florida, they focused on an experienced pastor just elevated to elder status. Born in North Carolina about 1797, Mack Steward had begun preaching as a youth. A member of the Methodist Church since 1812, he volunteered at the age of sixty-nine to face the peril of yellow fever on the Gulf coast. Pearce later would describe him warmly as "a man of faith and prayer, and full of good works." He added, "[Steward was] an Israelite indeed." At Apalachicola soon after the conference concluded, Steward founded St. Paul's AME Church. Until a sanctuary could be constructed, he gathered communicants in the humble surroundings of a local blacksmith's shop.[36]

12. As illustrated by this early drawing, Apalachicola's St. Paul's AME Church convened at first in a local blacksmith's shop. Courtesy Photographic Collection, Florida State Archives.

The Jacksonville problem was solved in the person of William S. Bradwell. Born at Darien, Georgia, in December 1822, Bradwell was a man of uncommon ability. A political opponent admitted later that he was "a very sensible fellow [who] has always borne a good character." During the Civil War he had "preach[ed] to his fellow slaves, though often flogged for doing so." In 1865, his brother Charles L. Bradwell had helped to organize the South Carolina Conference. "He seemed to be careful for nothing," a fellow minister mentioned of William, "all things seemed to work together for the good—for persecutions, rather increased his friends, and the threats and abuse of his enemies tended to replenish his storehouse." Now, in 1866 he sought admission to the conference as a preacher on trial. Payne and Pearce saw much potential in the man. They gave him the pastorate of Mount Zion with instructions to build a church.[37]

Pearce's program contained important elements beyond these five assignments. Until additional ordained ministers could be secured, the Florida church necessarily had to rely upon unordained local preachers. Henry Call and Jacob Livingston would help in Jackson County, as would Allen Jones in Gadsden. John Thomas remained active in Duval, while David Young of the Hope Henry Church at Lake City was admitted to the conference as a local deacon. There were a number of others, one of whom arrived at the Savannah conference by surprise. A native of South Carolina, Richard Brigadier (also Brigadaire or Brigadere) had been born about 1816. His owner had relocated him by 1860 to Columbia County, Florida. At war's end he was residing in the Mt. Tabor community, about ten miles southeast of Lake City near Olustee Creek. There he formed a Methodist congregation. In May 1866, Brigadier presented Mt. Tabor Church to the South Carolina Conference as a gift. It was gratefully received, and Dick Brigadier was accepted as an itinerant preacher.[38]

Pearce's work had only just begun with the conclusion of the Savannah conference. Soon, he turned to the North in search of further support. At the time, the elder felt an urgent need to open schools. For that work he needed teachers like Mary Miller. The *Christian Recorder*, the *Christian Herald's* successor, noted his presence at church headquarters in Philadelphia on September 8. He subsequently journeyed to New York. There he recruited at least three women for service with the church. They arrived in Florida by early October. Pearce would assign Martha D. Sickles (later Greenwood) to Robert Meacham's Monticello church. She organized a Sabbath school on her first Sunday there and began teaching a public school the following day. The elder reserved a Miss Day (later Mrs. M. E. C. Smith) and the third teacher for Tallahassee. Day's achievements echoed Miss Sickles's at Monticello. At the state capital, Day "labored incessantly for more than twenty years for the advancement of the Redeemer's cause."[39]

By the time of Elder Pearce's return to Florida in October 1866, the AME Church had begun to blossom. Pearce's energy had infused its spirit. The church also had benefited from a general surge of interest in religion among freedmen. "The negroes throughout the country have lately become very religiously inclined," reported a Tallahassee correspondent in early September. He added, "Revivals and 'big meetings' are the order of the day, or rather the night."[40]

13. This drawing of the Monticello AME Church, which was erected in the late 1860s by Robert Meacham, appeared on a "Birds Eye" map published in 1885. Courtesy Photographic Collection, Florida State Archives, Neg. No. 3570.

Nowhere was the progress more evident than at Monticello, where Robert Meacham had lent his considerable talents. On October 23 the newly ordained minister recorded the events of his first five months in that town:

> I arrived at the place of my appointment at Monticello, Fla., May the 30th. Finding no home we could worship in, and that we could call our own, I went to work immediately to erect a house for Divine worship. We bought a lot two hundred feet square, which is paid for and the deed drawn. The house is now erected, and I preached in it for the first time Sunday the 21st of this month; organized the Sabbath School in the morning at 9 o'clock, the house was crowded with little boys and girls and several adults. At 11 o'clock we had a prayer meeting which was well attended. And at 3 o'clock I preached to the congregation, which was very large. I took in thirty-five members. We rejoiced exceedingly and gave God all the praise for his love and kindness towards us.
>
> As we have no regular school house here, we organized a day school in the church, on the morning of the 22d at 9 o'clock. Our little ones

were so glad to commence school, that they thronged the place before the hour appointed. We have two good teachers that have taken charge of the school. Mr. Pembroke, from Baltimore, Md., and Miss Sickles from New York.

We intend to push on. We anticipate to have the [church] building completed and ready for dedication by the sitting of the next Annual Conference. So far, the debt is very small on the Church; we have a number of warm-hearted white friends in this town, some of whom are members of the M. E. Church South, and some of Presbyterian, and others are no members at all, only well-wishers of our effort in having a Church of our own; they have contributed over 250 dollars. Mr. Bird, of Monticello, gave us a large portion of the frame off his land, costing us nothing; Mrs. R. C. [Parkhill], of Monticello, furnished all of the other lumber, and delivered it on the spot for less than we could have got it elsewhere, besides giving money.

Meacham then turned to the meaning of recent events. "Truly our Church is prospering in this land. I have also been engaged in attending to the Churches around the county, during the time that we had no house of our own, and they are all prospering; so I am beginning to think that we are in the world, as well as other people, and feel that God is with us, and will crown our efforts with the best success."[41]

The AME advances were matched by setbacks for African Americans generally. The year had witnessed increased repression of freedmen and white southern Loyalists, with violence flaring in numerous locales. State-run courts often had balked at protecting basic rights and punishing outrageous crimes. By June federal authorities had declared martial law in Santa Rosa, Escambia, Levy, Madison, and Alachua Counties. The Freedmen's Bureau, under Thomas W. Osborn's conservative leadership, had proved a weak friend at best. This was so despite the efforts of the bureau's special counsel, Ossian B. Hart of Jacksonville. A leader of the state's southern Loyalists, Hart led a delegation to a Philadelphia convention held the week of September 3 to protest conditions in the South. Since Pearce was in the city about that time he may have attended some of the sessions, along with notables such as Frederick Douglass. Hart and his wife, Catharine, accompanied Elder Pearce and his wife, Ellen, as they returned from the North on the steamer *San Salvador*.[42]

The Philadelphia Southern Loyalists Convention may have helped spur an electoral revolution that, in turn, moved Florida's AME Church further toward the goals Elder Pearce had envisioned for it. Congressional voting in the fall of 1866 resulted in widespread victory for Radical Republicans, who demanded a Reconstruction policy that would offer protections to African Americans and Loyalists. A key demand was the vote for adult freedmen.[43]

As Elder Pearce's contemplations focused in late 1866 and early 1867 on the changes to come, he searched for the right direction for the church to follow. Bishop Payne's activism buttressed his own, of course, something that might eventually bring him into conflict with loyal southerners such as Hart who could be expected to assume control of state government. In those days of thought, one white northerner's words likely resonated ever more loudly for the elder. "We have conquered those Southern people," Daniel Richards was telling black audiences. "The aristocracy of the South was the cause of the struggle," he insisted. "The spirit of the aristocrats has been put down by the force of our arms, but this spirit is creeping up again, and unless it is met in time by us and crushed again, we shall have another and more bloody conflict." Daniels would conclude: "It therefore becomes our duty to unite, and to do all in our power to crush them and keep this spirit down. To do that it is necessary that we should get hold of the reins of government. It is our right and our privilege to legislate for these rebels and to hold the offices, and we will not rest until we have them—we must have them."[44]

3

THE FLORIDA ANNUAL CONFERENCE AND REPUBLICAN RULE, 1867–1869

An instrument in the hands of God
to lift our race up from degradation.

Following elections held in the fall of 1866, the U.S. Congress began early in 1867 to replace President Andrew Johnson's mild Reconstruction policies with ones far more harsh for the defeated South. For the first time, federal law mandated the vote for freed African Americans. Within a short time, black voters combined with northerners and southern Loyalists to seize control of Florida government under the banner of the Republican party. AME leaders stood at the forefront of this movement, a fact that spurred church growth within a population of grateful former slaves. The mantle of temporal power proved a heavy burden, though. Soon, the Republican party began to fracture. So, too, did the AME Church.

The southern political revolution commenced on March 2, 1867, when the U.S. Congress approved the First Reconstruction Act. Others quickly followed. The laws mandated military rule for most of the former Confederacy. That condition would end when new constitutions were adopted in each state and approved by the Congress. Delegates empowered to draft the charters would be elected by public vote. Military authorities would ensure that adult freedmen were permitted the franchise in those elections. Florida was one of the states directly affected.[1]

Euphoria gripped African Americans and southern Loyalists in Florida. "The Reconstruction acts made the great body of the people, black and white, radical," explained a correspondent. At Jacksonville, members of the black community gathered at an all-black Baptist church in mid-March to

14. The Reverend John R. Scott Sr. emerged as a key AME leader during the Reconstruction period. Courtesy Photographic Collection, Florida State Archives.

express their sentiments. Among their leaders were Mount Zion AME's minister William Bradwell and a lay associate, John R. Scott Sr. "There is now no distinction between the white and the black man on political matters," they proclaimed. "We now have a right to the ballot, but likewise the right to select the men that we choose to fill the offices." The group then nominated city officers. For mayor, it tapped southern Loyalist leader Ossian B. Hart.[2]

Although military officials short-circuited attempts to bring about a quick turnover of power such as occurred at Jacksonville, Elder Charles H. Pearce realized that the AME Church would be able to influence, if not control, the new state government in only a short time. To do so, though, the Florida church must organize itself in preparation. As he gathered his principal advisors together, Pearce understood that time was of the essence.[3]

The first concrete steps came during the week of March 30, 1867, when the South Carolina AME Conference, of which Florida remained a member, met at Wilmington, North Carolina. Bishop Alexander W. Wayman presided in place of Pearce's mentor, Bishop Daniel A. Payne. The change did not pose a problem. Wayman had valued a friendship with Pearce since both were young men in Maryland. The Florida delegation consisted of all but one of the ordained ministers assigned to the state, including Pearce, Apalachicola's Mack Steward, Quincy's Dennis Wood, Monticello's Robert Meacham, and Jacksonville's Bradwell. With the added influence of their Georgia colleagues, the preachers convinced the bishop and conference to set them free. On April 4 the new Florida Conference received final approval.[4]

That was not the only achievement at Wilmington. The Florida church was growing and required a host of pastors, who were, at the time, hard to come by. In the circumstances, its leaders desired the conference's seal of approval on local preachers they had decided to bring into the official church family. Gaining admission on trial were several men of ability, including Fuller M. White, Benjamin Quinn, Major Johnson, Jacob Livingston, Washington Rivers, Edward Trappe, and Allen Jones Sr. On April 3, the conference elected and ordained all of them, together with Richard Brigadier, as deacons. Ministerial appointments then illustrated the Florida church's new reach and its hopes for the immediate future. Pearce remained at Tallahassee, Bradwell at Jacksonville, Meacham at Monticello, and Brigadier at Mt. Tabor (Columbia County). Wood transferred to a new church at Palatka, while Mack Steward relocated to Marianna. Trappe received assignment to Fernandina; Quinn, Quincy; Johnson, Madison; Jones, St. John's Mission in Gadsden County; and White, Bethlehem Church in Jackson County. Listed as posts to be supplied were Pensacola; Apalachicola; Key West; Antioch, Springfield, and Campbellton in Jackson County; Concord (Leon County); Aucilla (Jefferson County); and Lake City.[5]

The Wilmington gathering not only armed the Florida church with a measure of control over its own affairs and a host of new pastors, it also armed it with militant policy. "Being firmly convinced that the African M. E. Church has been and is an instrument in the hands of God to lift our race up from degradation, we intend to use every means legitimate, honorable, and in our judgment pleasing to our Divine Master, to extend her principles and to build up her interests," its members resolved, "to unite our race into one great African Methodist family." A panel headed by C. H. Pearce ensured that thanks were delivered to those who had afforded the church the opportunities it now possessed to carry out those intentions. "We do hereby tender our profoundest gratitude to the . . . Congress for this noble act, which places her in just legislation in the front rank of any national government in the world," his report declared. "For this and other just measures enacted by the said Congress, . . . we renew our allegiance to the United States, and pledge to its protection our lives, our fortunes and our sacred honor."[6]

The Florida ministers returned to a state in which jubilation yet reigned among freedmen, and church affairs were bustling. African Americans had voted at Pensacola on April 1, setting off a new wave of excitement. At a single Gainesville rally three weeks later, three thousand individuals turned out to demand their rights. Robert Meacham addressed a crowd of two thousand at Monticello on April 30. In May, twenty-five hundred came together near Tallahassee. Pearce likely joined them. The gathering's tone sparked paranoia in at least one conservative white's mind. "The speeches, all of which, save one, were exceedingly violent, and harped so much on the evils endured by the race in slavery and the consequent obligation upon it to support the Radical party," he related, "that it is evident a very strong pressure has been brought to bear upon the colored population hereabouts by secret emissaries."[7]

As the excitement grew and the church's activist stance became more well known, hundreds, if not thousands, of new members flocked to the AME banner. In June 1867 a delighted Pearce would boast that total membership ran to 5,242, with twenty-five hundred children attending Sunday schools. "It really appears that God preserved the church in its afflictions until the AME Church came to her relief," he declared. "It is only necessary for us to name the AME Church to them, and they are willing to cast in their lot with us, and they are still coming by scores." At Allen Jones's St. John's mission late the same month, the presiding elder witnessed "a glorious meeting" attended by "over one thousand persons." He exulted in the occasion. "We are all looking forward to a glorious future," Pearce proclaimed.[8]

Tangible evidence of the progress could be seen in many places. At Quincy on May 10, trustees Lafayette Hargrett, Harry Crews, and Fred Hill purchased land upon which to construct a church. At nearby St. John's mission, Allen Jones had erected "a snug little church 80 by 45 feet." William Bradwell and his congregation were planning a sanctuary and parsonage for Mount Zion at Jacksonville, while Robert Meacham was continuing construction of the same facilities at Monticello. Other examples are available, but the prime one lay at Tallahassee. There on June 10, Elder Pearce and Bishop Wayman dedicated Bethel AME Church. "The church was crowded and many anxious hearers that could not get inside stood at the doors and windows," one minister reported. "Such a concourse of people was never seen in this city before," the bishop insisted, "they came from all parts of the country." Added Robert Meacham, "It was something new to a great many of the people to see one of the bishops of the AME Church."[9]

It was with these conditions as a backdrop that Bishop Wayman opened the first annual session of the Florida Conference, which was held at Talla-

15. Jacksonville's Mount Zion AME Church, seen here as it appeared in 1889, would surpass Tallahassee's Bethel AME as the denomination's largest church in Florida. Courtesy Photographic Collection, Florida State Archives.

hassee on June 8. Benjamin Quinn served as secretary. Twenty-two men received ordination, including those embraced at Wilmington. The names of thirty preachers now graced the Florida roster. The bishop created two administrative districts for the conference, one centered on Tallahassee with C. H. Pearce as presiding elder and the other headquartered at Marianna with Mack Steward in charge. Sixteen church buildings valued at $15,000 served the membership. The remainder of the congregations continued to meet in brush arbors or other locations. Temporarily, certain congregations in South Georgia were attached to the Florida Conference, as had been the case earlier with the ME Church South.[10]

Appointments announced in June 1867, most of them still located in Middle Florida, were:

Tallahassee District
C. H. PEARCE, PRESIDING ELDER
1. Tallahassee Station — C. H. Pearce
2. Tallahassee Mission — J. McCormick
3. Leon Co. Mission — George Vaughn
4. Quincy — Benjamin W. Quinn
5. St. John's Mission — Allen Jones Sr.
6. Chattahoochee Mission — David Foster
7. Monticello Station — Robert Meacham
8. Concord Mission — H. E. Bryant
9. Aucilla Mission — Solomon D. Stewart
10. Turkey Scratch — Emory Foreman
11. Madison — Major Johnson
12. Live Oak Mission — Levi Taylor
13. Lake City — David Young
14. Mt. Tabor — Richard Brigadier
15. Jacksonville — William Bradwell
16. Palatka Mission — Dennis Wood
17. Sanderson — Samuel Morgan
18. St. Augustine — John Smith
19. Valdosta — J. W. McDougal
20. Bainbridge — John Thornton

Marianna District
MACK STEWARD, PRESIDING ELDER
1. Marianna Station — Mack Steward
2. Bethlehem — Fuller White

3. Antioch — Smart Livingston
4. Springfield — Jacob Livingston
5. Campbellton Mission — William Clemmings
6. Apalachicola — Washington Rivers
7. Calhoun Mission — Peter Spears
8. Woodville Mission — William Ely
9. Holmes' Valley — C. Baker
10. Holmes' Valley Mission — Jacob Rusk.[11]

The expansive vision of June 1867 contemplated far more growth than these thirty appointments suggest. In the Tallahassee District, Pearce saw the need to exploit fertile opportunities for recruitment of members in Jefferson County (Monticello Mission), Gainesville, Fernandina, New Smyrna, Mosquito River, and Key West. The Marianna District considered possibilities at Sim's Harbor, Greenwood, Mount Vernon, Oak Hill, and Pensacola. On the other hand, the success of the ME Church in some of these places, such as at Gainesville and Fernandina, continued to pose obstacles for AME missionaries. The state's two largest towns, Key West and Pensacola, offered a similar but different concern. In both, the African Methodist Episcopal Zion Church had established itself, and its congregations were prospering. Such problems notwithstanding, Pearce could do little for the time being due to a lack of qualified ministers. So, the conference categorized all of these appointments as "to be supplied."[12]

16. Bishop and Mrs. Alexander W. Wayman. Courtesy Photographic Collection, Florida State Archives.

Issues of church expansion naturally thrilled those who attended the first annual meeting of the Florida Conference, but politics offered the major source of excitement. The organization formed by Pearce, Meacham, Steward, Bradwell, and others stood ready to enter the fray. It represented the sole organizational structure in the African American community that could touch a majority of black voters. White conservatives (Democrats), as well as several factions of white Republicans, had begun to court AME leaders for support. Until the Tallahassee meeting, the direction of church sympathies remained unknown. Now, one message came into the political arena clearly. "The most exciting question is, what party shall we vote for," explained Robert Meacham, "but the answer from all quarters of the State is the Republican party."[13]

William Bradwell, and through him the Florida church, learned immediately that a price would be exacted by conservative whites for AME support of Republican political ambitions. Bradwell and other church leaders had stayed at Tallahassee for extended meetings following adjournment of the Florida Conference. At Bethel on the evening of June 17 he preached "a sermon against slavery in Church or State." Robert Meacham described what then occurred. "After church there was a mob came out with staves and sticks, and went to the parsonage, and inquired of brother Pearce where brother Bradwell could be found," he wrote. "Just at that time brother Bradwell came up and said to the mob, that he had heard that there was a mob out after him for preaching against slavery, and said he was ready for them," the minister continued. He added: "The mob was composed of colored men. When brother Bradwell spoke to them, they denied their intention of mobbing him. These men were members and well-wishers of a church that is under control of the M. E. Church South, which speaks plain for itself why they wished to mob one of the ministers of the AME Church." Meacham concluded, "After he spoke to them they seemed to lose their courage, and went quietly home without anything happening to him (Bradwell)." The black men who formed the mob later would separate themselves from the ME Church South for what would become known to many as the "rebel" or "the old slavery church." Others knew it by the name Colored Methodist Episcopal Church (CME) in Florida.[14]

The June 17 incident foretold tragic times to come, but its meaning was lost in the exhilaration attendant upon the rise of Republicanism. Pearce and his allies determined to put themselves in position to broker power within the new party. They did so, as one Republican faction, led by Freedmen's Bureau personnel and its state director, Thomas W. Osborn, organized its own rank and file through Middle Florida's black Baptist churches. That so well regarded a figure as longtime minister James Page would associate himself with the Osborn faction gave it immense credibility with the region's black voters. This occurred at a time when Baptists were eyeing warily the new AME organization and its expansion. Osborn sensed an opportunity for leverage from that fact. According to one commentator, he and his men "taught [the Baptists] that the members of the Methodist churches were opposed to the Baptists getting any of the offices, which caused much bitterness and much fighting among themselves." So AME competition with the Baptist Church would extend beyond religious conversions to political ones as well.[15]

Jockeying between the various Republican factions came to a head at the Republican state organizational convention held at Tallahassee in July 1867. The southern Loyalist Ossian B. Hart had spearheaded party development as chairman of the state executive committee. Osborn, with assistance from other factions, moved to oust Hart from party power. A northern man named Liberty Billings, who had control of a faction based in Fernandina along with Daniel Richards, assisted. Billings blasted Hart, arguing that "a southern man could not be trusted." Furious southern Loyalists and some black Baptist leaders battled back. For his part, Charles H. Pearce attempted to pour oil on troubled waters. "Our interests are identical, and we are all aiming at the same thing," he proclaimed. "God made of one blood all the nations of the Earth; we are all brothers, and as such should work in harmony together," Pearce proceeded. "We meet here not to abuse each other, or to stir up strife and dissension, but to form a platform upon which all the loyal people can stand, and we must begin by making no distinction between the black and white."[16]

The purge of Hart from Republican power succeeded, and Pearce's choices for alliances diminished somewhat. He had admired the social equalitarian and other activist teachings of the white northerner Daniel Richards. In August he drew even closer to the man who represented Radical Republicanism in Florida. That month, the Republican congressional committee dispatched to the state a black orator to assist Richards and Liberty Billings. One man described William U. Saunders as "happy in the use of language." So he was. A stirring orator, he was said to be "excellent in appeals to passion or prejudice." Here Pearce saw a chance for real victory for African Americans and the AME Church. He agreed to a coalition with

Richards, Billings, and Saunders, which soon came to be called the "Mule Team." Reportedly, Mule Team plans called for Billings to become governor and for his two partners to go to the U.S. Senate. They agreed to back Pearce for lieutenant governor or, more likely given the AME commitment, superintendent of schools.[17]

Elections held in the late fall for constitutional convention seats gave the Mule Team what appeared to be a clear victory. Initial tallies showed eighteen of forty-six delegate race victors to be African Americans. Four of them were Pearce, Bradwell, Meacham, and their fellow AME minister Major Johnson. At least six others—Owen B. Armstrong, Auburn H. Erwin, Emanuel Fortune, Frederick Hill, Anthony Mills, and John W. Wyatt—were AME laymen, several of whom would become ministers. Highlighting the AME contribution to the win, the Mule Team leaders designated Pearce to open the constitutional convention in January 1868 as temporary president. They then organized the body and started writing a constitution that embodied their desires and ideals.[18]

Where the Mule Team leaders went wrong was to assume that the narrow majority they controlled early in the convention would hold up. Their radical agenda scared most white Republicans such as Thomas W. Osborn and President Andrew Johnson's local man, Harrison Reed, not to mention white conservatives. These elements recruited Ossian B. Hart to figure out how to wrest control of the convention from the Mule Team. That was accomplished in early February with the expulsion from the assemblage of Pearce, Richards, Billings, and Saunders on the grounds that they had not lived in Florida long enough to qualify as residents. Pearce had achieved a major goal, though. Even the less radical constitution subsequently drafted and accepted contained language calling for a legitimate public school system, something quite new and daring for Florida. "It is the paramount duty of the State to make ample provision for the education of all the children residing within its borders," the clause read, "without distinction or preference."[19]

All these events were happening at the same time as the church was opening its doors to increasing numbers of adherents. When the constitutional convention ended its business in February, AME membership in Florida had climbed to 7,610. This represented an almost 50 percent jump since the previous June. Thirty-three churches and twenty Sunday schools now operated. Sixty-six local preachers and forty exhorters helped to fill them. As Bishop Wayman would remark, "The Conference was in its infancy, yet it presented considerable promise."[20]

17. One-time Florida slave Thomas Warren Long served in the state senate while building churches deep into the peninsula. Courtesy Photographic Collection, Florida State Archives.

What with politics stirring and church affairs flourishing, the second session of the Florida Annual Conference, scheduled for Tallahassee on March 4, 1868, promised happenings of dramatic proportions. It did not disappoint. Bishop Wayman arrived late and presided beginning on the second day. He asked those assembled to elect his young protégé B. T. Tanner of the Baltimore Conference as conference secretary, and they did so. In turn, the bishop found himself astonished at the progress worked by the church's leaders, whether religious, social, or political. "These men seem imbued with the Holy Spirit," he informed readers of the *Christian Recorder*. "There is also a beauty of eloquence to be seen in the most of the men, that would astonish the world, in view of the many disadvantages under which they have had to come up."[21]

The meetings saw the church's ranks reinforced to meet its growing challenges. Its successes and its activist agenda had spurred individuals of substantial ability to opt for membership in its clergy over other opportunities. Fifteen preachers were admitted to the conference, among them John

Thomas, William G. Stewart (back from South Carolina), Thomas Warren Long, S. D. Stewart, Robert Watson, John Churchwell, Lafayette Hargrett, King Stockton, Simon Boggs, Adam Small, Richardson Harrison, Peter Dyer, John Pope, and Smart Livingston. Long, Thomas, Churchwell, Watson, Stockton, Boggs, and Hargrett achieved ordination as deacons, while William G. Stewart, Major Johnson, David Young, H. E. Bryant, Peter Spears, Fuller White, Samuel Morgan, and Noah Graham became elders. The conference also selected Pearce, Mack Steward, Bradwell, and Meacham as delegates to the Thirteenth General Conference, planned for Washington, D.C., in early May.[22]

These enhancements to the roster of preachers permitted Bishop Wayman, with urging from presiding elders Pearce and Mack Steward, to assign pastors to churches and missions that could not previously be serviced. In the Tallahassee District, the Monticello Mission would receive Joseph Alexander; Gainesville, Richard Brigadier; Ocala, Samuel Morgan; the Houston Mission, Simon Boggs; and the Centerville Mission, Frederick Barton. Out of the Marianna District came John Pope for Sim's Harbor, William Ely for Greenwood, Caesar Elby for Dry Creek, and, most importantly, David White for Pensacola. Much remained to be done, but the appointments constituted a serious step forward.[23]

These steps must have seemed tiny ones, though, compared to the political steps that were under consideration at the Second Annual Conference. Elder Pearce fumed at the Mule Team's defeat in the constitutional convention and vowed to carry the fight to the nation's capital. His anger rose to white hot when he considered the charter's provisions on legislative apportionment, which effectively denied African Americans any chance to control either house of the state legislature. He convinced enough conference members of his positions that they approved a series of resolutions aimed at the national public and the Congress. They declared that indifference or silence under the circumstances would be "criminally untrue to the great practical principle of right and justice which God has put into our hands, and to make of our religious professions but sounding brass and tinkling cymbals, as unblessed as any that ascend from Pagan altars." The resolutions then declared, "We are justly indignant at the attempt to reconstruct the State upon principles of most unequal representation in the law-making branch of the government as deceitful in its conception, as it would be disastrous in its results." They then rejected the proposed constitution and called upon the Congress to continue Florida under military rule.[24]

Pearce accomplished his political goals at the conference, although at the cost of creating a potentially ruinous split in the church. Robert Meacham opposed the presiding elder's resolutions and supported the constitution as the best possible under the circumstances. "Brother, this is wrong," he informed Pearce in a letter to one of Jacksonville's and one of Washington's leading Republican newspapers. "You are working an irreparable injury to our people, to our party, and to our State." He added, "Ministers of the Gospel, if they enter the political arena at all, should be found on the side of right, laboring for the temporal as well as spiritual welfare of the flock of whom they are the shepherds." William Bradwell came to Pearce's defense, insisting that the feud went back to the moment in 1866 when Pearce dispossessed Meacham of Tallahassee's Bethel AME and dispatched him to build a new church at Monticello. Whatever the case, the church found itself confronted by dissension from within.[25]

The intrachurch rift festered in April and May as other problems beset church leaders. For one thing, conservative whites reacted with violence and threats of violence to the fact that any Republican constitution had been drafted. According to a friend, Pearce traced "these threats of mob-violence to parties who certainly mean what they say." In early April, what may have amounted to an attempt on the presiding elder's life came up short. A local man noted that "a vile woman was found in the room with a loaded revolver" during one political meeting chaired by Pearce at Bethel Church. "It is more than suspected," he averred, "that she was expected to shoot some one of the speakers at said meeting." Two weeks later a former Republican ally challenged Pearce's integrity. William U. Saunders had dropped his opposition to the constitution. Some of its supporters enlisted him to change Pearce's mind. On April 20 Saunders offered a bribe to the churchman by way of a check drawn on the account of a prominent white conservative. Pearce rejected the overture. "I should not be surprised if Saunders has to leave the State," reported Daniel Richards. "Bishop Pearce will give him no quarters and will at the very first opportunity publicly expose his villainy."[26]

Undeterred, Pearce pursued his crusade against the constitution in Washington during May, just at the time President Andrew Johnson was undergoing trial in the U.S. Senate after his impeachment by the House of Representatives. Richards sent with him a letter of introduction to leading Radical Republicans in the Congress. "He is a man of great ability, worth and power; and he is doing a noble Christian work among and for these people," the party organizer commented. "When all around him were faltering and turning back, his regard for his people and his race was above all temptation, above price," he continued. "Through the stormy existence of our Convention, [he was] as true to the interests of his people as the needle to the pole, and up to the very last battled manfully to save his race and our state from the terrible calamity of the Rebel-Reed Constitution." Attempting to help Pearce overcome publicity about his quarrel with Meacham, Richards also stressed the church's position in Florida political life. "The Conference is of the most vital importance on the colored people," he informed Congressman Thaddeus Stevens. "They regard it as an oracle of their religious persuasion and a guide to their political conduct."[27]

Pearce's Washington quest and related events portray just how astute a leader the presiding elder could be. Determined to void the proposed constitution (he failed), Pearce nonetheless engaged the church fully in the races for elective office that were being run that spring, under the assumption that the constitution would go into effect. As a result, he, Bradwell, and Meacham won election as the twenty-four-seat state senate's only African American members. The house of representatives consisted of fifty-three members, seventeen of whom were black. At least eight were AME pastors or laymen. It was not the political start that Pearce had anticipated, but it was a start.[28]

The beginning of state Republican rule in June and July 1868 then ushered in an era of political infighting that would embroil the AME Church, among other groups, an eventuality that no one had foreseen in the heady days of constitution making. Basically, the Republican governor, Harrison Reed, offered relatively weak leadership that vacillated according to the needs of the moment between support for white conservatives and for African Americans. Still, the constitution made Reed a powerful figure because he controlled appointments to most state and local offices. Thus, the governor necessarily stood at the center of one key faction or "ring." Thomas W. Osborn headed an opposing faction. Elected to the U.S. Senate, he controlled federal patronage and money. Quickly, the two rings were tearing at each other for pre-eminence. Pearce considered Osborn treacherous, and, besides, the senator had based his support among black Baptists, not African Methodists. The AME Church, then, was left with only Governor Reed to support.[29]

The relationship between the church and the governor suffered trials from the beginning. AME policy, as guided by Elder Pearce especially, called for state protection of civil rights and support for public education.

Reed proved lukewarm to the latter and vetoed one measure that addressed the former. As his proposals languished in the legislature, Pearce saw white friends of Reed and Osborn undermining his position. "Every appeal for my race has been voted down by the Conservatives," he thundered, "aided by these weakkneed Republicans." In October the governor struck another blow. He hit directly at the church's influence by attempting to remove Meacham from the state senate. Reed's gambit worked temporarily, but Jefferson County voters returned the clergyman to the senate at a special election held in December.[30]

On the other hand, Reed occasionally acted in the church's favor. He had given Pearce, for instance, the office of Leon County school superintendent, and the elder's subordinate, Thomas W. Long, received appointment to the same position for Madison County. At the time, the state's population of 155,000 or so included about 72,000 African Americans (46 percent). Leon County contained 15,000 persons, making it by far the state's most populous subdivision. Just under 12,000 Leon Countians were black (17 percent of the state total). Madison's population amounted to 11,000 (6,300 were African Americans). Following his re-election in December, Meacham requested that Reed confer upon him the superintendency for Jefferson County, a wish that the governor granted. Jefferson held a few over 7,000 persons, including roughly 4,600 individuals who were black. Thus, by early 1869 Reed had given direct control of school systems covering approximately one-third of all African Americans in Florida to the AME Church. It was no small matter.[31]

The church rewarded the governor fully. When the Osborn ring attempted in late 1868 to depose Reed, Pearce and his allies rode to the rescue. "Mr. Pearce ... had great influence with the colored people throughout the State," explained a leading black political figure. "He was enlisted as an active agent and furnished with money to visit the various counties where trouble existed and quiet the apprehensions of the freedmen," he continued, "and he rendered great service in Leon, Gadsden, Franklin, Hamilton and other counties, in allaying the fears of the colored masses." The man concluded, "This move on the part of Governor Reed had the effect of mustering most of the colored ministers to his support." The impeachment controversy came to a head in January 1869. The northern-born white lieutenant governor was compelled to resign, and Senator Meacham temporarily replaced him as presiding officer of the state senate. Before long, the Osborn ring men gave up the fight. In appreciation of the labors of his champions, the governor threw a party in the supreme court room of the state capitol. There, Pearce, Bradwell, and friends enjoyed "a very happy interchange of sentiment" with Reed. "It was not till 'the wee, short hours ayant the twelve,'" an account noted, "that the pleasant party separated, with mutual assurance of friendship and goodwill."[32]

It clearly was more than a coincidence that, days before the impeachment attempt collapsed, the legislature finally passed with the governor's support a bill to implement fully the constitutional mandate of a uniform system of free public schools. As the AME Church insisted, it contained no restrictions on racially integrated classrooms nor any mandate for racially segregated school sessions. Senator Meacham had shepherded the bill through the senate by January 25. The house concurred the following day, and Reed signed the bill on January 30. Doubtless, Pearce and his colleagues celebrated this, their first grand legislative victory.[33]

Many were the causes for AME celebration in early 1869. The church's involvement in politics yet generated excitement among the state's African Americans, and its congregations were experiencing continued growth. By March, eleven thousand names crowded church rolls. At Jacksonville, African Methodists were enjoying the new Mount Zion Church building, erected the previous year. Pastor Bradwell maintained his family nearby in a new and comfortable parsonage. At Madison, Thomas W. Long had improved the sanctuary and constructed a parsonage. "The Lord has blessed my labors," he reported. The same story replayed itself any number of times. Bradwell summed up the general feeling. "We are progressing finely," he observed.[34]

The progress came, in part, because women had begun to exercise a larger and more influential role in church affairs. Women held the majority in southern church membership during this period, including that of Florida's AME Church. Congregations and the church at large depended on their financial contributions, as well as their work on behalf of the church. The Thirteenth General Conference, held at the nation's capital in May 1868, had recognized that fact. Its members had authorized creation of a new agency in the official AME organizational structure to be called the Board of Stewardesses. Many local congregations, if they had not already done so, soon copied the model.[35]

The presence of so relatively many educated women working closely with local pastors ranked as an important element in the gender equation. The AME Church had committed itself to the cause of education. Its houses of worship often hosted schools or else its congregations sponsored them. Accordingly, congregations actively recruited female teachers. Philadelphia's Mary Still provides an example. Teaching at Jacksonville's Mount Zion in 1868, she helped to spread the word "up North" about Florida's needs. "Our schools are doing well, but we want more teachers," she related in the *Christian Recorder*'s columns. "Young women can contribute more to building up their race out here than they can in the North," Still added. "They should not be afraid to come, as all are safe now." The teacher concluded, "There is a great deal to be done."[36]

While Florida's church leaders appreciated women's contributions and listened to their input, the institution remained male dominated in 1869 and evidenced little desire to work for guarantees of women's rights. William Bradwell expressed the sentiments of most church fathers. His words were spoken upon the presentation of a gift for his labors to raise funds to enlarge Mount Zion. Charles Pearce sat behind him as chairman of the meeting. "Ladies, I can only say to you, though you are deprived from going to the ballot and giving a vote to either party, you are also deprived from the Legislative halls, and many other places where you cannot go as men do," he began. "Yet I feel gratified to find that you are engaged in the cause of human rights, that your hearts beat with those who are fighting your battle," the minister continued. "Let me say to you, ladies, go on, be found in every good work. Crown your lives with virtue, usefulness, industry, and intelligence, which make woman lovely."[37]

Still, the Florida Conference waxed prosperous in early 1869. At its third session, convened at Jacksonville on March 20, members happily gathered under the superintendence of a new bishop. John Mifflen Brown, a man of fifty-two years, had been elevated to the episcopacy months before. He was a man of extraordinary talent and ability. Born in New Castle County, Delaware, on September 8, 1817, he ranked among the great leaders of African Methodism during the late nineteenth century. As a youth, he spent two years with William Seals, a Quaker, who taught him the importance of the work ethic. At age twenty, he learned the trade of barbering, and around that time he joined the AME Church. He also attended various schools as a youth. In 1838 he prepared for college by attending the Wesleyan Academy in Wilbraham, Massachusetts. From 1844 to 1847, pursuant to Bishop Morris Brown's appointment, he served as pastor of the AME church in Detroit, Michigan. During the same period he entered Oberlin College in Ohio, studying religion there for about four years. Brown married by 1852, to Miss M. L. Lewis. Eight children subsequently were born out of the union. From the late 1830s to the late 1860s, Brown occupied many positions in the AME Church until the general conference elected and ordained him a bishop in May 1868. With his background, training, knowledge, and experience working within the AME organization, Brown was prepared to take on the leadership of the southern district.[38]

As a man wise beyond his years, the new bishop steered clear of divisive problems in Florida. The unfortunate animosities of the previous year seemed, for the time being, distant memories. For the conference's eight days, the ministers conducted church business in a leisurely fashion, enjoying hospitality provided by the Daughters of the Conference, headed by Mary Still and Sarah Allen. Twelve petitioners were received as preachers on trial: Alexander Lofton, George Witherspoon, John Peterson, Levi Taylor, Henry Brown, George Anderson, Frank King, William Cole, Thomas T. Thompson, Josiah Armstrong, Frederick Barton, and Peter Dyer.[39]

Only a few problems seemed apparent. The political activity of the previous year had taken valuable time away from the process of church building. Some of the plans adopted for expansion in 1868 had proved too ambitious under the circumstances, and recruitment of preachers had not proceeded as expeditiously as hoped. This meant that important pastorates

18. Bishop and Mrs. John Mifflin Brown. Courtesy Photographic Collection, Florida State Archives.

19. Future AME bishop Josiah Haynes Armstrong began his ministry in Florida, where he sat from 1871 to 1875 in the state's house of representatives. Courtesy Photographic Collection, Florida State Archives.

such as Pensacola, St. Augustine, Sanderson, New Smyrna, and Mosquito River were left "to be supplied." New initiatives were few, although the Long Swamp and Lake Griffin areas of the central peninsula would receive attention, and John Thomas would be sent down the frontier line to the remote region of Tampa Bay. Otherwise, much catching up was left to do, including the development of some ideas the bishop had about education of the clergy. Conference members decided to meet again at Quincy in December, ignorant of what a difference the passage of nine months would make.[40]

4

CONNECTIONS AT LIVE OAK, 1869–1872

*African Methodism
is about to rule Florida.*

As the 1860s ended and the 1870s began, Florida's AME leaders persisted in attempting to balance their time between their ministrations to the spiritual and related needs of the church and its members and their active engagement in Reconstruction politics. Although the church was blossoming in size with the passage of time, political realities drove its leaders to devote ever greater portions of their days, weeks, and months to the messy business of temporal rule. By mid-1872 their long struggle seemed near to reaching its crest so far as political power was concerned. Real accomplishments could be toted up, but they came at a high cost. Tensions shook the church, and fissures appeared in the foundations that underlay its ability to serve its members.

A hint of the types of problem with which the church soon would deal arose out of the Third Florida Conference, meeting at Jacksonville in March 1869. The Tallahassee District's presiding elder, Charles H. Pearce, effectively ruled the conference in the bishop's absence. Yet Pearce was a busy man. In addition to pastoring Tallahassee's Bethel AME Church and supervising his district, he also served as Leon County's state senator and superintendent of schools. The public offices and associated political duties took up a great deal of his time, so much that Pearce found himself neglecting what he considered nonessential church duties. The problem became acute late in 1868 when Pearce unsuccessfully ran for Florida's congressional seat against the incumbent backed by U.S. Senator Thomas W. Osborn. As a result, the minister failed to press forward with fund-raising

20. Presiding elder Charles H. Pearce. Courtesy Photographic Collection, Florida State Archives.

for Bethel, and the church faced mortgage foreclosure early in 1869. New bishop John M. Brown learned of the problem at the annual conference in March and delayed reappointing Pearce to the pastorate. Pearce apparently could not reassure Brown to the degree required, for the bishop subsequently acted against the pastor. Brown gave Bethel—then the banner church of the Florida Conference—to his own young protégé William D. Johnson of the Baltimore Conference. Resentment stirred in Pearce's mind, a fact that did not bode well for church affairs.[1]

Typically, though, Pearce reacted to crisis by intensifying his efforts, as had been illustrated by his actions following dismissal from his pastorate. He remained presiding elder, and he determined to organize and revitalize the Tallahassee District. His principal new strategy for doing so involved protracted camp meetings. These sessions lasted one week or more, permitting rural residents easier access to religious services. Since Florida remained overwhelmingly rural and agricultural, this technique served his purposes well.[2]

21. Poet, newspaper editor, legislator, and AME layman John Willis Menard. From the collection of Canter Brown Jr.

Pearce chose for his first camp meeting experiment the tiny town of Live Oak, the county seat of Suwannee County. It offered a new field for church recruitment (no AME sanctuary yet graced the town), as well as important transportation advantages. It lay roughly half way between Jacksonville and Tallahassee, but that was not all. "Live Oak is a pleasant little town," explained a local resident in February, "located at the junction of the Pensacola and Georgia Railroad of Florida, and the Georgia and Florida branch road, connecting the Pensacola and Georgia Road with the Atlantic and Gulf Road of Georgia, thus having daily communication with Savannah, Georgia, and the principal cities of Florida."[3]

Live Oak's depot and rail connections were so important in the 1860s and 1870s that they would become legendary within the AME Church, attaining a prominence even greater for Floridians of the time than that of Atlanta's airport for modern travelers to and from the South. After the Florida Conference's First Annual Session in 1867, Bishop Alexander W. Wayman "left for the North, passed by Live Oak where I had to remain until night, and then took my uncomfortable car for Savannah, Georgia." The next year, his encounter with the town made a deeper impression:

When we reached Live Oak the supper-bell was ringing; and Brother Weaver was anxious to go in and get us a cup of tea, but he said "he would not go into the kitchen."

When the landlady came he asked for tea, and she gave us a side-table. I got through first, and stepped to the landlady and asked what was her bill? She said, "One dollar." I gave it to her. Then came Brother Weaver, and he asked what was his? She said, "A dollar." Brother Weaver said, "A dollar?" "Yes," she said, "you put yourselves on an equality with white people [by not going into the kitchen], and you must pay what they pay." My friend got very tired paying a dollar for supper. Brother Tanner enjoyed it very much indeed.[4]

African American editor and public official John Willis Menard even left a delightful poetic description of the Live Oak experience, which he called "Waiting at Live Oak":

Of all the minor woes,
A mortal undergoes,
'Tis waiting in shawl or cloak
Seven hours at Live Oak!

Waiting from nine to four,
Seven hours, sometimes more,
Amid box-cars and logs,
And the music of the frogs.

Musquitos, bugs and fleas,
Vile dust or raging seas,
Inflict, by far, less pain,
Than waiting for a train.

Ye gods of Rome and Greece,
When shall this waiting cease—
This waiting in the cold and rain
For the Savannah train!

I'd much prefer to take
A ride o'er Great Salt Lake—
The mountains of the moon,
Or to the grand Ty-coon,

Than wait in rain or cold,
With minor woes untold,
Wrapp'd up in shawl or cloak,
Seven hours at Live Oak!⁵

Live Oak's location and transportation facilities seemed ideal to Pearce, but others had begun openly to question his judgment. The elder's run-in with Bishop Brown had left him subject to criticism from within the Florida church. Barbs could not yet be directed at him personally, but details of his programs were fair game. Pearce refused to allow the second-guessing to blunt his determination to go ahead. "A great many of our friends told the Elder that it was no use for him to have a camp meeting at such a small place as Live Oak," a church member reported, "but the Elder's reply was, that he would try it."⁶

In the end, the Live Oak experiment proved a healthy success, confounding Pearce's critics. The meeting lasted eight days. One man who attended insisted that "the citizens, both white and colored, were not willing for us to break it up, but the Elder thought that he could not stay longer with them." Reportedly, average daily attendance ran about one thousand. Pearce graciously invited his Tallahassee successor, William D. Johnson, to preach. Thomas W. Long, Thomas Thompson, William Bradwell, and Pearce himself occupied the pulpit, as well. Thompson, whom Pearce had sent to Live Oak to build a church, counted at least fifty new members in his congregation. "The best harmony and much religious enthusiasm prevailed," an attendee proclaimed. "We had a heavenly time," recounted another, "the people all say they have never before heard such good preaching and seen such a loving and orderly set of Christians together."⁷

In 1869 and subsequent years the church needed ever more urgently the religious enthusiasm generated by the Live Oak camp meeting and its successors. Although the AME organization had coalesced in Florida before most of its competition had reached that point, the competitors had begun to catch up. On April 22, 1869, for example, the Florida Conference of the African Methodist Episcopal Zion Church organized at Pensacola. Its principal churches lay at Pensacola, Milton, and Key West, where the AME Church had yet to make substantial progress. The AMEZ ministers prepared, though, to spread their message throughout the state.⁸

More significantly, rumors circulated that the remaining African American members of the Methodist Episcopal Church South would withdraw to form their own church. The Colored Methodist Episcopal Church, in fact, would see life in 1870. AME leaders viewed this act as a betrayal of promises made by ME South officials to turn over church property to African Methodists. They labeled the CME Church the "rebel church" and the "old slavery church" because it maintained close ties to the white southern Methodists. Eventually, the AME Church would, as one church historian put it, "campaign to destroy the C.M.E. Church." He added, "To say, then, that the A.M.E. Church perceived the C.M.E. Church as an enemy would be an understatement." The Florida Annual Conference of the CME Church would not hold its first session until November 5, 1873. For AME Church fathers, though, the threat seemed immediate years earlier.[9]

To expand the reach of African Methodism while combating competition from these three—the AMEZ Church, the CME Church, and the ME Church—required a large corps of dedicated, trained ministers, something that the Florida AME Church lacked in 1869. From its advent in the state four years before, it had depended on a cadre of untrained local preachers, many of whom barely could read and write if they were literate at all. The South Carolina Conference had attempted to address the point in 1867 by adopting guidelines for a four-year course of study to prepare ministers for admission to full connection in the soon-to-be-created Florida Conference. The program included:

FIRST YEAR—The Bible, English Grammar, Modern Geography, Discipline of the A. M. E. Church.
SECOND YEAR—The Bible, Sacraments, Wakefield's Christian Theology, first and second part.
THIRD YEAR—The Bible History and Chronology, Wakefield's Christian Theology.
FOURTH YEAR—Review of the whole course pursued in the three previous years, and Vinet's Homiletics or the Theory of Preaching.[10]

As a stopgap measure, this course of study aided church leaders but did not solve their long-term needs for an educated clergy. Elder Pearce and his mentor, Daniel A. Payne, long had advocated more extensive training, and at the March 1869 annual conference meeting Bishop John M. Brown added the weight of his authority. Thus, at the next annual conference questions of ministerial training would rank high on the list of concerns.[11]

A second item of concern to be addressed grew out of Pearce's district-building efforts and the success of the Live Oak camp meeting. Pearce believed that the church was ready to begin contesting areas of the state in which the AMEZ and ME churches enjoyed strongholds. In the former case, this meant Pensacola and surrounding areas, Key West, and the settled portions of the Southwest Florida frontier. In the latter case, it meant Gainesville and Fernandina, among other places. Only recently, for instance, ME minister Isaac Davis of Gainesville had informed AME minister Thomas W. Long "that no African church should be built in that city." At Fernandina, AME initiatives had met with so little success that the assigned pastor, Voss Neal, had fled the town. William Bradwell insisted that he did so "to the rescue of his family, who were literally starving." He added, "Fernandina was not the best place in the world for a minister to get support."[12]

With these and other needs to be addressed, the Fourth Annual Session of the Florida Conference opened at Quincy on December 31, 1869. Bishop Brown was delayed in his arrival, and Elder Pearce convened the gathering. Sadness marked the occasion as word of the deaths of Smart Livingston and William Commends was received. Pearce then stunned his colleagues by asking, for reasons not entirely clear but that subsequent events may help to explain, that he be given one year's relief from his church duties. According to conference minutes, the request, "after a prolonged discussion, was withdrawn." That day and the next routine business occupied the forty men in attendance, including the work of committees appointed by Pearce. The assembly then adjourned until Monday, January 4, 1870.[13]

Bishop Brown sat in the chair when the conference reconvened. Pearce soon secured its concurrence in his plan to appoint a missionary to organize South Florida. A few other matters received attention during the day. Importantly, conference members admitted ten new preachers. Among them were Henry Call, who had attempted to found the state's first AME congregation during the Civil War, and John R. Scott Sr., who with Call would emerge as one of the church's great leaders. Also admitted were William D. Johnson, Benjamin Nathan, Joseph Broadinax, Peter Crooms, Amsley Hall, David Wilson, James Gaskins, and King Stockton.[14] But bigger events were on the immediate horizon.

That evening Bishop Brown sermonized on "Ministerial Education." His protégé William D. Johnson thereafter delivered a report of the conference's committee on education that spoke to "the necessity of instituting a theological seminary for preparing young men for the ministry." Johnson moved that the report be adopted and that the new school be named Brown Theological Institute in honor of the bishop. Those present who were elected as the proposed institute's trustees were Bishop Brown

22. Jacksonville's William W. Sampson. Courtesy Photographic Collection, Florida State Archives.

(chairman), C. H. Pearce, W. G. Stewart, William Bradwell, Josiah H. Armstrong, George W. Witherspoon, Thomas W. Long, Major Johnson, Robert Meacham, and W. W. Sampson. They also authorized new missions at Brooksville, Clay County, Lake George, and Bellville before adjourning, at Governor Harrison Reed's request, to reconvene at Tallahassee.[15]

The bombshells began falling when the conference regrouped at Tallahassee's Bethel Church on Saturday, January 9. As the first order of business Bishop Brown distributed his appointments to a stunned audience. Acting to consolidate his own authority, he had taken Pearce's plans for church expansion and reworked them to reduce substantially the presiding elder's authority as well as that of Mack Steward, the Marianna District head. In Steward's case, most of Florida west of the Apalachicola River save Jackson County was assigned to a new Pensacola District to be led by Washington Rivers. For Pearce the loss ran even greater. All of the Tallahassee District east and south of Madison County now belonged to a Jacksonville District. Senator William Bradwell, Pearce's colleague and the pastor of Mount Zion

Church in Jacksonville, was passed over for the office of presiding elder in favor of Thomas W. Long. In fact, Bradwell was transferred out of the district entirely. He replaced Senator Robert Meacham at Monticello. In turn, Meacham received demotion to the Aucilla Circuit. Newly ordained deacon John R. Scott Sr. took Bradwell's place at Mount Zion with concurrent responsibility for Fernandina.[16]

Then the furor erupted. As noted by a reporter present, "some discussion arose concerning the disposition of the people" before the bishop's appointments were accepted for inclusion in the conference minutes. Brown insisted that the changes had more to do with fund-raising than anything else, although William Bradwell challenged him on the point. As time passed, a motion was offered to memorialize deceased pastors. With emotions frayed, even that sparked an argument. A short while later, Pearce attempted to deflect sanctions against Fernandina's runaway pastor Voss Neal, and another fight flared. Thomas W. Long branded Neal a deserter and demanded that he be suspended. Bradwell lurched to the defense of Pearce and Neal. Long countered. Pearce thereupon "made another most touching appeal in [Neal's] behalf." At that point the bishop took the floor to mock the presiding elder. The reporter described the scene.

> The Bishop wished to warn the Conference against the seductive oratory of the gentleman who had just sat down. He was a most wonderful man; had astonishing powers of speech. He was just the man to stand up before a jury and have every one of them saturating their handkerchiefs with lachrymal fluid in a few minutes; he ran away with their sympathies, could make them believe the vinegar was sweet as molasses, and make compassion for the individual usurp the supremacy belonging to reason and judgment. He wished to see the member suspended.
>
> The Elder arose to defend himself, but the Bishop was inexorable, and would not listen, and matters began, at this juncture, to put on a belligerent aspect, but the meekness of the Elder triumphed over the situation, and prevented an unpleasant termination of the morning's session.[17]

The struggle for power within the Florida Conference played itself out, while across town the state government was embroiled in a power struggle of its own. The governor's fortunes had waxed and waned during 1869, but by year's end the faction centered around Senator Osborn and known as the

Osborn Ring once again was attempting to remove Reed from office. He begged the AME Church for its assistance during the annual conference, and many of the ministers responded positively. Led by newly ordained state representative John R. Scott Sr., AME public officials provided the margin that defeated the impeachment effort.[18]

Where the church demanded support for civil rights, public education, and social services as the price of its support for Reed, others were not so high-minded. Money seems to have changed hands in large amounts. The governor also committed his support to all sorts of get-rich-quick schemes then pending in the legislature that ultimately would cost the state a fortune. Reportedly, additional bribes greased the wheels of the legislative process to move the schemes toward passage. An odor of corruption oozed from the state capital, and the authority and credibility of the Republican party suffered yet another blow.[19]

Before the year was out the atmosphere of venality would be manipulated by Elder Pearce's enemies to discredit the church leader, but, in the late winter and spring of 1870, excitement reigned as the AME Church launched itself on the grandest journey of its short life in Florida, the "Great Revival of 1870." This was the culmination of "Bishop" Pearce's year-long planning effort begun after Bishop Brown ousted him from the pulpit of Bethel AME. The initiative would bring back together the conference's two most powerful and respected men—Pearce and Robert Meacham. It would portray African Methodism as the church militant in the African American community, shunting aside the competition of rival denominations and setting the stage for the church to exert significantly enhanced political muscle in elections scheduled for the fall.

Plans for the Great Revival seem to have unfolded smoothly. They included the opening up of Southwest Florida and portions of the central peninsula. For that assignment, Bishop Brown had selected Thomas W. Long, newly appointed presiding elder of the Jacksonville District. His missionary territory took in Columbia, Alachua, and Marion Counties, but he concentrated that spring on Levy, Hernando, Sumter, Hillsborough, and Monroe. His son Charles Sumner Long recalled that his father covered much of the vast expanse on foot and that the harsh frontier conditions challenged his father's faith:

> Between Brooksville and Tampa, while passing through a swamp, he saw a panther cross the road just a-head of him, closely pursuing a deer. The vicious animal in hot pursuit of its prey, did not see him. He

walked hurriedly for three or four miles with tears and great fears. Then he began to ask himself, "What am I doing out here? If some wild beast should destroy me, my wife and children would never know what became of me." Then it was that he heard the voice of God out of heaven, clear and distinct, saying, "Be of good cheer, lo I am with you always, even unto the end of the world." He dried his tears, his fears all left, and he reached Tampa while the sun was yet an hour high.[20]

Elder Long left churches at each major stopping place on his frontier journey. Likely in May he brought together the worshippers who, within two years, would organize Mt. Pleasant AME of Sumter County. From there he traveled to Brooksville, where he may have undertaken missionary work the previous year. There, Mt. Zion AME resulted. On June 10 at Tampa, St. Paul AME saw its beginnings. An AMEZ congregation had been meeting there since 1865. Levy County came next on the elder's itinerary, where Mt. Pleasant (Adamsville), Mt. Olive (Montbrook), Mt. Zion (near Raleigh), and Grant Chapel (Cedar Key) all formed. By steamer, Long then departed for Florida's largest city, Key West. On that island, the AMEZ Church had entered the state. Now, Long organized Bethel Church there. He also recruited a local preacher, J. I. Lowe, to return with him to the mainland and assist in other church endeavors.[21]

With Elder Long busily engaged in missionary work, other Jacksonville District ministers fueled the fires of the revival in upper East Florida. They brought together new congregations, including Sweet Canaan at Wacahoota in Alachua County; Mt. Zion at Green Cove Springs in Clay County; Ebeneezer near Ocala in Marion County; and Fort Union and Shiloh in rural Suwannee County. In July, Francis Carolina—newly licensed by Long—pushed back ME Church resistance at Gainesville. He built a sanctuary for Bethel AME before aiding L. A. Anders in doing the same for Mt. Pisgah at Archer. Others also built churches. John R. Scott led trustees John Bird, Ray S. Delaney, Harry Young, and William Young to purchase land and erect a thirty-by-fifty-foot building with a sixteen-foot ceiling for Macedonia at Fernandina. At Jacksonville, Scott superintended construction of St. Paul at LaVilla, a suburb. Within the city, he set work in motion on what "bids fair to be a very fine chapel, 40 x 70 and 20 feet from floor to ceiling." By September, Scott was claiming eight hundred new members for district churches. "Thank God we are making progress religiously and morally," he declared.[22]

23. Tampa's St. Paul AME Church, seen here as it appeared in 1892, was founded by the Reverend Thomas W. Long. Courtesy University of Tampa Press.

Although East Florida's preachers could claim progress, the Great Revival's real excitement came in Middle Florida, where Elder Pearce retained control of the Tallahassee District. He organized an April tour of the region by a group that included all three of the state's African American (and AME) state senators—himself, William Bradwell, and Robert Meacham. As an added attraction, the program featured the well-known evangelist, poet, and women's rights advocate Frances Ellen Watkins Harper of Maryland. Through area towns they traveled, drawing thousands of listeners to hear calls for adoption of a fifteenth amendment to the U.S. Constitution, for better schools, and for the AME Church. Together under AME leadership, Florida's black citizens could, as William Bradwell put it, "turn back Pharaoh's army" before it was too late.[23]

To benefit from the appearances, local ministers slated revivals and camp meetings. "During the spring of 1870 we were blessed with the greatest revival known in the memory of the oldest inhabitant," recorded William D. Johnson, pastor of Tallahassee's Bethel AME. "On one Sabbath we baptized 63 of those received on probation." William G. Stewart of Quincy may have surpassed all others. The crowds that he drew and the heights of emo-

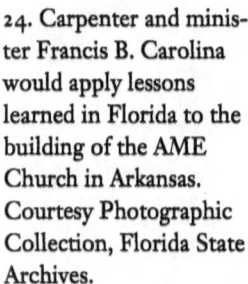

24. Carpenter and minister Francis B. Carolina would apply lessons learned in Florida to the building of the AME Church in Arkansas. Courtesy Photographic Collection, Florida State Archives.

tion he reached were recalled with amazement decades later. At one session the pastor grew so enraptured that he slipped into some sort of trance. "The spirit remained with him at one time for three days," a friend related, "and when he came to himself again he told the people of Quincy that he saw in his visions an epidemic and that hundreds died with the disease." The vision sadly proved accurate, but in April 1870 only joy filled the air at Stewart's services. When D. J. Phillips died at Jacksonville in 1894, his family still remembered his conversion by Stewart during "the great revival of 1870" as the most important turning point of his life. Stewart "commenced a revival," recalled another man, "day and night he worked to convert sinners to repentance, and when the revival ended he had five hundred converts."[24]

The results of the Great Revival in the Tallahassee District came as an answered prayer for Pearce, but the good news also set him again on a collision course with Robert Meacham. By late June the presiding elder could report the addition of 1,518 new members, with almost $4,000 raised for church purposes. That he chose to make the figures public at Meacham's home church in Monticello proved an ironic twist, for within weeks, Pearce and Meacham would announce against each other in the campaign for Florida's sole congressional seat. Both hoped to take advantage of the newly energized church with its enlarged membership. Angry at Pearce for failing to support his choices for office, Senator Osborn endorsed Meacham. When the nomination convention deadlocked in August, Pearce refused to withdraw in favor of his AME colleague and, instead, backed Alachua County's state senator Josiah Walls.[25]

Walls narrowly prevailed in the November 1870 elections to become Florida's first African American representative in Congress, but Charles H. Pearce soon discovered that his temerity in defying Osborn would exact a heavy penalty. Osborn planned to oust Governor Reed from office in January 1871 and now knew that he could not gain Pearce's support. So the senator decided to rid himself of the problem. He arranged for two of his allies to allege that Pearce had offered a bribe to a fellow state senator during the legislative wheeling and dealing earlier in the year. A Leon County grand jury reported an indictment. A former Confederate official whom Reed had appointed circuit judge presided over a quick trial. Found guilty, Pearce received a prison sentence that was suspended while he appealed. This dark cloud hung over the elder's head for well over one year.[26]

The AME Church came out of the elections of 1870 in much better shape than did Elder Pearce. A white southern Loyalist who received church support assumed the lieutenant governorship. Of seventeen African Americans elected to the state house of representatives, four—Josiah H. Armstrong, Noah Graham, John R. Scott Sr., and John W. Wyatt—were AME ministers. Alfred Brown Osgood of Madison County, who later would join the AME clergy, numbered among church layman in the lower chamber. In the state senate, Robert Meacham returned to represent Jefferson County and Frederick Hill led the vote in Gadsden. Pearce also won re-election. Baptist minister James Page, with Osborn Ring encouragement, had battled Pearce for the Leon seat. As it turned out, the AME minister bested the Baptist preacher by a margin of two to one. Not many months later, William G. Stewart summed up the prevailing wisdom among church leaders. "I am glad to inform you," he commented to the *Christian Recorder*, "that African Methodism is about to rule Florida."[27]

So it was an optimistic assemblage of clergy and laypersons that convened for the Florida Conference's Fifth Annual Session at Madison on December 15, but, once more, shock confounded them. Early in the proceedings, the church feud exploded with added rancor. It began when Bishop Brown attacked Pearce, Meacham, and others in all but name. The bishop likely had reflected deeply on the troubles experienced by other AME clergymen, particularly those endured by Henry McNeal Turner in his attempts to hold a seat in the Georgia legislature. As the minutes noted, the bishop "made some cutting remarks against the ministers engaged in politics." He then declared that he would have no sympathy for excuses made by politicians who had not fulfilled their church duties. The sentiments expressed attitudes directly opposed to those of Bishops Payne and Wayman, but they were ones that increasingly were gaining credibility within the church, given the unsavory nature of political life. Further facts about the meeting are scarce. It appears to have lasted only a short time before the bishop announced appointments and the conference adjourned.[28]

As soon as the bishop had left the state, Florida's clergymen began to mull over the church's future, given the rift that yawned between the bishop and his friends and the political preachers and theirs. Nothing could be accomplished during January and February 1871 because of the legislative session. In March, though, the church fathers acted. Twenty-one leading ministers, including the four presiding elders, issued a call for a general church conference to be held at Tallahassee on June 15. Its purpose, they stated, was "to take into consideration matters appertaining to the general interest of our people." Every minister and six laymen from each district were requested to attend. Although the bishop's name appeared on the call, his support for the meeting likely was lukewarm at best. When the time arrived, he insisted that pressing church business kept him elsewhere.[29]

Meanwhile, seeds planted by the Great Revival of 1870 began to bear beautiful fruit. On April 8, Elder Long and Francis Carolina laid the cornerstone for Gainesville's new church. Sixteen days later Long joined Allen Dean to perform the same function at Key West. "I was much surprised when I saw the rapid progress the pastor had made with his church," the elder reported. "The church is in fine condition at this time," William Bradwell observed from Monticello on April 13. "The Lord is here with us." Five months later that town's sanctuary would be dedicated with suitable ceremonies led by Pearce. By May, Palatka's parsonage neared completion and a church site had been cleared by the congregation's eighty-five members. Soon, Tallahassee began to plan a new and grander church. Other examples abounded. "Six years ago we had not a single member in the State of Florida, and not one church," Pearce declared from Tallahassee on May 5, "now we number in from 13 to 14 thousand members, 57 churches, valuing about $39,793.00, 48 Sabbath schools, and 2,500 children in attendance, also 13 parsonages."[30]

With the church reveling in its bounty and with the bishop absent, Elder Pearce found little difficulty in directing the Tallahassee general conference of June 15 to 17 to his liking. Numerous dignitaries attended, including Governor Reed and Congressman Walls. Delegates selected Pearce's friend William W. Sampson as their president, with Pearce and William G. Stewart as vice presidents. They debated and took positions on pressing issues of church and state, including racial violence, education, the evils of alcohol and tobacco, immigration, and "industrial and political interests." Then, the delegates rebuked their bishop. With William Bradwell's cosponsorship, the gathering adopted the following resolutions, among others:

> *Resolved*, That the sympathies of the A. M. E. Church are heartily with those who heartily stand up for us as a Church and as a race.
> *Resolved*, That politically our sympathies are with the Republican party.
> *Resolved*, That we will not be the tools of any politician, but we hold sacred the right to speak out in the pulpit and elsewhere in support of what we consider right, and in denunciation of what we consider wrong.[31]

The resolutions set the scene for a new act in the ongoing drama of the bishop and the presiding elder. It opened at Apalachicola on December 7 with the start of the Florida Conference's Sixth Annual Session. The first night, Elder Pearce preached from a text of 2 Tim. 4:2–5: "Be instant in season, out of season; reprove, rebuke, exhort with all long suffering and doctrine." The next day John R. Scott Sr. asked the conference to thank Pearce for his "instructive" and "able discourse to the members of this Conference." Apparently the bishop took this as an endorsement of Pearce in the face of his episcopal authority. Tension hung in the air as routine business ensued over the next several days. Consideration of educational issues prompted spirited discussions. Later, memorials for pastors Mack Steward and John Lewis—both recently deceased—were listened to with quiet respect (Fuller White succeeded Steward as the Marianna District presiding

25. St. Paul AME Church, LaVilla, as it appeared in 1889. Courtesy Photographic Collection, Florida State Archives.

elder). William D. Johnson, John R. Scott, Thomas Thompson, George W. Witherspoon, Henry Call, Adam Fort, George Anderson, John H. Peterson, Lafayette Hargrett, and Francis King were ordained as elders. Benjamin W. Roberts, Primus Gowens, William Jones, Allen Jones Jr., Henry Hall, Wiley P. Williams, Alfred Brown, John D. Haynes, Leonard Hill, James Edwards, and Warren Woods received ordination as deacons. The Reverend Long Taylor appeared at the door, joined the church, and was admitted to the conference.[32]

As the final day's business wound down, the bishop had his way in the contretemps with Pearce and the conference's other leading political preacher, Robert Meacham. In Meacham's case, Brown directed the preacher to tend to the less than prestigious Turkey Scratch Circuit. As to

Pearce, the bishop took the Tallahassee District away from its presiding elder and handed it to William Bradwell. At the same time, the bishop created for Pearce a fifth district, to be headquartered at Live Oak. The move distanced the elder from formal power in the Florida Conference, since the new district was a poor one with few members and little potential for fundraising.[33]

The genius in Brown's maneuver lay in the fact that it allowed him to use Pearce's commitment to educating the clergy as a justification for separating him from church power. That this was so stemmed from events that began in May 1870, when the trustees of Brown Theological Institute, presumably at the bishop's behest, had rejected Pearce's proposal to place the school at Jacksonville. Instead, they had chosen Live Oak for its rail connections and general location, probably citing in support of their decision the success of Pearce's camp meeting the previous summer. Someone then donated ten acres for a site, but little else occurred. In September 1871, though, the Bethlehem Baptist Association announced intentions to build their own "College of instruction for our ministers and children," largely through the encouragement of Pearce's two principal African American nemeses in Leon County politics, the Reverends James Page and John N. Stokes. It would not do to let the Baptists gain the upper hand, so enthusiasm for quick action ran high at the annual conference meeting in December. The ministers changed the school's name to Brown's Theological and Classical Institute, and they asked the bishop to appoint a financial agent to collect necessary funds. Brown convinced Pearce to accept the job, then dropped him as presiding elder of the Tallahassee District, citing all the travel and work involved in his new duties.[34]

Whatever else might be said of Charles H. Pearce, it must be acknowledged that he possessed determination and persistence in great quantities. Rather than sit idly by letting his wounds heal, he attacked his many problems head on. During the legislative session of January and February 1872, he blazed away at Osborn Ring opponents and finally abandoned his support for Harrison Reed. The hapless governor stood impeached and was, for a few months, suspended from office. Lieutenant Governor Samuel Day, whom Pearce had supported, assumed the executive office. Before adjournment, Senator Pearce also secured enactment of a charter for Brown Theological Institute. In March, he overcame his separation from the Tallahassee District in a creative way, by holding with William Bradwell joint meetings of their two districts. On April 10, the political warrior helped his church allies seize control of a Republican party convention in defiance of Reed and Osborn. One week later he suffered a setback. His appeal of the 1870 felony conviction was denied by the Supreme Court of Florida on a technicality. Then an old friend and subsequent political opponent came to his aid: Justice Ossian B. Hart, the southern Loyalist leader, convinced other officials on the state pardon board that Pearce had been victimized. They granted him a full pardon.[35]

Elated by the turn of events, Pearce redirected the focus of his attention. Now he set his sights on the church's Fourteenth General Conference, scheduled for May, and on the financial needs of Brown Theological Institute. John M. Brown's four-year term as the Seventh Episcopal District's presiding bishop neared its end. At the Nashville, Tennessee, general conference, Pearce lobbied to ensure a more congenial appointment. For the new Fifth District of Georgia, Alabama, Florida, and Mississippi, the assignment went to Bishop T. M. D. Ward. After the meeting's adjournment, Pearce traveled the North seeking funds for the Florida seminary. He succeeded to the point that, in his absence, work could begin. Caleb Simpkins of Augusta, Georgia, received the contract. Pearce returned to Florida in mid-June and declared himself "in possession of sufficient means to carry the work forward to a successful termination." Within one week a Jacksonville newspaper could report that AME friends were "engaged raising the roof of their college at Live Oak."[36]

With construction progressing quickly, Pearce announced that dedication ceremonies for the institute would be held at Live Oak on July 4. About one thousand people attended. They included a host of dignitaries, from the governor (Reed had recaptured the office) on down. Many were jockeying for AME support in the upcoming fall elections. Pearce presided in the bishop's absence. Masonic delegations performed appropriate ceremonies as the cornerstone was laid. It read:

ERECTED FOR EDUCATIONAL PURPOSES,
July 4th, A. D. 1872
BY THE A. M. E. CHURCH

REV. CHAS. H. PEARCE, P. E., FOUNDER.[37]

A hint of the future then occurred, in the form of an event that seemed insignificant at the time but that would resonate with importance before too many months had passed. Pearce called to the platform Ossian B. Hart, requesting that the justice say a few words immediately after Pearce's own address. Hart, it was reported, "returned thanks for the honor conferred on him and touched upon educational matters." Little did anyone know that the AME Church was about to help install the one-time slaveowner in the governor's chair and that, with his leadership, many of its long-cherished hopes for civil rights protections and education would be realized.[38]

5

ACTS OF GOD AND MAN, 1872–1876

*The times has been so very hard
with my people this year.*

In 1872 Florida's AME Church stood ready to ascend to the pinnacle of political and religious power in the state. It scored that November the greatest of its Reconstruction-era electoral triumphs but discovered in its aftermath a curious fact. The church's spirit and direction had begun to change. Still, optimism remained high until a series of unforeseen circumstances cast the church into turmoil and cracked the foundations of its hard-won power. Within four years, a mostly united and determined institution found itself broken apart and struggling to find its way.

The background to much of what occurred during the early to mid-1870s concerned politics. Specifically, under "Bishop" Charles H. Pearce's leadership, the Florida church had committed itself to political war against U.S. senator Thomas W. Osborn and his Republican allies. They were known as the Osborn Ring. The principal exception to this church position was Senator Robert Meacham of Jefferson County, whose political ambitions the Ring had backed. Meacham was a good man attempting to represent African Americans in Florida as best he could, but the Ring saw in his candidacies something else. They offered an opportunity for the Ring to rend the AME block and, in the process, undermine Pearce's authority. The two most influential men in the Florida church, Meacham and Pearce, had found themselves at odds for a good part of the time since 1866.[1]

As an alternative to backing the Osborn Ring, the AME leadership had buttressed Republican governor Harrison Reed. This came despite Reed's wavering support for AME causes and his sometimes blatant appeals to former Rebels. Having saved the governor from impeachment and removal on several occasions, by early 1872 disenchanted church leaders had begun to look elsewhere for promising leadership. They found it in the person of southern Loyalist leader Ossian B. Hart, a former slaveholder and now associate justice of the state supreme court. The Reverends John R. Scott Sr. and Josiah H. Armstrong led the clergymen and their supporters against Reed men, the Osborn Ring, and Senator Meacham to capture control of the Republican gubernatorial nominating convention of August 1872. "They wanted Hart and intended to have him," a spectator commented.[2]

Thanks in good part to AME demands, Hart captured the Republican party nomination for governor. Although white Republicans split their votes between the southern Loyalist and the Democratic candidates, the church energized its membership behind Justice Hart. In November, he triumphed in what even his opponents admitted was a fair election surprisingly free of violence or corruption. "Elder C. H. Pearce saved this state to the Republican party," declared newspaperman J. Willis Menard after the votes were counted. "He has been hound down and victimized by a few unscrupulous and money-making politicians since the beginning of reconstruction," Menard continued, "simply because he steadfastly refused to wear their collar and make himself their pliant tool for the advancement of their own interests and schemes." The newspaperman added, "Florida is destined to become the negro's new Jerusalem."[3]

The electoral season, in fact, had seen Pearce "hound down and victimized." The Osborn Ring and many of Leon County's black Baptists had combined in an attempt to deny the elder reelection to the state senate. Their candidate was Baptist minister John N. Stokes, a close ally of Pearce's previous Baptist adversary James Page. Pearce necessarily diverted much of his time to the state campaign, although a loss in Leon might have delivered a death blow to his political career. One newspaper put it this way: "Pearce and Stokes—one or the other of them will be laid on the shelf to day." As it turned out, the voters shelved the challenger. "Stokes was routed horse, foot and dragoons," a local editor reported. The victory, it was said, upset the previously confident Baptists. "The Stokes men," the editor added, "are very much disgruntled at their defeat."[4]

The causes for celebration extended well beyond the Hart and Pearce wins. In Marion County, Thomas W. Long achieved election to the state senate, to join Pearce, Meacham, Frederick Hill, and Washington Pope. William G. Stewart took one of Leon County's chairs in the state house of representatives. Church stalwarts Daniel M. McInnis and John R. Scott Sr.

26. Bishop and Mrs. Thomas M. D. Ward. Courtesy Photographic Collection, Florida State Archives.

of Duval County fought back concerted opposition from Baptists organized by Cataline B. Simmons to regain their house seats. "Elders C. H. Pearce and T. W. Long are the moving powers in the Senate, while Hon. John R. Scott and Wm. G. Stewart hold the balance of power in the House," observed black leader J. Willis Menard. "Mr. Scott will likely be the next speaker."[5]

The enthusiasm bubbled as the Seventh Annual Session of the Florida Conference convened at Monticello on December 28. Governor Hart's inauguration and the opening of the new legislature lay only days away. Earlier clashes between Elder Pearce and Bishop John M. Brown now seemed only memories, as the clergymen prepared to welcome Bishop Thomas M. D. Ward, who was expected to arrive at any time. Who was Bishop Ward? He had been born in Pennsylvania around 1823. His parents left Maryland and settled in Pennsylvania, where the youngster converted to the AME Church. Unfortunately, little is known about Ward's formative years or his family life as husband or father. He was said, as an adult, to be a small-framed man with a sharp narrow nose, large forehead, and sunken eyes. Licensed to preach by the AME Church, Ward presided over congregations in Philadelphia and New England and on the Pacific coast. In the latter area, he became a bishop in 1868. After four years there as prelate, he received assignment to the southern district in 1872, which had brought him to Florida.⁶

With the bishop's advent anticipated but not yet a reality, Pearce, then the Live Oak District's presiding elder, gaveled the session to order with the approval of the seventy-two ministers present. Also with their assent, he consolidated control over the gathering by appointing committees dominated by his friends Josiah H. Armstrong, William Bradwell, and William G. Stewart. On the second day, Pearce preached to his colleagues on the theme "Behold I send you forth as sheep in the midst of wolves: be ye therefore as wise as serpents and as harmless as doves." The political undertones hardly escaped the minds of his audience.⁷

The delivery of reports heightened the festive mood. The Florida Conference had grown to encompass 36 elders, 57 traveling deacons, 24 licentiates, 250 local preachers, and 12,280 members. Church prosperity radi-

27. The Florida Senate in 1875. Thomas W. Long stands in the front row holding his hat, while Frederick Hill appears directly above Long and to the right. Robert Meacham looks out from the second row from the top, third man from the right. Washington Pope apparently is the man immediately to the right of Meacham. Courtesy Photographic Collection, Florida State Archives.

ated in the hall, a great contrast to conditions of only a few years earlier. "The ministers appear to have been pretty well cared for on their missions, if we are to judge from the shining appearance of their broad cloth and fine boots," an onlooker observed, "and each one seems to take great pride telling around to his fellow ministers, what his people have done for him."[8]

It may have come as quite a surprise to the ministers that their new prelate brought with him his predecessor, Bishop Brown. They arrived about January 1, 1873, although surviving accounts provide little information beyond noting "several able and interesting discourses" delivered by the two bishops, Elder Pearce, and several others. Apparently, Ward carefully watched Elder Pearce's actions while striving to avoid reopening old wounds. Nonetheless, he succeeded in establishing his episcopal authority. The gathering would thank him for "the able and dignified manner in which he presided over the conference this session," although it did not offer thanks to Bishop Brown for his presence. Of symbolic importance, Brown's protégé William D. Johnson accepted transfer to Georgia at Bishop Ward's request. Also at the new bishop's initiative, Pearce agreed to step down from his position as presiding elder in order to concentrate all his time on collecting funds for Brown's Theological and Classical Institute, then under construction at Live Oak. Josiah H. Armstrong succeeded him.[9]

With the conference's adjournment, the church's political preachers hied themselves to Tallahassee in anticipation of great advances to come. The legislature already had convened when Governor Hart took the oath of office on January 7. Political infighting in the Republican party unfortunately denied Representative Scott the speaker's spot. On the other hand, the general assembly—which in those days elected U.S. senators—refused re-election to Thomas W. Osborn. At the same time, the legislators opted to block former governor Reed's bid for the position. Robert Meacham showed strength in balloting, before the northern Republican who bested Scott for speaker (Simon P. Conover) eventually took the honor. Meanwhile, Representative Dan McInnis's proposed civil rights act proceeded to passage with the governor's assistance. It became the first law signed by the new chief executive, capping almost five years of AME church effort.[10]

Other AME prayers found their answers. Fulfilling church desires, Hart placed Florida's emerging public school system in the charge of an African American, Dartmouth- and Princeton-educated Jonathan C. Gibbs. The governor then pushed for substantially increased funding for the schools and initiated programs for the mentally ill. He also revamped state finances and the tax collection system in order to pay for the new programs. Additionally, on January 29 Hart approved a bill of personal interest to Elder Pearce. It changed the name of Brown Theological Institute. Reflecting the new optimism of the AME church, the school henceforth would be known as Brown's University of the State of Florida.[11]

The benefits accruing to the church from the new administration continued after the legislature's adjournment. The constitution permitted the governor to appoint almost all local officials, and Governor Hart proceeded to rework Florida's corps of public servants. He stressed in doing so the importance of giving African Americans the chance to serve. AME clergymen and laymen received a wide range of offices. Hart reappointed Robert Meacham to tend to Jefferson County's public schools, for example. Governor Reed earlier had removed him. Other examples are plentiful. Hart turned to William Trapp (Alachua), Emanuel Fortune (Duval), and Fuller White (Jackson), for instance, to hold office as county commissioners. Hart entrusted Francis Carolina with the position of Columbia County tax assessor. The venerable Henry W. Call assumed the responsibilities of Walton County justice of the peace. And the list continued from there.[12]

The advances of early 1873, in an unexpected twist, set in motion a train of events that would lead the AME church away from politics and toward a purer or more rigid sense of its own role and identity. The change came about in this manner. For a time in 1873 and early 1874 it appeared to Florida's African American population that the Civil War finally had been won, with the state now the guarantor of civil rights and the committed sponsor of public education. The state also now ensured the peace. Terrible violence had beset the countryside during Governor Reed's administration. When the threat arose at Lake City in the spring of 1873, the new governor declared martial law and garrisoned the town with black militiamen. The threat dissipated, and a point had been made. "The strife is over; the antagonists have measurably expended their force," wrote an ME minister in March, "the elements are settling into closer harmony." A few months later the *New York Times* would report: "Political peace has come to the state." The release of tensions, in turn, facilitated the rise of new ways of thinking within the church. Before they could take hold, though, circumstances required that "Bishop" Pearce suffer personal embarrassment and loss. Only then could Bishop Ward lead his clergy in another direction.[13]

For those inclined to believe in such things, omens of ill tidings had begun appearing in the fall of 1872. Drought and caterpillars had attacked crops in Middle Florida, to cite two occurrences. Farmers black and white found themselves suffering hard times as a result. In the peninsula, incessant rains pounded dry soil into mud, while flooded prairies and fields bred mosquitoes in numbers beyond count. Many residents, as well as candidates in the state elections who traveled through the region, sickened from fevers. So badly was O. B. Hart affected that supporters feared he would die from pneumonia. Such annoyances, inconveniences, and worse persisted into 1873. By late that year James D. Spencer, the AME minister at Marianna, would note, "I am glad to say, though the times has been so very hard with my people this year, yet they stood by me."[14]

Had Elder Pearce read the omens correctly, he might have been able to forestall the ill luck that was about the befall him. He had collected and paid out almost $1,500 during 1872 in aid of construction at Brown Theological Institute. Charged by the bishop and conference in December with finding money to finish the job and fund the newly conceived "university," he appealed to white politicians, some of whom were not so savory in reputation. "We have nothing narrow or exclusive in our plan," he told the men, "we have no prejudices of caste or color, all will be freely admitted into our institution, whatever their profession or their race." By March 28, 1873, Pearce had $7,000 raised and was attempting to add an additional $25,000. All but $5,000 of that sum he managed to secure in the form of railroad bonds and state scrip from former Union general Milton D. Littlefield, a railroad developer then knee deep in scandal and anxious to establish strong ties with the powerful AME church.[15]

Catastrophe followed. In early April fire struck Pearce's Tallahassee home, causing damage that totaled $2,500, uninsured. "Everything he had burnt up," the local newspaper reported. The conflagration crippled Pearce financially, but it also reduced his fund-raising success to smoke. Littlefield's bonds and scrip could not be found in the ashes. Presumably they burned along with the elder's other nondisbursed collections. Townspeople held a "festival" to raise funds for Pearce's family. In the meantime, they speculated on the disaster's cause. Many believed it the work of an arsonist. As a newspaper soon would comment, "There seems to be somebody around here who has a devilish spite against Bishop Pearce." Coincidentally, Milton Littlefield watched in July as his Jacksonville properties were sold to satisfy debt. The connection of this event with the fire, if there was one, is unknown.[16]

In May, a bad situation for Pearce grew worse. A second cornerstone-laying ceremony for Brown's University took place at Live Oak. Naturally, discussion of the fire losses dogged the elder during what should have been a gala day. Unfortunately for Pearce, that was not all. His young protégé George Washington Witherspoon, then assigned to the prestigious church at Monticello, had just been accused of adultery. The accusation had come to the circuit court at Live Oak because Witherspoon earlier had pastored there. According to an AME resolution, the state attorney who propounded the charges also had slandered the church "by saying the Church was corrupt, and its ministers were all guilty of adultry." All of the charges seemed to stem from political motivations, but they angered AME clergymen while further embarrassing Pearce.[17]

Hard on the heels of these happenings, the Live Oak District meeting convened on May 22 at Madison, with Bishop Ward presiding and numerous visiting ministers from other districts in attendance. The clergymen lambasted "wicked politicians" who would attack the church and create the "fountain of wickedness" that Florida politics sometimes seemed to be. The bishop reserved his ire for Pearce. He relieved the elder of his responsibilities as financial agent for Brown University. Instead, Ward designated teams of ministers from each district to collect funds. They included John R. Scott Sr., William Cole, and Singleton Coleman for the Jacksonville District; Robert Meacham, Tally Denham, and Benjamin W. Roberts for the Live Oak District; and Allen Jones Sr., Thomas Thompson, and John H. Peterson for the Tallahassee District. Within a few months, Ward openly was criticizing ministers who strayed too close to the political life. "All men have reason to dread the professional politician," he declared.[18]

The level of anger and frustration displayed at the meeting appears from this distance all out of proportion to the problems of the moment. State affairs had enjoyed marked improvement, while church growth continued unabated. By May 1873 the Tallahassee, Live Oak, and Jacksonville districts alone counted 15,641 members exclusive of those at Tampa and Key West. This amounted to a jump of more than 25 percent in six months. In excess of eight thousand persons attended Sunday schools. Outreach in the form of a mission to the Bahama Islands seemed timely and received authorization. The cause of education, so dear to the church, prospered beyond expectation. Presiding Elder Josiah H. Armstrong reported as much from Lake City on May 14. "On closing our day-school we had an exhibition and pic-

90 ◃ Laborers in the Vineyard of the Lord

28. The Reverend Singleton H. Coleman. Courtesy Photographic Collection, Florida State Archives.

nic," the future bishop recounted enthusiastically. "About two hundred children attended, with other well wishers, and a few of the militia," he continued. "The day was fine and the children all neatly dressed formed before the AME Church and marched thence through the principal streets." Armstrong concluded, "We are improving morally and intellectually."[19]

What had occurred was this. The immediate need for the kind of political commitment and activism personified by Charles H. Pearce seemed to many church people to have passed. This permitted long-simmering resentments of political preachers and of the church's detour away from religion to resurface among the clergy and influential members of the laity. These sentiments rarely found voice at times when the need to address political crises took precedence. In those periods Pearce remained virtually all-powerful within the Florida church, as he eventually had demonstrated during his conflict with Bishop Brown. Recent events, though, had changed all that. Bishop Ward had proved it so by displacing Pearce—with little opposition—from his presiding eldership and then from his position as financial agent.

These changes, coming about almost without notice, turned the church's gaze inward. As the proceedings of the Live Oak District meeting illustrated, issues of temperance, tobacco use, and education now received greatly enhanced priority. This especially was the case with respect to the clergy itself. Moral rectitude replaced political adroitness as a quality that commanded high esteem (and rewards within the church). "Now I will tell you what we want in Florida," Josiah Armstrong informed readers of the *Christian Recorder*. "Preachers and teachers who have good morality to teach our people not only by precept but by example; and in ten years time the AME Church will have a power that will surmount all that oppose it." Armstrong and his peers equated such strong morality with good education. At Madison, they declared, "We believe the hour has come when we as a church must either encourage sanctified learning or be blotted out as a church."[20]

Thus, the turnabout in church focus reinforced the AME commitment to building and maintaining a seminary. The ministers at Madison accepted without question that this meant carrying out plans already made for an institution grander than a mere school for preachers. They pledged to pursue "every available means to complete and endow Brown's University at Live Oak, Florida," and they set out to do just that. One large event, a camp meeting at Gainesville in early September, seemed to bode well for the project.[21]

At that point disaster struck again, this time with double force. On September 19 the New York banking firm of Jay Cooke and Company collapsed, sparking a national economic depression so severe that its impact still would be felt decades afterward. History would remember it as the Panic of 1873. On the same day, much of Florida found itself dealing with another kind of blow. A massive hurricane swept into Middle Florida, laying waste towns, farms, and churches. Newly commissioned Tallahassee postmaster William G. Stewart lost his recently completed home. At Live Oak the winds destroyed cotton in the fields, blew down fences, and ripped up buildings. One of them was the almost-completed Brown's University. "A gentle little zephyr from some unholy locality came wandering down to Florida for its health; a stupid little zephyr, unable to distinguish between a house dedicated to the Lord and one dedicated to the service of the devil," said one resident in an attempt to see some humor in the catastrophe, "so it let the [Live Oak] barroom alone, probably the whisky was too strong for it and tackled the seminary." He continued, "It tugged and pulled and then spit on its hands and pulled agin, until this skeleton of a proposed preacher factory tumbled to the ground in ruins, and the zephyr, not quite satisfied, picked up the fragments and scattered them unto the four points of the compass."[22]

Bishop Ward reacted to the tragedy by opting to place responsibility for raising funds required for rebuilding the university in the hands of a white ME minister, Dr. R. O. Sidney. Their agreement entitled Sidney to 15 percent of all money he raised, an arrangement similar to Pearce's earlier understanding. The clergy rallied around the minister, inviting him to attend all manner of church functions. Sidney found the way hard going, though, a fact that might have tipped off church leaders that they had distanced themselves from their membership. At Station One in late October, for example, thousands turned out for a camp meeting headlined by William Bradwell. Their contributions to Brown's University totaled a mere twelve dollars.[23]

Other signs of problems also appeared. After the surge in membership that followed the elections of 1872, new converts came few and far between, while recent additions melted away from local congregations. At the Station One camp meeting, only nine persons came forward out of thousands. By December, presiding elders would report fewer than eleven thousand members supporting 119 churches. What with ruined crops, hurricane damage, and the beginning effects of national economic depression, times for many had turned hard. Victims possessed few dollars for church support. The drop-off also may have represented resistance to the recent trend in church policy. Moreover, a separate dynamic probably came into play. AME championship of the race as evidenced by its political activism had drawn many a convert to its banner. With the victory apparently secured, the allure may have faded.[24]

The falloff in membership mirrored a slump in AME political fortunes. At special elections held in November 1873, particularly those in Duval County, voters telegraphed disenchantment. "There was no political principle involved in the contest," noted a Jacksonville newspaper, "but it was, practically, the AME Church against the field—and the field won." The *Florida Union* added: "The AME Church in this county, under the leadership of [John R.] Scott, has been for years endeavoring to control the county as the AME Church at large, under Pearce, Scott, and other political ministers, has been endeavoring to control the State."[25]

Another circumstance that should have caused church fathers to reconsider their situation came as a legacy of the 1872 campaign. Governor Hart, who had never really recovered from the pneumonia he had contracted then, left the state in June to convalesce in the North. In his absence Lieutenant Governor Marcellus Stearns, a one-time member of the Osborn Ring, held the executive authority. Some unruly whites took the opportunity to reassert their own power, particularly after news arrived in late summer that Hart neared death. Violence flared thereafter in isolated instances.[26]

The violence touched the AME Church and its members. Cornelia McPherson, considered "the mother" of the church at Starke, was shot and killed in one such event. Minister Richard Brigadier reported the October 24 incident.

> She and myself and her husband and two of her sons were sitting at the supper table on Thursday night about 7 o'clock, and there came a posse of armed men and fired a pistol. They aimed to kill David, her son; they missed him, and the ball almost scalped me. They fired again with their double-barrel shot guns three times. David called to his mother to shut the door. She ran to do it, and received seven buckshot in her body. Her son was also killed instantly. She lived about two hours, and before she died, she called to her Lord and said, "Oh Lord come, and come quickly."[27]

Although not with such fatal results, Bishop Ward experienced the unsettled conditions personally following adjournment of the annual conference meeting in December. "On our way from Conference a band of rowdies who had got on the train promised to give us some trouble," he recorded. "After breaking and smashing in its glass windows they began to fire off pistols, the balls flying in a direction I didn't much like." Unbowed by the assault, the bishop acted to end the unpleasantness. "I thought it was about time to advance on the enemies' works, and therefore gave the command," he concluded. "We silenced their guns, took one prisoner, gave him into the hands of Presiding Elder [William W.] Sampson, who will attend to his case in Jacksonville."[28]

The confidence evidenced by Bishop Ward's actions, though few recognized it at the time, added to the church's mounting but unappreciated problems. He was the type of individual who could project confidence, filling others with reassurance. "Bishop Ward was one of the most eloquent men the Church ever produced," Charles Sumner Long averred. "He had a

29. Wilberforce University graduate Benjamin W. Roberts held public office at Key West while ministering to the community. He later contributed as a church builder in Texas, where he died in 1904. Courtesy Photographic Collection, Florida State Archives.

voice like a lion; and in the pulpit, or on the platform, he had few equals in his or any other generation." Long continued, "His spirit was like a great magnet, it drew and thrilled all that came in touch with him." The problem arose from the fact that, while Ward's personality and talents permitted him to transmit confidence to others, his experience had not prepared him to understand the reality of conditions in the South. Born a free man in Pennsylvania in 1823, he had spent his long church career in New England and on the Pacific coast. The bishop had little direct contact with slavery, southern politics, or racial violence. In the circumstances, he misunderstood the potential gravity of conditions brewing in Florida during late 1873.[29]

Still, Bishop Ward felt great confidence and inspired many of his colleagues with it during the Eighth Annual Session of the Florida Conference, held at Gainesville on December 20. "We had a glorious time," the bishop declared. A total of 104 ministers attended. The gathering had grown so large that it could not fit inside the town's sanctuary. So, as Ward observed,

"We adjourned to the woods and ordained nine Elders and thirteen deacons." The former group included J. D. Harris, Austin McGriff, Benjamin W. Roberts, Allen Jones Jr., Wiley P. Williams, Warder Wood, William Cole, and Allen Dean. The latter contained Herbert B. DeVaughn, Washington Jones, William Jones, John Speight, Asa Dudley, Singleton H. Coleman, Sidney Powell, Abram Grant, and Milton Trapp. The meeting spent little time formulating plans for new programs to combat membership losses in Middle and East Florida or to prepare for political contingencies. Rather, the bishop pressed for missionary work in West Florida, where the church had yet to prosper. Ward designated John W. Wyatt, a former legislator known for a take-charge attitude, to spearhead the assault.[30]

As the year 1874 began, apparent peace lulled church fathers. Governor Hart had returned to the state late the previous year—ailing but better—and had reassumed power. Perpetrators of the recent acts of violence desisted. When the legislature assembled in January, the governor proudly exclaimed, "It is . . . very gratifying to know that the spirit of political hatred and bitterness, which was the fruit of the great rebellion, is well nigh extinguished, and that the people of all parties are more united and harmonized than they have been for many years." He reported that the state now operated five hundred free public schools for eighteen thousand children. With solid support from AME legislators, Hart secured additional funds for school construction and teacher pay. The days passed quickly, as the governor expanded his administration's program of reform, reorganization, and extension of government services. "This legislature is the best we have had to be sure," concluded one observer.[31]

Malignant storms then struck, one after another, beginning March 18. That day Governor Hart died suddenly at his Jacksonville home. The Republican party separated again into warring factions. Political chaos soon prevailed. Meanwhile, as the fallout from the Panic of 1873 grew in magnitude, the Freedmen's Bank at Jacksonville failed. It ceased paying depositors in May and closed the next month. The Tallahassee branch followed. The closings bankrupted hundreds of depositors, many of whom were AME ministers and laymen. More bad news arrived in August. At the state capital, Superintendent of Public Instruction Jonathan C. Gibbs collapsed and died. By then Gibbs stood as the most well-respected African American political figure in the state. Many Florida blacks had depended on the Presbyterian minister to lead them out of the confusion in which they suddenly found themselves.[32]

As if this were not enough, the church suffered several additional calamities. A heavy wind storm hit Live Oak in mid-May, apparently inflicting damage to the Brown's University construction. About that time, the financial agent, Dr. Sidney, absconded. "He collected more than three thousand dollars from the people as his receipts showed," Morris Marcellus Moore related. "He failed to pay the carpenters; used the money for self aggrandizement and ran away," the bishop continued, "but for his dishonest deeds to the people who had just been made free, was over taken in a storm, and the great God of the Heavens strangled him to death beneath the maddening waters of the Atlantic, to await the judgement trumpet of the Arch Angel."[33]

At a Jacksonville District meeting in June, Bishop Ward wrestled with his own embarrassment and disappointment. "A rich man who will borrow dollar money from poor traveling preachers and then forget to return it, is unworthy of either private respect or public confidence," he thundered in anger, although whether his target was Sidney or the Freedmen's Bank officers is not known. The subject of the university had become a sensitive one, and he stepped away from his support for it. Instead, he expressed frustrations at what he now saw as pretensions on the part of young, educated clergymen, indirectly challenging the necessity for persisting in the development of an institution such as Brown's University. "Many of our young men both in and out of the ministry will not kneel in the house of prayer for fear of getting dust marks upon their shining broad cloth," he commented. Almost with a sigh of resignation, he added, "The moral and intellectual work to be done for our people in the South is simply Herculean; and nothing short of the power of God will accomplish the collosal task."[34]

Henceforth, the bishop placed his emphasis on stern morality, rather than on building up a university. He made the point by disciplining a young minister for "neglecting his wife." Defensively, Ward asserted, "He had a fair trial and the judgment of the meeting was that he must support his wife." A greater point was at stake, though. "This is the fight which is now raging between the forces of Liberty, and the minions of oppression," he argued, "and the war will not cease until moral worth and mental excellence shall be the criterion by which men will be measured." As far as grand edifices were concerned, Ward articulated his view by what he did not include in his report of the meeting to the *Christian Recorder*. After consecrating the banner church of East Florida African Methodism, he observed

30. Governor Marcellus Stearns greets *Uncle Tom's Cabin* author, Harriet Beecher Stowe, on the steps of Florida's capitol in April 1874, the month following Governor Ossian B. Hart's death. State Senator Robert Meacham and his family may be seen standing to the far right on the capitol's upper level. Courtesy Photographic Collection, Florida State Archives.

simply: "Sunday morning, June 21st. Mount Zion AME Church was dedicated to the worship of God." All details of the event and its participants were omitted.[35]

In the succeeding months of 1874, happy reports from AME congregations became rare. Only at Marianna and Pensacola, it seems, did the spirit of joyful progress prevail. "Our church is doing well," acknowledged Joseph Spears from Marianna. "We have a good time now." John W. Wyatt had arrived at Pensacola in February to discover "eighteen persons just forming a church." He commenced building a sanctuary measuring fifty-two by thirty-four feet. By August he claimed at least a partial victory. "Though the sinners was before me, of the [AME] Zions on the one side and the Baptists on the other," Wyatt insisted, "'but having obtained help of God we continued unto this day.'" He asked as a reward that the bishop bring the year's annual conference to his city. "Our people are coming home at last in Pensacola," Wyatt concluded.[36]

Anxious for the comfort and support of any shining light, Ward acceded to Wyatt's request and called the Ninth Annual Session of the Florida Conference for Pensacola on December 26. The conference did not go well. To the good, the slide in membership had been arrested, at least temporarily. Although the number of churches had dropped from 119 to 111, an addition of 240 names to the rolls had upped total membership to 10,913. Also to the good, Wyatt had rushed construction on the Pensacola church (Allen Chapel) so that the bishop could dedicate it during the conference. The effort cost the minister $1,000 of his own money. Ward saw the structure as "a good building," noting also that it boasted "a bell in the tower that can be heard five miles off." He rewarded Wyatt by backing his election as an elder. On Sunday, December 27, the ministers fanned out through the town to preach and to impress the residents with the strength and size of the AME Church. "The preachers having kindled a fire at Pensacola...," the conference secretary reported, "as to make the Pensacolians realize a lasting impression of the success and importance of the AME Church."[37]

The positive news failed to outweigh the negative. Membership remained depressed. The bishop attempted to put as pretty a face on the matter as he could by asserting that the Florida preachers "now control over 40,000 souls." Recent elections had produced more ill tidings. Republican losses meant that the Democrats might well organize the legislature, while the church's political preachers had confronted each other personally and in support of candidates that they all might have opposed two years earlier. A despondent Charles H. Pearce left the state senate for good. Meanwhile, his protégé George W. Witherspoon battled Robert Meacham for supremacy in Jefferson County. Meacham, in turn, narrowly failed to secure a congressional nomination that Pearce also had wanted. At the Pensacola conference, the remote location and the nature of church finances combined to produce a low turnout of ministers. The town's several dozen African Methodists found themselves swamped trying to accommodate those who did attend. By Monday, the somber mood had convinced conference members to adjourn, pending reassembly at Tallahassee on February 20 after the legislative session's close. Perhaps by then, it was hoped, some solutions might have appeared.[38]

They did not. Exhaustion, more than anything else, brought some sense of comfort to the Tallahassee meeting. The ministers had spent their energies stemming the tide of defections, fighting the political wars, ministering in increasingly difficult circumstances, and simply getting to and from church conferences. Optimistically, Bishop Ward believed that, at least within the church, differences could begin to be laid aside. "Much of the spiteful feeling, the offspring of political differences were I trust forever buried," he hoped of the meeting's outcome. Elder William Bradwell's request, subsequently granted, for a transfer to the Georgia Conference seemed to suggest otherwise.[39]

Through 1875 the church endured a slow bleeding. Almost two thousand members quit its ranks (leaving a total of 8,947), despite missionary efforts primarily in East Florida that increased the number of churches by 18, to 129. As Henry Call mentioned, "In many portions of the [Pensacola] district, there were no permanent organizations of our church whatever." John Wyatt by midyear delighted in claiming that the Pensacola church remained "alive." The once-thriving Fernandina outpost slumped badly. "Our church here has been surrounded by unfavorable circumstances from its organization," commented preacher J. J. Sawyer, "except a period of two years when elder John R. Scott had charge of the congregation, and built the house in which we now worship, which is in every way what we want when it is finished." Similarly, at St. Augustine just sixteen members continued their affiliation, prompting Scott to remind others that the town was "the home and strong den of Roman Catholicism." Middle Florida found itself mired in the doldrums. "There seems to be very little Union among the leaders in that once leading district in the state," Scott commented. "Now it stands far behind."[40]

As the church bled, Brown's University lay moribund. Once Dr. Sidney fled with its funds, all hopes were transferred to Congressman Josiah Walls. In December 1873 he had introduced a measure in the Congress to grant the institution one million acres of public lands. It died in the Forty-third Congress, but the bill could have been resubmitted in late 1875. Walls chose not to do so, though. Instead, he spent much of his time fighting attempts—ultimately successful—to remove him from his seat. Bishop M. M. Moore told the rest of the story. "The people became disheartened and refused to give any more money toward the building," he recorded, "the carpenters sued the board of trustees and obtained a judgement in the court; the building was sold to the highest bidder, the timber and other material was disposed of, and thus ended Brown Theological Institute and Brown University."[41]

Watching these developments from Jacksonville, Presiding Elder John R. Scott and his friends increasingly resented what they saw as Middle Florida failures dragging down the East Florida church. Scott believed that almost all the membership drop had come in the old plantation counties where political and personal squabbles went on unabated. He also resented the mess at Live Oak. To the elder, a Jacksonville home for Brown's University would have ensured its success. He looked around him at Jacksonville, which was growing by leaps and bounds and where African Americans were prospering, and saw only bright promise for the future. "We have Jacksonville well fortified now," he observed in September. "Rev. Abraham Grant commands East and West, with marked success," he added. "Rev. Thomas Higginbotham commands North and South, in every way creditable for a young man." The outcome of large camp meetings in July and August encouraged his perceptions. They would not soften with the passage of time.[42]

Unsettled and troubling, then, were conditions when the Florida Conference celebrated its first decade of existence at Jacksonville on February 26, 1876. Bishop Ward opened the Tenth Annual Session, which would be the last of his four-year term. He and Charles H. Pearce must have debated the conference's problems at length prior to the gathering. The old antagonists now displayed a newfound sense of cooperation. Pearce offered a prayer and "addressed the throne of grace." Within days, the bishop had returned Pearce to his former position of authority, the presiding eldership of the Tallahassee District. Perhaps the old warrior could breathe new life into the Middle Florida church. Through the conference, Pearce's East Florida colleague Scott watched and, for the most part, kept his own counsel about matters of concern. Whatever his personal feelings about Pearce, he likely assessed the elder's chances of success as poor. It would take something else to satisfy Scott, something that the coming general conference and a new bishop might be able to accomplish. His plans dealt little with mending the Florida Conference. Rather, he had decided to divide it.[43]

6

REDEMPTION AND THE EAST FLORIDA CONFERENCE, 1876–1880

*Where are now
the hopes I cherished?*

When the Reconstruction era ended for Floridians in 1877, important elements within the AME Church already had begun to view political activism as a corrupting influence, to be abhorred by its clergy. As the church backed away from political involvement and instead stressed tenets of stern morality, its membership totals coincidentally plummeted. Important leaders in East Florida blamed the shortcomings of old-guard Middle Florida ministers for this development and demanded that the Florida Conference be divided. But the old warriors had not yet given up on their commitment to political victory. With the church's missionary efforts stagnating in many areas of the state, they launched a renewed assault on Democrats and white Republicans alike, hoping to capture, at last, real temporal power for African Americans and for the church.

Reconstruction's days were numbered when the Tenth Annual Session of the Florida Conference met at Jacksonville's Mt. Zion Church on February 26, 1876, but participants could not yet discern that fact with any clarity. True, the Republican party had split again into garrulous factions, but upcoming elections still could be won. African Americans retained many positions of power. AME elders Robert Meacham and Thomas W. Long remained in the state senate, along with laymen Frederick Hill and Alfred Brown Osgood. Eighteen African Americans held seats in the house of representatives, including Josiah H. Armstrong (Columbia County), Joseph E.

Lee (Duval County), and George Washington Witherspoon (Jefferson County). Additional scores of AME members served in county and municipal offices. Moreover, a number of church members and clergymen occupied federal offices, such as postmaster and deputy marshal positions. John R. Scott Sr. held one of the highest ranking U.S. government jobs in the state; since 1873 he had run U.S. revenue collection operations at Jacksonville.[1]

At the same time—through a complicated mixture of violence, other forms of intimidation, fraud, frustration, and disenchantment—black men in the United States gradually were losing access to the ballot or else declining to run for office at both the regional and the state levels. Florida followed the trend. Its results alarmed many AME preachers, but the situation did not inspire them sufficiently as a group to bring about a reversal of the church's recent movement away from direct political involvement. Even if the state government fell into Democratic hands, the churchmen reasoned, they could take comfort from the fact that, the previous year, the federal government had promised to safeguard their rights. The Civil Rights Act of 1875, in fact, had spoken of "the equality of all men before the law" and the obligation of the U.S. government to "mete out equal and exact justice to all, of whatever nativity, race, color, or persuasion." The measure specifically had assured "all persons within the jurisdiction of the United States" that they could take "full and equal enjoyment" in all public, quasi-public, and private accommodations that served the public (theaters, inns, railroad cars, etc.).[2]

Of course, some of the ministers rejected the prevailing trend of thought and insisted that, church policy notwithstanding, they must help lead the state out of the storm clouds they feared lay on the horizon. Elder Charles H. Pearce, for example, would opt by mid-1876 to back Governor Marcellus Stearns as the lesser of evils, despite Stearns's credentials as a former Osborn Ring member. At the February annual meeting, though, Pearce had felt it necessary to offer a resolution "providing that no one be admitted hereafter into the Conference as members who were involved in political pursuits." The circumstances suggest that he was attempting to head off a stronger measure that might have affected him. They also hint that he believed that he had found a powerful ally. Just before Pearce acted, Dr. Henry McNeal Turner, a future AME bishop and renowned Georgia political activist, was introduced to the assemblage. Pearce's motion, after "a warm discussion," gave Turner the opportunity to suggest "that the Conference should not commit itself, neither pro, nor con," and to advise the elder "to withdraw the motion." Likely with a sigh of relief, Pearce complied. The minutes noted that "much time was saved" thereby.[3]

Other church leaders agreed with Pearce on the need for political involvement. William G. Stewart aided Elder Pearce while serving as Tallahassee's postmaster, a position that gave him influence over all postal operations in the state. John R. Scott Sr. maintained close ties to Republican U.S. senator Simon P. Conover and organized Duval County for the party. Robert Meacham sat on the Republican state executive committee and kept one eye on the possibility of a congressional seat. With the other eye, he watched the doings of Pearce's protégé George W. Witherspoon, then ministering at Monticello in Meacham's Jefferson County. Witherspoon was beginning to emerge as an activist of more radical stance than that of his mentor or any other AME political preacher.[4]

Even among those who accepted the need for politically active preachers, a marked difference of opinion existed with respect to what issues merited the involvement of clergymen. Many believed that the basic political fights of Reconstruction had been fought and either won or else lost for good. This especially seemed plausible following enactment of the Civil Rights Act of 1875. In line with the recent trends of church thinking, they felt that moral issues deserved priority over governmental ones. Although tobacco use constituted one matter of great concern, the issue that would spark the most passion was the use of alcohol.

The temperance movement pre-dated the Civil War, and the issue had been a matter of discussion within the Florida Conference from its earliest days. At its Fourth Annual Session, for instance, William G. Stewart had crafted for conference members a resolution on the subject. "We believe the use of intoxicating liquors is an evil and ought not to be used by any minister of the Gospel," it read, "that no preacher who feels the importance of his high and holy calling, can for a moment, we believe, think of indulging in the use of this unholy fire, which so often sets the tongue on fire of hell." It concluded, "If it is not good for the minister, then it cannot be good for the membership."[5]

The 1869 meeting's minutes are unclear as to whether the conference adopted the Stewart report, but the "Convention of Ministers" held at Tallahassee in July 1871 picked up the same theme in a statement scripted by William Bradwell.

> Your Committee on Temperance beg leave to report that we deprecate the use of intoxicating drinks and tobacco among our people, as

defacing God's image in the soul of man, despoiling the intellect, depraving the moral sentiment, and fitting him for degradation and vice. In view of the flood of misery and wretchedness that has swept over our people, as ministers of the Gospel we will resolve ourselves to look not upon the cups of intoxication, to give no countenance to its use in ourselves or others, or to its traffic; that we will in no wise be partakers in this destructive evil, and that among our members we will increasingly call attention to the first clause of the eleventh statutory law in our Book of Discipline, page 170, twelfth edition, and urge that it become the duty of each minister in charge of the several churches to organize Temperance Societies, that in this also we may present our lives and bodies an acceptable sacrifice to God.[6]

The words set a high standard for AME adherents and tended to be honored more in the breach than church fathers would have preferred. Temperance men persisted in trying to make the cause a paramount church priority, although they met with little success by the mid-1870s. Even with stern morality taking a front seat by 1876, the annual conference shied away from committing itself too strongly on the issue. A temperance committee composed of B. W. Roberts, Thomas W. Long, and N. B. Sterritt proposed "total abstinence from spirituous liquors, as well as tobacco." No vote was taken on the measure. Rather, those present "discussed very ably" the temperance cause. In the end, "there were a good many acknowledgments of the good the former efforts against the two evils had accomplished."[7]

While in 1876 the Florida Conference could avoid an issue as divisive as total abstinence, another day lay around the corner. One major impetus for the change arose out of the creation of temperance societies that were independent of, but closely associated with, the church. Particularly, later in 1876 the International Order of Good Templars (IOGT) Grand Lodge of England of the Right Worthy Grand Lodge of the World authorized the creation of subsidiary lodges in Florida. This initiative came as late as it did because earlier attempts had centered on the Templars Right Worthy Grand Lodge (RWGL) of the United States. That body had balked at associating black Florida lodges on equal terms with white lodges. In 1873 a Jacksonville group had received a charter, but it had arrived with the standard clause erased that authorized representation with the grand lodge. Lodge members saw it revoked a year or so later, according to AME layman Joseph E. Lee, "because WE WERE COLORED PERSONS." A Key

31. AME minister, state official, federal official, and attorney Joseph E. Lee lived in Jacksonville until his death in 1920. Courtesy Photographic Collection, Florida State Archives.

West request simply met rejection. "The I.O.G.T. was only established for *white* people," a white officer informed Lee. Subsequently, Lee spearheaded efforts to secure a nondiscriminatory charter from the Grand Lodge of England.[8]

Once established in Florida's African American community, the IOGT under Joseph E. Lee's leadership enjoyed substantial success. Within two years, four separate lodges operated at Jacksonville with encouragement from Lee, John R. Scott Sr., A. W. Walker, and J. C. Waters. Additional lodges existed at Key West, Pensacola, Tampa, Ocala, Mandarin, St. Nicholas, LaVilla, Magnolia, Darbyville, Baldwin, and Monticello (where George W. Witherspoon preached). Funds that otherwise might have supported an AME Church badly in need of them poured instead into the new organization. At Jacksonville, for example, supporters erected an impressive Good Templar Hall measuring sixty by thirty-three feet. Yet much, if not all, of the initiative involved in spreading the order came from within the church's East Florida region. "I am glad to see that the Order is being spread, north and south, among the colored people, chiefly by the ministers of the AME Church," reported a Key West backer. "A nobler mission they could never engage in."[9]

The church's national organization supported the Good Templars as enthusiastically as did the preachers of East Florida. The order's principal historian, David M. Fahey, concluded, "AME clergy and laity joined the RWGL of the World in disproportionate numbers." Bishop Daniel A. Payne became just one of many church leaders to associate themselves with the order. By 1878 the *Christian Recorder* had become, in some respects, an IOGT organ. Sentiment ran warm for the organization not only for its antialcohol stance but also for its racial one. IOGT news appeared in the *Christian Recorder* under the RWGL of the World's seal, which displayed a black man and a white man shaking hands. After attending one international gathering, Joseph E. Lee summed up the feelings of many. "*For the first time in my life* I took as a *brother* the hand of the Englishman, the Irishman, the Welshman, the Scotchman, the American, and the African," he declared, "feeling that I was in truth a man."[10]

What then did the Good Templars have to do with the Florida AME church's political involvement? Two points should be made. First, of the church's political preachers who served in the legislature after 1876, the real energy came not from old warhorses such as Pearce, Meacham, Long, and Bradwell, but from younger men such as John R. Scott Sr., Joseph E. Lee, and George W. Witherspoon. Rather than fighting what they saw as hopeless political causes, they often concentrated in their legislative work on moral issues such as temperance. Lee made the point in a letter to international lodge officials. "Being a member of the Legislature of this State, and having introduced, at its last sitting, a Bill the object of which was to make the *liquor seller* from whom *any* intoxicated person might obtain his liquor pay the damage that such person might incur, or be put to, or cause to be incurred," he proudly informed them, "I became pretty generally known in this state as a Temperance advocate."[11]

The second political ramification of the temperance cause that would affect the AME church involved the use of alcohol or the toleration of its consumption as a weapon for political attack. This did not so much apply against church outsiders as it did against church insiders. The main case in point arose in Jefferson County, where George W. Witherspoon engaged in continuing conflict with Robert Meacham over religious and political supremacy. With the Good Templars rise spurring the temperance cause by 1878, Witherspoon would direct the ire of fervid converts onto his fellow churchman. The event happened as Meacham sought a congressional seat despite Witherspoon's opposition. With the political heat rising, the Mon-

32. Bishop Daniel A. Payne served as mentor for Isaiah H. Welch, seen here during his student days at Wilberforce University. A Civil War veteran of the famous 54th Massachusetts Volunteers, Welch remains known in Florida in good part because of his church activities at Tampa and Pensacola. Courtesy Photographic Collection, Florida State Archives.

ticello congregation put Meacham on trial for intemperance and ejected him from its pulpit. "Poor fellow!" blared a Democratic Tallahassee newspaper, "politically and religiously dead! dead! dead!" It added, "'Where are now the hopes I cherished?' &c."[12]

Importantly, though, the temperance cause's powerful impact on the Florida church still lay somewhat in the future in 1876, leaving other matters at the forefront of consideration during the Tenth Annual Session. Questions of politics, it seems, found no airing, although former governor Harrison Reed attempted to raise the issue. "He referred to the past history of our connection in the State," an account noted, "and said he hoped that the same course would be pursued for the common good of the State and country." The ministers declined to take the bait. Rather, education "became the special business of the conference." Elders Pearce and W. W. Sampson, with others, pleaded for renewal of the commitment to Brown's

University. In future years Bishop Thomas M. D. Ward would proclaim, "If we neglect our educational matters we will go to the wall as sure as God sweeps the seas with the tempest." Now, he temporized in the face of depleted membership rolls and empty coffers. This left Dr. Henry McNeal Turner with little room for giving counsel. "His advice was for the young men to study, for the advance of the people would soon demand an Educated ministry," recorded the conference secretary. Turner singled out English grammar as one key subject to pursue. Isaiah H. Welch, with support from Elder Scott, anxiously hoped to save the school. He introduced a resolution to move it to Jacksonville. After a "lengthy and spirited debate," the conference agreed, but, for all intents and purposes, the great dream had died aborning.[13]

Naturally, the conference admitted new ministers, including N. B. Sterritt, Walker Swain, Scott Roberts, Edwin Pinckney, Aaron Hammond, C. L. Hadley, Edmund Williams, Thomas S. Delaney, and Nelson Watson. Readmitted were Alfred Brown, Sidney Powell, John Speight, Robert Eppes, Abram Grant, Jacob I. Lowe, B. W. Roberts, M. A. Trapp, Tally Denham, W. L. Jones, Dennis Fuller, Moses Robinson, Asa Dudley, Samuel Jackson, John Tyler, Walter Glimp, and Primus Gowens. All were accepted as deacons, plus Edmund Smith, John Taylor, James Edwards, Ben Williams, George Washington, Washington James, Richard Hays, W. A. Brise, Leonard Hill, Silas Marshall, A. J. Kershaw, J. R. Robinson, S. Barnes, Thomas Higginbotham, Jacob Sutton, Anthony Davison, A. Lofton, King Stockton, G. Reed, Simon Boggs, Francis Lavette, Alexander Godwin, and E. Campbell. Sterritt also received elder's orders.[14]

The infusion of so much new ministerial blood ran somewhat counter in logic to the church's declining popularity, but, to the good, it permitted the bishop latitude to reorganize the conference in order to address the membership problem. The need for such changes had become apparent after the state took a census in 1875. While most areas showed modest growth, population totals for Northeast Florida and the St. Johns River valley had begun to soar. Thanks to northern capitalists such as William Astor, Henry S. Sanford, Lewis Lawrence, Henry A. DeLand, and Josiah C. Eaton, new towns were springing up and tiny villages were expanding close to the St. Johns. They extended upriver as far as Orlando in Orange County. During the decade Florida's total population would increase by 43.5 percent to 269,493, of whom 126,690 were African Americans (47 percent). By contrast to the statewide growth, Duval County boasted a 63 percent rise; St.

Johns, 73 percent; Putnam, 64 percent; Bradford, 66 percent; Volusia, 91 percent; and Orange, 302 percent. Steamboats offered access to this dynamic region. Until railroads provided easy transportation, though, actual numbers of peninsular residents would remain relatively low. Still, rumors of planned construction circulated widely by mid-decade.[15]

Faced with these facts, the bishop implemented a schedule of districts and appointments in 1876 that committed the bulk of the church's missionary resources to the peninsula and away from Middle Florida. He increased the five existing districts (Tallahassee, Marianna, Jacksonville, Pensacola, and Live Oak) to eight. The additions all came in East Florida and the Bahama Islands. The location of districts and the range of pastoral assignments offer insight into the bishop's (and the church's) forecast of a future that encompassed all of Florida and at least a portion of the Caribbean:

Jacksonville District

W. W. SAMPSON, PRESIDING ELDER

1. Jacksonville Station	James C. Waters
2. LaVilla and Mount Olive	Abram Grant
3. Duval County Mission	Thomas Higginbotham
4. Green Cove Mission	Samuel Jackson
5. Palatka Circuit	Francis Carolina
6. Enterprise	J. R. Robinson
7. Fernandina	J. I. Lowe

Live Oak District

JOSIAH H. ARMSTRONG, PRESIDING ELDER

1. Live Oak Circuit	W. L. Jones
2. Jasper Circuit	Peter Crooms
3. Bellville	Adam Fort
4. Madison Circuit	Thomas Thompson
5. Cherry Lake	Tally Denham
6. Gum Swamp	Edmund Williams
7. Monticello Station	J. J. Sawyer
8. Monticello Mission	George Anderson
9. Thompson Valley	George W. Witherspoon
10. Lake City	W. R. Woods
11. Aucilla	Robert Meacham
12. Wakulla	John R. Weir
13. Houston and White Springs	Simon Boggs

14. Ellaville Mission	Scott Roberts
15. Springfield Mission	Henry Hall
16. Mt. Tabor Mission	Allen Jones Jr.

Marianna District

JACOB LIVINGSTON, PRESIDING ELDER
1. Springfield and Magnolia	Joseph H. Spears
2. Bethlehem	Fuller White
3. Jerusalem	Edmund Smith
4. Pope Chapel	Anthony Davis
5. Apalachicola	John Churchill
6. Aspalaga Mission	Alexander Groom
7. Greenville Mission	Asa Dudley
8. Antioch Mission	John W. H. Gilbert
9. Marianna Station	Wiley P. Williams

Island District

BENJAMIN W. ROBERTS, PRESIDING ELDER
1. Key West	Benjamin W. Roberts
2. Harbour Island	William Cole
3. Nassau, New Providence	T. B. Anderson
4. Orange Creek	Washington Jones

Gainesville District

M. G. JOHNS, PRESIDING ELDER
1. Gainesville	M. G. Johns
2. Archer	William Jones
3. Garden Circuit	Primus P. Gowens
4. Micanopy	C. L. Hadley
5. Mt. Zion Mission	Darcey Hamilton
6. Newnansville	David Young
7. Starke	Richard Brigadier
8. Pineville	Kelley Moses

Ocala District

THOMAS W. LONG, PRESIDING ELDER
1. Hopeville	Jacob Sutton
2. Long Swamp	Robert Eppes
3. Ocala Circuit	Thomas W. Long
4. Leesburg	Alfred Brown
5. Sumter County	Walter Glimp
6. Tampa Bay	Isaiah H. Welch

Pensacola District

JOHN H. WYATT, PRESIDING ELDER
1. Pensacola Station	John W. Wyatt

2. Holmes Valley Mission Washington Spears
3. Milton Circuit John Taylor
4. Campbellton Circuit John Speight
5. Lime Sink Alex Godwin
6. St. Johns and St. Lukes Henry Call
7. Navy Yard Station Walter Anders

Tallahassee District
CHARLES H. PEARCE, PRESIDING ELDER
1. Tallahassee Station George C. Christburgh
2. Concord (Gadsden County) J. W. Rickes
3. Wakulla Mission Benjamin Williams
4. Lake Jackson Francis Lavette
5. Concord (Leon County) Samuel Rose
6. Iamonia Slough Walker Swain
7. St. Johns Allen Jones Sr.
8. Quincy Station S. L. Mims
9. Rock Comfort J. D. Haynes
10. Walker Mission Lafayette Hargrett
11. Liberty County Mission Herbert B. DeVaughn
12. Chattahoochee Aaron Hammond
13. Midway Mission William A. Bird.[16]

33. Albert Julius Kershaw grew up a slave in Leon County. His grandson Joe Lang Kershaw became the first African American in the modern era to serve in the Florida legislature. Courtesy Photographic Collection, Florida State Archives.

34. William A. Bird ministered at "Mother Midway" church following the 1876 Florida Conference sessions. Courtesy Photographic Collection, Florida State Archives.

This reorganization presaged a parting of the ways of the East Florida church and the Florida Conference. For almost one year John R. Scott Sr. and other area leaders had been laying out their case for the robustness of the AME cause in the east, as opposed to conditions existing in Middle Florida. The same men had been urging limitations on political preachers, the enforcement of strict codes of morality for the clergy, and the cause of temperance. Often rebuffed, they had run out of patience. The men now saw going their own way as their only real alternative. At the Fifteenth General Conference, held in Atlanta during May 1876, they received authority to proceed at the next annual session of the Florida Conference. At the same gathering, Jabez P. Campbell accepted appointment to oversee the split as the new bishop of the Sixth Episcopal District.[17]

As was true for that of a number of his episcopal colleagues, Bishop Campbell's background reflected a life molded early on by the temper and culture of the Middle Atlantic states as they existed in the early nineteenth century. Born in Delaware about 1815, Campbell experienced a life-altering episode when his father mortgaged him to another man and then failed to repay the debt. Fearing that he would be sold into slavery as a result, Jabez Campbell ran away to Philadelphia where his mother resided. Otherwise, little is known about his personal or family life. At Philadelphia, Campbell participated actively in AME Church activities. Bishop Morris Brown licensed him to preach, after which he presided over churches in Philadelphia, New York, the New England states, and Maryland. In May 1864, during the Civil War's final year, he achieved election and ordination as a bishop.[18]

Nine months elapsed after the Fifteenth General Conference and Bishop Campbell's appointment to Florida before the details of the Florida Conference division could be worked out. Eventful ones they were. Politics dominated the headlines. As one of three southern states still in the hands of a Republican-run government, Florida endured a bitter and sometimes violent electoral campaign in the fall of 1876. Individual political preachers, with Elders Pearce and Meacham taking their customary lead, pitched in without the church's institutional support. Meacham nearly paid the ultimate price when an assassin shot twice at him while the senator stood on his front porch at Monticello. Meacham, who was wearing a pistol, fired back. All parties avoided serious wounds. The same could not be said for the Republican party. The Florida supreme court eventually gave the close gubernatorial election to the Democrats, while permitting the state's three presidential electors (including Pearce and Thomas W. Long) to cast Electoral College ballots for Republican Rutherford B. Hayes. The legislature also fell under opposition control. Democrats called their takeover Redemption, believing that they had redeemed the state from the "evils" of Reconstruction. The era of Republican government in post–Civil War Florida had ended.[19]

Meanwhile, pastors endeavored to maintain the strength of their congregations in the face of apathy. Some even attempted to increase the numbers. In March, Jacksonville's St. Paul's Church, under Abram Grant's pastorate, celebrated its dedication by Bishop Ward. John Thomas organized a twenty-seven-member congregation at Baldwin in July. "They have erected a temporary building," he reported, "which they are using until they can do better." Three other congregations—Thomas (at Molino, Escambia County), Kirsey (thirteen miles north of Tallahassee), and Wesley Chapel (ten miles west of Ocala)—trace their origins to this year. Then, in January 1877 church builder Abram Grant helped to dedicate Jacksonville's Mount

Olive sanctuary. The services would constitute one of Jabez Campbell's first actions as bishop of Florida.[20]

Most news did not arrive in so pleasing a form. W. L. Jones's Live Oak experiences may have been more typical than anyone cared to admit. A yellow-fever scare threw a camp meeting into disarray during September. "But in God whom I trust," Jones declared, "I have gone on up to this date." As the minister neared the end of his first year in the town, he reported, "I have been trying to do all in my power to build up my work. I had a trying time since I have been here and am undergoing some of it now, on account of the unwatchfulness of the pastor whom I succeeded." Education and politics ruled his thoughts. "I am praying and looking to see the time when the Bishop will send me where I can spend some time in school," he continued. "Brethren who know the good and power of education, please pray that I may get to some place where I can spend my leisure time in preparing myself more for the elevation of my people, as a minister of the Gospel." Jones concluded, "The Floridians of color are very much excited, and down hearted thinking that after all it seems as though the State is about to go into the hands of the Democrats, or is already."[21]

The long months of waiting for conference division ended on February 2, 1877, with the opening of the Florida Conference's Eleventh Annual Session at Monticello. Bishop Campbell sat as presiding officer, then sixty-

35. Bishop and Mrs. Jabez P. Campbell. Courtesy Photographic Collection, Florida State Archives.

36. Future bishop Abram Grant spearheaded efforts to build Tallahassee's Bethel AME Church from 1877 to 1879. This photograph was likely taken following the 1878 Florida Conference meeting. Courtesy Photographic Collection, Florida State Archives.

two years of age. Campbell had been born in Delaware, and much as had been true of Bishop Ward, his church work, distinguished though it was, had been undertaken elsewhere than in the South. He was, though, "a great preacher," and, according to J. C. Waters, "most acceptable." Campbell shared his predecessor's commitment to strict enforcement of moral strictures on the clergy. He quickly made the point, overseeing the expulsion from the conference of Tallahassee's George Christburgh for "gross immorality." The conference secretary observed, "The worst wounds the Church of Christ receives is often given by those who say they are called to promote its interests and strengthen its stakes." He added, "Put down brakes all along the line."[22]

Other than to decide the particulars of separation, the conference entertained few weighty issues. A report written by Elder Scott recommended establishment of a conference high school in lieu of the defunct Brown's University. Although the report received approval, its implementation awaited another day. As church historian Charles Sumner Long explained,

"Nothing was done about the school under Bishop Campbell." Otherwise, the gathering decided to split the conference at the Jefferson-Madison county line. Perhaps as a condition of the agreement, Elder Pearce requested a boon. Bethel AME at Tallahassee needed an able church builder to oversee construction of a new sanctuary. Campbell assigned the best such man in East Florida to do the job, Abram Grant. So efficient did Grant prove to be that cornerstone-laying ceremonies were held in December. Governor George F. Drew declined to attend the event for reasons that are not known, although he sent Secretary of State William D. Bloxham in his place. U.S. Senator Simon P. Conover participated, as well. "On the whole you see that our Church is on the road of progress," Grant observed.[23]

For the Florida Conference in 1877 and the years that followed, the road of progress passed through difficult terrain. It convened its reduced personnel at Quincy (Twelfth Annual Session) on February 13, 1878, and at Apalachicola (Fourteenth Annual Session) in February 1880. The date and place of the 1879 annual session are not known. Revivals early in the period spurred membership, but the excitement soon cooled as church fathers grappled with the beginnings of a population drain from Middle Florida. Democratic rule, coupled with harsher conditions, prompted many to look elsewhere for a safer and more secure future. The emigrationist ideas of the time, including the Back to Africa and the Exodusters movements, complicated the situation. Already by 1878, Bishop Campbell had to plead with members not to abandon their homes. "[He] has been giving his brethren some very good advice," commented the *DeLand Volusia County Herald*, "such as to go to work, the men with the plow and hoe and the women with the wash bowl and ironing table." The account continued, "He took occasion to tell those who had ideas of emigrating to Liberia that any who had money enough to buy farming implements and provisions might go and thrive, but that nation did not want an importation of paupers from this country."[24]

The Pensacola District's presiding elder, Henry Call, writing in 1880 of "the most discouraging situation" he found in the western Panhandle, looked for sunshine through the clouds. "With my feeble efforts I thank God for the consolation of having accomplished a small portion of the gigantic work that remains to be done in West Florida." Call could count some progress, however modest. A church building stood near the Pensacola Navy Yard after a decade's effort, and John Taylor had "wielded a great power in advancing the cause of Christianity in Washington County

Circuit." Francis Lavette's small Walton County congregations were "working faithfully to free themselves from all temporal obligations such as usually raise contentions, retard the good that might be going on." On the other hand, trials outweighed successes. Dernard Quarterman of the Santa Rosa Circuit, for example, "had a pretty rough time of it, being compelled when he reached [Milton] to sleep in the church." Call concluded:

> This work requires men of strong will power, men who will go forward fearless of the glittering temptations of vice; men of virtue; men of pure Christian morality who will stand up for Jesus amid the very storm of the most powerful opposition that Satan can present to combat with the Christian band. With such men, our banner will no longer trail in the dust of vice, ignorance and immorality.[25]

Nowhere did the Florida Conference contend with greater disappointments than at Pensacola. In 1873 John W. Wyatt had brought optimism to the mission. A church building had been started, and a core membership had been recruited. It took less than six years for his work to crumble, illustrating the key role individual ministers played in church development. Evidence came on December 27, 1878, when the almost new church burned in the midst of controversy. Wyatt had died the previous April. Insisting that the congregation owed $1,000 advanced by her husband for construction costs, the widow took the matter to court. "The suit resulted in her favor, whereupon she closed the edifice, which created much ill feeling," reported the *Pensacola Advance*, "and it is supposed the burning is an act of incendiarism, as the church was unoccupied."[26]

Bishop Campbell reacted to the Pensacola crisis by dispatching another East Florida church builder, Isaiah H. Welch, to the scene to begin the process of healing and rebuilding. The results were not exactly what the bishop expected, although initial reports indicated qualified improvement. By 1880 Presiding Elder Call could report, "Elder I. H. Welch, pastor, hopes to complete the building and liquidate the debt before the [1881] annual conference convenes." But Call felt the need to add a few sobering words. "Owing to the general condition of affairs when I made my round to this station," he continued, "I could not administer the sacrament and the information concerning the debt of the church was very indefinite." By the time Call voiced these sentiments, Welch had acted without the presiding elder's knowledge to help Pensacola detach itself from the Florida Conference, just as he had aided in the creation of the East Florida Conference. At

St. Louis in May, he successfully petitioned the Sixteenth General Conference to attach the Pensacola District to the Alabama Conference. Furious Florida Conference ministers protested. They ultimately managed to have the action reversed.[27]

Even the conference's flagship church at Tallahassee suffered the vicissitudes of the times. Pastor Abram Grant proceeded with construction of the new Bethel AME as quickly as finances permitted. By May 1878, the seventy-by-forty-foot structure was well along, and Grant expected its completion by December. Work remained to be completed in March 1879, when word arrived that Bishop Campbell, an ardent advocate of the church's missionary work in Texas, had transferred Grant to San Antonio. Bethel's board of trustees, headed by Henry Jones, pleaded for reconsideration. Builder Joseph White, plasterer John Sheppard, and Governor Drew, who had loaned funds to the congregation, were threatening to act on the debts. "To have him removed would demoralize and discourage our people," Jones insisted. Campbell declined the request. Church finances teetered so precariously that in July the church had to sponsor a festival to raise funds "for the purpose of bringing hither the new Pastor's family."[28]

All the unforeseen tribulations undermined the ability of ministers in the Florida Conference to command respect from area residents. This prompted Allen Jones Sr. to deliver a sermon that became legendary among his colleagues. He chose as his topic "So we preach, so you believe." At a service held in connection with the Tallahassee District meeting in May 1878, he argued "that faith cometh by hearing." Jones continued:

> How can you hear without a preacher? And how can he preach without he is sent? When he is sent he must preach the pure word of God; and when the word of God is preached, so you, my congregation, must believe. I was once young, but now I am old; my head is blossomed for the grave. I don't know whether I will be permitted to preach to you again, so I say to you this evening, repent of your sins, come unto God, who only is able to deliver you.[29]

In East Florida from 1877 to 1880, the church fared far better than in the Panhandle, although the giddy days of fast-paced growth were far behind. Seventeen churches trace their origins to those years: in 1877, Columbia County's Mt. Pisgah (Lake City) and Putnam County's Pleasant Grove (Georgetown); in 1878, Duval's New Hope (Jacksonville) and Volusia's Bethel (DeLand); in 1879, Clay's St. James Chapel (Orange Park); and in

1880, Alachua's Bethel (La Crosse), Columbia's Shiloh, Lake's St. Stephen's (Newtown, near Leesburg), Levy's New Hope (Bronson), Marion's St. John's (Citra), St. Paul (Ocala), and Shiloh (south of Ocala), Nassau's Mt. Bethel (Callahan), Seminole's Mt. Tabor (Forest City) and St. James (Sanford), Suwannee's King's Chapel (Wellborn), and Volusia's St. Paul (Garfield).[30]

The East Florida Conference organized itself at Palatka on February 27, 1878. Thirty-seven members attended the sessions chaired by Bishop Campbell. They included presiding elders Josiah H. Armstrong, M. J. Johnson, Thomas W. Long, John R. Scott Sr., and Benjamin W. Roberts; traveling elders W. W. Sampson, J. J. Sawyer, Francis Carolina, J. C. Waters, J. I. Lowe, John Thomas, Samuel Jackson, T. C. Denham, Thomas T. Thompson, W. R. Wood, Peter Crooms, Allen Jones Jr., Washington Jones, Richard Brigadier, W. C. Cole, Adam Fort, David Hamilton, Alfred Brown, Joseph C. Crews [La Cruse], and Primus G. Gowens; traveling deacons E. J. Brookens, Walter Glimp, R. Epton [Robert Eppes?], J. R. Robinson, Thomas Higginbotham, J. Sutton, Simon Boggs, Edmund Smith, King Stockton, James Edwards, Alexander Chambers, and C. L. Hadley; local elders Cupid Wilson and Dennis Wood; and local deacons Alexander Lofton and Dennis Fuller. Admitted on trial were R. B. Brookins, Romulus Spencer, Auburn Erwin, Lewis Johnson, A. A. Cromartie, J. W. Bowen, F. H. Chisolm, and J. Tyler. Brookins, Spencer, and Erwin achieved election to deacon's orders and were ordained. Richard Brigadier, tired from long labors, asked to be retired.[31]

Subsequent sessions of the conference followed at Ocala on February 7, 1879, and at Madison on March 2, 1880. Minutes of the Ocala meeting have not come to light, but at Madison W. W. Shells, Richard Chadwick, H. F. Chisolm, S. H. Coleman, and Jacob Williams were ordained deacons, while members elected R. B. Brookins and J. R. Robinson to elder's orders. Goodbyes also were said. Most notably, John R. Scott Sr. had died suddenly at Jacksonville on March 7, 1879, leaving a tremendous leadership vacuum for the conference to fill. Adding to the vacuum, Bishop Campbell furthered his support for Texas missionary work by dispatching Josiah H. Armstrong to join Abram Grant. Both men eventually would achieve election as bishop. Also leaving Florida for Texas were T. C. Denham, William Buggs, J. H. Watson, and Jerry Grimes.[32]

Membership totals for East Florida seem to have risen modestly in line with the new churches brought into the conference. A reported eight thousand persons belonged in early 1878, although that number likely reflected a rosier than justifiable estimate. In most cases, converts probably were hard won, given the times and prevailing conditions. Allen Jones Jr.'s experience at Lake City is illustrative. When Jones arrived at the town on March 17, 1878, he "found the spiritual prospect low, and the cloud was heavy and dark." The church was in debt, with few alternatives for payment. Within months, the talented young preacher had found the money, rejuvenated the congregation, and begun building a new sanctuary. Money always loomed as a serious concern, though. A visitor noted that fall, "[Pastor Jones] seems to be laboring under some financial embarrassment." He added, "May God hear his cry for pecuniary assistance."[33]

East Florida's clergymen, generally speaking, did not face the same degree of indifference or disrespect that sometimes was the case in the Florida Conference, and, unlike many of their Panhandle colleagues, they celebrated numerous highpoints. Bishop Campbell's dedication of Macedonia Church at Fernandina on February 23, 1878, certainly counted as one of those events. Members credited the achievement, occurring in one of the cities most resistant to AME incursions, to Pastor J. I. Lowe. "He told the congregation [in 1876] that his mission here was to lite up the banner of African Methodism that had been trailing in the dust," wrote one parishioner, "and, by the grace of God assisting him, he did not intend to leave the place until he had accomplished his mission." The man added: "Suffice it to say that he is a minister of whom no congregation need be ashamed. He is a Christian, a gentleman, a church builder and a good preacher."[34]

Perhaps the East Florida Conference did share one important consideration with the Florida Conference. While each had turned its back on active engagement in politics, a number of individual members had persisted in seeking political office and political solutions to the race's enhanced problems in Reconstruction's aftermath. This factor, in turn, had diminished time spent on building up the church in the respective regions. To add to the problem, increasingly the political preachers lost their election bids. Robert Meacham, to cite just one example, fell short in another congressional bid in 1878. His last session as a state senator followed in 1879.[35]

By the beginning of the 1880s, at least in Middle and West Florida, enough politically directed energy remained among the preachers for one last great push. Accordingly, in 1880 George W. Witherspoon took up the reins of political leadership. With assistance from elders C. H. Pearce and William G. Stewart, he wrested a Republican congressional nomination away from the white claimant. Campaigning to "Africanize" Florida, he likely won the election, although white Republicans "counted him out" in the U.S. House of Representatives. With the deck so stacked against the race, opposition to the political preachers intensified as the decade progressed. As it did, the church itself and some of its ministers changed in unexpected ways. A new era dawned for Florida and for the church. And, with it, the membership rolls began to grow at long last.[36]

7

BISHOP WAYMAN'S RETURN, 1880-1884

*African Methodism is gaining
grandly on this work.*

The early years of the 1880s saw Florida and its AME church changed by rapid developments in transportation, immigration, urbanization, and politics. In negotiating its way through the thicket of change, the church benefited from the guidance of a gifted leader. Where Jabez Campbell's 1876–1880 tenure as bishop of the Florida and East Florida Conferences had witnessed troubles within the church, Alexander Wayman's softer touch would help to smooth troubled waters and aid the institution in preparing to meet greater challenges. A time of transition, to be sure, but also a time of advance and accomplishment.

The elections of 1880 had signaled some of the transitions that were beginning to impact the state and the church. For one thing, they pointed out that a new and different generation of leaders was emerging in the African American community. Thomas W. Long's race in Marion County offers an example. Essentially a self-educated man, the presiding elder had immersed himself in the rough-and-tumble world of frontier church building and Reconstruction-era politics for well over a decade. His style, which reflected his experiences, had proven effective and led him to high church position as well as the state senate. In April 1880 when Long announced for re-election, he likely expected an easy time of it in a county dominated by black voters.[1]

To Long's surprise, he discovered serious opposition at the county's Republican nominating convention. His opponent, Henry Wilkins Chandler, offered a dramatic contrast to the senator. Chandler had resided in Marion for only a few years and had never held public office. The newcomer nonetheless commanded respect for his educational attainments and personal polish. A teacher and lawyer, the Maine native had graduated from Bates College with a B.A. degree in 1874, taught at Howard University during 1874 and 1875, and studied law at that institution up to June 1876. Now, the ideals and styles that each candidate represented clashed so boldly that their supporters "got into a row, and broken bones and bloody faces prevailed; pistols and knives were drawn and a scene of great disorder prevailed." Chandler captured the nomination, but Long's men battled back for months. They accused the nominee of being "a political adventurer" and insisted that he was "dishonest in his political pretensions." The attacks failed to sway Marion's voters. On Election Day they retired the senator in favor of the new man.[2]

Henry W. Chandler's election illustrated dynamics then at play beyond the loss of political office by old-line AME ministers. To some extent it demonstrated the growing strength of towns and cities in a state previously rural. At the Civil War's beginning, neither of the two largest communities (Key West and Pensacola) held as many as three thousand persons. Twenty years later Key West contained almost ten thousand, with Jacksonville and Pensacola trailing, respectively, with about seventy-five hundred and seven thousand. Thanks to growth during the 1880s, at least nine other towns would claim more than twenty-five hundred residents by 1890. They included Tallahassee, Apalachicola, Fernandina, St. Augustine, Palatka, Ocala, Gainesville, Orlando, and Tampa. At the same time, Key West boasted eighteen thousand inhabitants, Jacksonville seventeen thousand, and Pensacola almost twelve thousand.[3]

Railroad construction fueled much of this urban growth. Especially, Connecticut-born Henry Bradley Plant opened up a large part of the northeastern and central peninsula during the early 1880s. With backing from wealthy northerners such as the Standard Oil Company's John D. Rockefeller and Henry Flagler, Plant gobbled up small lines and laid new track at a rapid pace. By January 1884 his trains had reached as far as Tampa, until then little more than an isolated frontier village. Along the way, he had left Jacksonville, Lake City, Gainesville, Ocala, Green Cove Springs, Palatka, DeLand, Sanford, Leesburg, Orlando, Kissimmee, and other places prospering. The flip side of the coin saw the old Middle Florida AME heartland depressed, with little in the way of rail construction or development. In the first half of the 1880s, Hamilton, Madison, Jefferson, and Leon

37. This view of Tallahassee drawn in 1885 illustrates the proximity of Bethel AME Church (upper right) to the state capitol (lower left). Courtesy Photographic Collection, Florida State Archives.

Counties lost population. By early 1884, more than six hundred laborers had departed Jackson County alone to perform construction work on a single line, Plant's South Florida Railroad.[4]

Growing towns lured African Americans with high-paying jobs and other business opportunities, just as railroad construction lured into the peninsula black workers from Middle Florida and out of state. The expanding economy bolstered an emerging black middle class of teachers, contractors, carpenters, government employees, hotel workers, merchants, and professionals. Literally, skilled black craftsmen often built the bustling new cities. As they did, Jacksonville became the financial and spiritual heart of an increasingly urban Florida. Meanwhile, African American town officials had helped and continued to help guide the state's urban destiny. The men often belonged to the AME clergy or laity, although such service became less common for ministers with the passage of time. Still, Francis B. Carolina served as a councilman at Lake City and Palatka; George Washington sat as a founding member of Bronson's policy-making board; Joseph J. Sawyer presided as Palatka's clerk and tax assessor; and Oliver J. Coleman influenced his fellow councilmen at Madison, while Thomas T. Thompson and Primus Gowens did the same, respectively, at Live Oak and at Henry W. Chandler's home base of Ocala.[5]

Few, if any, individuals represented the growth of the black middle class better than did Jacksonville's John E. Onley. A "master builder" by profession, he already had reached lofty economic heights by the 1880s. "Ten years ago Mr. Onley was a poor man, but by perseverance, combined with business tact he is now in comfortable circumstances, possessing a first-class home, eight houses on rent besides, and keeps from 25 to 40 men employed on contract work," reported a Key West newspaper in 1884. Among his friends, Onley counted Bishop Daniel A. Payne, who had begun spending his winters at Jacksonville early in the decade. The bishop savored memories of the "many delightful evenings" he spent at the Onley home, where his "Reading Circle" met. Payne particularly admired Annie Onley, his host's daughter. A Stanton Institute teacher and a gifted vocalist and musician, Annie's "articulation" was, according to Payne, "as correct and distinct as her voice is full, round and sweet." Sadly for the bishop, he could not attend Annie's wedding to Henry W. Chandler on October 2, 1884. Sadly for the AME Church—as too often was proving the case among the middle-class families—the ceremony took place in an ME church and was presided over by a Presbyterian minister.[6]

The groom, on the other hand, belonged neither to the ME nor the Presbyterian Church. Senator Chandler was a Baptist. His 1880 victory also symbolized a significant change in Baptist strength relative to African Methodism. Even the denomination's old-time and conservative political preachers, such as Charles H. Pearce's frequent foe James Page, enjoyed blessings from the Baptist resurgence. "It must be gratifying to him in his declining years," a Tallahassee newspaper mentioned of Page in 1882, "to see his labors so abundantly blessed in the conversion of sinners."[7]

Beyond that, the situation also hinted that Baptist Church leaders had accomplished a good deal more in certain areas of great concern and sensitivity than had their AME counterparts. A sense of dynamism previously identified with its Methodist rivals adhered by the early 1880s to the Baptist Church. One aspect of the dynamism caused AME leaders particular embarrassment. Where their plans for Brown's University had hit the shoals of hard luck and eventual apathy, the Baptists had succeeded in building an educational institution for their clergy and members. Located at Live Oak and known as the Florida Institute, the school opened on October 1, 1880. During its first year ninety-one students enrolled, seven of whom were preparing for the ministry. In 1882 the institute's trustees added a dormitory for girls, and two years later a boys' dormitory followed.[8]

AME people heard the message of their educational shortcomings loud and clear. They began to emphasize more emphatically their pride in educated members of the clergy and laity. Included among those often mentioned were Isaiah Henderson Welch, valedictorian of the Wilberforce University class of 1870, and Joseph E. Lee, who joined the AME ministry in 1881 as a graduate of Philadelphia's Institute for Colored Youth and the Howard University Law Department. Men such as Welch and Lee certainly felt no educational deficiency relative to the likes of Senator Chandler. Students at and graduates of Wilberforce held a special place in the hearts of Floridians because of the school's close connection with Bishop Payne. "We have had three young men to struggle through difficulties and get to Wilberforce, viz: Thomas D. Scott, John R. Scott [Jr.], and William Cole," R. B. Brookins proudly reported in mid-1882. "Mr. Thomas D. Scott has graduated from the scientific department with the highest honors of his class," he continued. "The other two still remain at Wilberforce studying how to battle against sin and satan." Brookins added expectantly, "God grant that they become great leaders of their race."[9]

AME supporters realized, as well, that the time had long since come for development of a school for the church's clergy. Many were the preachers desirous, as R. B. Brookins put it, "of improving themselves in their studies, that they may become efficient laborers in the vineyard of the Lord." One minister, Joseph J. Sawyer at Palatka, had attempted in 1878 to act on his own to carry out the report adopted at the 1876 Florida Conference in favor of a conference high school. When Bishop Campbell showed little support for the effort, according to M. M. Moore, "His project died aborning." Sawyer did not give up. As East Florida Conference secretary in 1880, he carried the clout to secure approval of a resolution "in favor of holding an educational conference at Live Oak, Fla., on the 20th of October, 1880" with "the co-operation of the Florida Conference (proper), and invite Bishops Campbell and [John M.] Brown to be present with us and all the good friends who may like to come."[10]

The results of the conference are not known, but the climate for commitment to greater educational opportunities soon changed. By the time the East Florida and Florida Conferences met in 1881, Campbell no longer presided. In his place sat a fervent education advocate, Bishop Alexander W. Wayman. And what a difference Wayman's presence would make!

38. Robert Burns Brookins championed higher education for Florida's AME clergy. Courtesy Photographic Collection, Florida State Archives.

Wayman's early life resembled that of Bishop Campbell. A native of Caroline County, Maryland, Wayman came into the world in September 1821. His father, a farmer, put his son to work when he was still "a little boy." The bishop attributed his adult appearance—large, muscular physique, large forehead, and broad nose—to that fact. "My father put me to ploughing when I was young," he explained, "and made my muscles expand, and therefore I grew large." Little information remains about Wayman as a husband or father. At age sixteen he joined the AME Church; by the time he was twenty-two, the Philadelphia Conference already had assigned him to various positions. After being stationed by the church in Philadelphia, Baltimore, and Washington, D.C., he became a bishop in 1864. Besides obtaining the church's highest office, Wayman also received the Doctor of Divinity degree from Howard University. It was such a man who oversaw a time of transition and ensured that it would become a time of advance and accomplishment.[11]

Wayman's influence quickly manifested itself. With episcopal power now weighing in to support the measure, the East Florida Conference in February 1881 endorsed building Sawyer's Palatka high school. "The [Baptists] have their high schools going on in this State," observed T. C. Denham. "While we can boast of our number, we have nothing to speak of in that direction." He added, "Brethren of the East Florida Conference, come to the front at once; delays are dangerous." Although minutes are not available for the Florida Conference held at Marianna in November, the gathering likely followed East Florida's lead. Financially, though, the times had not yet improved sufficiently. The church needed to build itself up before it, in turn, could build up a school.[12]

The Florida church found the right man to help it rebuild and expand in the person of Alexander W. Wayman. One biographer described him as "a man of very great character, earnest and powerful as a preacher, and . . . universally beloved by both white and colored people, in all walks of life." He felt strongly the call of the South and its people, refusing at one point even to consider service in Haiti or Africa. "I said never would I consent to go, or assist in sending any one there," the bishop asserted, "until I could go all over the South to see my brethren." Wayman summed up his philosophy in words from the Book of Genesis, "I seek my brethren." Howard University awarded him a doctoral degree, but honors failed to change him. Wayman never lost the human touch or forgot the simple lessons he learned as a boy on his father's Maryland farm.[13]

One of the secrets to Wayman's eventual Florida successes derived directly from those early lessons. In addition to other initiatives, the bishop repeatedly took church campaigns to the people rather than waiting for the people to come to him. While allowing those whom he encountered to bask in the glory of his episcopal status, he related with them as one human being to another. "Bishop Wayman was a great commoner and traveler," recounted Charles Sumner Long. "He went through the rural sections preaching and gathering in members," the church historian continued. "People would gather along the road to see the Bishop pass by. They would take their children, some would line the fences along the fields just to see a Bishop."[14]

One of Wayman's itineraries has survived. The trip occurred after the February 1882 East Florida Conference sessions at Fernandina. From that

39. The Reverend Reuben B. Brooks. Courtesy Photographic Collection, Florida State Archives.

point, the bishop traveled to Ocala, Gainesville, Cedar Key, Starke, Baldwin, Monticello, Gum Swamp, Waukeenah, Concord, Mount Olive, and points in between. He consoled Thomas W. Long, encouraged J. R. Robinson, visited with the retired Richard Brigadier, joked with R. B. Brooks, expressed regret at the illness of George W. Witherspoon's wife, rode with Milton A. Trapp, praised A. B. Dudley, and preached with J. H. Spears. Wayman reported overflow congregations at many stops. "From what I have seen there is no doubt but what African Methodism has the State of Florida," he reported. "These last named places that I visited the people had never seen any of our bishops before and the ministers are of the opinion that it will greatly help the Dollar Money collection."[15]

Wayman also felt no reluctance about pressing his friends into service. Capitalizing on Bishop Payne's winter residence in the state, he dispatched the prelate to tour some areas even before Wayman's first conference meetings. In January 1881, Payne visited Palatka, Green Cove Springs, and St. Augustine "at the request of his colleague." As James C. Waters noted, "Bishop Payne has made himself useful to our church, preaching and lecturing etc." Wayman also transferred his longtime friend Charles H. Pearce to East Florida. The prelate placed the elder in charge of what had become the new banner church of African Methodism in the state, Jacksonville's Mount Zion. In doing so, Wayman gained a steady ally who knew the ins and outs of church and state. "He has scarcely got straight yet, but will soon be all right, for he is fully able to hold the fort," Waters commented of Pearce in March. "Though over sixty years old he is one of the most powerful and acceptable preachers in the State." Waters added, "May he live long and at last may his sun set without a cloud."[16]

The energy, drive, determination, and common touch that Wayman brought to bear quickly paid off for the church. New congregations coalesced, most of them in the peninsula. In 1881, they included Marion County's Mt. Olive (Anthony) and Orange County's Mt. Olive (Orlando). The next year came Alachua County's Allen Chapel (High Springs), Duval's Wayman Chapel (Jacksonville), Jefferson's Greenville Church (near Ashville), Putnam's Payne's Chapel (near Palatka) and Bethel (San Mateo), Suwannee's St. James (near Rixford), and Volusia's Mt. Zion (Orange City). The year 1883 saw the beginnings of Gadsden's Mt. Zion (near Mt. Pleasant), Marion's Mt. Pisgah (Summerfield), Volusia's Mt. Olive (Glenwood), and Walton's Mt. Pisgah (near Freeport). And 1884 ushered in Lake County's St. Joseph's (near Leesburg) and St. John's (Tavares) and Orange County's St. James (Kissimmee).[17]

Of even greater importance than the new churches, many old congregations grew and prospered. As early as the spring of 1881 signs of rejuvenation had begun to sprout. At Micanopy, Henry Hamilton almost tripled his membership in a few months. The same Gainesville church that M. A. Starkes described as in "deplorable condition," "irregular," and "poorly attended" in the winter had become a prosperous congregation of 121 before summer. Starkes already was planning a new sanctuary. R. B. Brooks at Starke added a bell and organ. Soon, Bulley Wiley reported overflowing Sunday schools in the Osceola District. At Callahan members purchased land to erect their first church. And at Tampa, Washington Jones boasted

40. The Reverend Bulley William Wiley tended churches in many parts of the Florida peninsula until his death at Plant City in 1909. Courtesy Photographic Collection, Florida State Archives.

"the largest congregation and membership of any colored church in South Florida."[18]

The resurgence swept out of East Florida into the Panhandle. Fuller White commenced revivals in Jackson County during April that generated ripples of optimism through Middle Florida. Dozens of converts joined the church, many of them young. "Truly I can say that 'God moves in a mysterious way,'" White recorded, "'his wonders to perform.'" From the Marianna District, J. H. Spears wrote, "We have had glorious revivals and many added to the church." He continued, "The people have experienced a very hard way to live in this district up until now, and everything looked gloomy at first, yet God has blessed us abundantly." In northern Leon County W. C. Hamilton held a meeting for two weeks, as a result of which "forty-seven souls professed a hope in Christ." The Centerville pastor kept busy erecting two new churches. Even in West Florida the hard going seemed to ease. A September camp meeting near Pensacola netted "twenty-three souls from the enemy's ranks." The gains permitted Benjamin W.

Roberts to declare, "I am glad to say that Allen Chapel AME Church is alive."[19]

The new year brought more good news. Members attending the Fifth Session of the East Florida Conference in February 1882 learned of important financial advances. "The 'almighty dollar' seems no longer to be a burden in the East Florida Conference," T. C. Denham observed, "and we can truthfully say that we are rapidly rising in the scales of means and intelligence." At Live Oak, one hundred new members graced the congregation. "The opposition here has been very strong, but the Lord has promised, and surely will perform, to lead Israel," commented D. W. Gillislee. In the process of erecting a $3,000 parsonage, A. P. Miller of Lake City wrote, "I am glad to say 'we are rising' and we shall continue to rise higher and higher in proportion as the sun of righteousness lifts us up out of sin, self and ignorance." Thirty new members were added at Ocala by Walter Jones, and Thomas W. Long brought in one hundred at Palatka. From Key West came word of paid-off debt and "recent revivals [that] have been the means whereby many souls have been converted to God."[20]

New sanctuaries and related structures rose in many parts of the state. At long last the rebuilding of the Pensacola church neared completion after Bishop Wayman preached there in April. "Forty-eight souls came forward to be prayed for," B. W. Roberts related. "The bishop, by his affable and obliging manners, freed from all *officious* pedantism," he continued, "charmed the ear, and gained the heart of Pensacola." At Gainesville, a sanctuary built to seat "eight or nine hundred persons" came into use. "African Methodism at this point is alive," M. A. Starkes concluded. John Speight supervised construction of a parsonage at Apalachicola, while Archer's new church stood ready for dedication. Singleton H. Coleman, more than any other minister, assumed Abram Grant's mantle as the great church builder. In 1882, he first opened a twenty-four-by-forty-foot chapel that he saw as "the best church in Sanford." By October he had finalized construction of Orlando's Mt. Olive. "Thus you see African Methodism is gaining grandly on this work," he declared.[21]

One new factor, when added to the benefits of a growing economy and the energy derived from Bishop Wayman's presence, spurred the intensity of interest in the church that blossomed in 1882. It concerned Bishop Daniel A. Payne. Associated since 1865 with church work in Florida, the bishop had taken up part-time residence at Jacksonville. When in February 1882 he boarded a train for Fernandina to attend the East Florida Confer-

41. This view illustrates the appearance of Key West's Bethel AME Church during the 1880s. Courtesy Photographic Collection, Florida State Archives, Neg. No. 421.

ence, he came face-to-face with the state's growing practices of racial discrimination. A conductor ordered the internationally acclaimed educator and cleric out of the car in which he was sitting and to "a colored car." Payne refused, insisting that "I will not dishonor my manhood by going into it." The conductor put him off the train at the next station, and the seventy-one-year-old senior bishop of the AME church walked five miles back into Jacksonville carrying almost thirty pounds of baggage.[22]

The incident provoked outcries of protest and indignation from around the nation and the world to the point that, as events took their course, the controversy reintroduced into the public mind the concept of the AME Church as Florida's activist African American religious institution. Payne spoke out early and often, labeling the order for his removal a "relic of the barbarous system of slavery." He would add, "The order is barbarous, its execution is barbarous, and all who apologize for it are equally barbarous." The bishop demanded, "Why should I be treated like a dog in my native land?" So profound was the reaction that attempts to implement schemes of racial discrimination on Florida's railroads were set back for years. Already a hero to African Americans, Payne emerged as a greater one. His church benefited, as well. Without stooping to the level of electoral politics, it had wielded its clout on a political matter of very real concern. As a result, new members flocked to its ranks.[23]

The positive fallout from the Payne crisis helped carry the church through several of its own crises in 1882. From August to December the plague of yellow fever afflicted residents of West Florida coastal areas. Quarantines blocked ports as the pestilence spread. "Yellow fever was worse that year in Pensacola than it had ever been, or has ever been since," one resident recorded. Pastor B. W. Roberts wrote of the results to Florida Conference members meeting at Monticello. "I regret that I must inform you that I can not meet you all this Conference on account of the epidemic that visited our city, which left destitution, poverty and death in its wake," he stated. "Yet we can say, thanks be to God," Roberts continued, "who saith to his people, we are left here to suffer a little while longer." He added, "We are all anxious for the Bishop to visit us as soon as possible." All told, 2,350 individuals took sick at Pensacola and 197 died.[24]

As West Floridians succumbed to the fever, Middle Florida's residents endured a different natural calamity. In early September a monstrous hurricane blasted ashore southwest of Tallahassee. Wakulla, Leon, Gadsden, and Jackson Counties bore the brunt of its wind and water. Pine forests were swept down, while a structure as well built as Tallahassee's new brick Episcopal church was "seriously injured." AME churches, many of them simple log structures, stood little chance. In the Tallahassee District, casualties included Midway and Chattahoochee. To the west in the Marianna District, the destruction engulfed the church at Marianna and two churches of the Campbellton circuit. Throughout the region, AME sanctuaries survived only at the cost of extensive damage.[25]

The Florida Conference's annual session convened on November 29 with both of these disasters serving as major topics of interest. Bishop Wayman sat as chair, directing the course of events. Delegates prepared to act in the face of the natural disasters and to take advantage of the new spirit brought to Florida by the bishop. At that time, sixty-seven itinerant preachers, 142 local preachers, and fifty exhorters served fifty-six churches directed from forty-seven stations. Conference membership totaled 4,555, plus 808 probationers. Bishop Wayman continued the basic organizational structure adopted following creation of the East Florida Conference. At that time a Monticello District had been created for Jefferson County, which had been split off from East Florida's Live Oak District. Presiding

42. Pensacola's tall-steepled Allen Chapel AME Church as it appeared in 1885. Courtesy Photographic Collection, Florida State Archives, Neg. No. 4690.

elders as of the conference were A. Henry Attaway (Monticello), Fuller White (Tallahassee), Thomas Moorer (Marianna), and W. L. G. Jones (Pensacola).[26]

Personnel changes naturally received a great deal of consideration. S. W. Frazer, G. W. T. Wynn, and C. L. Lane received ordination as deacons, with Forney Jones and Berry Cromidy becoming local deacons. New elders included Isaac Buggs and E. W. Johnson. The delegates accepted a decision to transfer Elders S. L. Mims, J. H. Gilbert, and Benjamin W. Roberts to Alabama, but they attempted to overturn an order to send M. M. Moore to Georgia. Harris Humphreys, John Dash, Henry Starks, A. B. Collins, K. P. Neal, Fagan Peters, and Charles Spires were admitted on trial, while S. W. Frazer, P. Johnson, James Clark, W. Washington, J. E. Roberts, Serry Lewis, Noah Randolph, R. Raymon, L. W. Allen, G. W. Wynn, F. J. Thompson, and W. A. Burch remained on trial. B. C. Gibbs, J. P. Campbell, E. R. Robinson, W. C. Hamilton, C. L. Lane, and S. C. Clary were admitted or readmitted to full connection. R. H. Munroe was dropped from the rolls.[27]

Noticeably, political questions found no place on the agenda. As one conservative white had noted of the previous conference meeting, "The annual assembling of this body was once closely watched by designing politicians..., but those days died with carpet-bagism." He added, "The ministers and delegates now seem to confine themselves to their church work and nothing more, which is gratifying to all christians." Another change came in the meeting's tone. Several decisions taken by delegates suggested that Bishop Wayman had signaled a relaxation of the standards of stern morality demanded of the clergy under Bishop Campbell. Particularly, certain charges against A. R. Hansberry and Milton A. Trapp were dismissed rather than pressed.[28]

The matters that captured the passions of ministers present related to temperance and education. The conference report on drinking and tobacco written by A. B. Dudley insisted that "a good many of our children are walking the streets, half naked—no hat nor shoes upon their heads or feet; yet their mothers and fathers can always find money to buy tobacco, cigars, pipe, snuff, or a bottle of whiskey." Dudley added, "We are sorry to say that the bottle has destroyed more souls than even the cannon or the sword, yet ministers of Christ are seen drinking that awful cup of hell." The report concluded, "Leave it; oh, leave off now and forever," but it recommended no sanctions in aid of enforcement. The conference remained too weak to draw too tight a line as of yet.[29]

On education, the Florida Conference accepted a responsibility to act, although the path toward fulfillment of goals remained murky at best. M. M. Moore assaulted his fellow delegates on the subject: "Brethren, your Committee would have you hear the sound of the trumpet. It reverberates through the land, 'Educate!' 'Educate!' 'Educate!' Hark! do the Florida Conference not hear our sentries—Payne, Wayman, Lee—cry, 'To the work!' 'To the work!'" Delegates consented to push the cause in a general sense and to "do all we can towards aiding and sustaining Wilberforce University, and our other connectional educational interests; and, at the same time, work earnestly to establish a College, or Conference High School, in this State."[30]

Bishops Wayman and Payne wanted educational matters to go further, and they prevailed upon the East Florida Conference to become the engine that would drive the cause. This occurred at the conference's annual session begun at Gainesville on February 21, 1883. The delegates, feeling their newborn prosperity, agreed to open a "theological school," although they opted for Jacksonville over Palatka as its location. William W. Sampson consented to become conference educational agent in charge of raising funds. The name chosen was the East Florida Divinity School, soon to be known simply as the Divinity High School.³¹

To operate the conference school, the bishops selected William Preston Ross, a graduate of the Unitarian Theological Seminary at Meadville, Pennsylvania. The young man was due to arrive in March from the Pittsburgh Conference to assume the pulpit at Jacksonville's Mt. Zion Church. The opening had occurred, apparently, because Charles H. Pearce and the congregation had not seen eye to eye, a situation that had resulted in the elder seeking transfer to Fernandina. Bishop Payne, particularly, saw a potential for greatness in Ross. "He evidently made good use of his advantages," the bishop recorded in April, "and if he maintain a pure and high Christian character, I predict for him a career of great usefulness as an expounder of the Holy Scriptures." Others came to agree with Payne's assessment. "He was educated, bold and fearless; would move at once to strike down the wrong and defend the right," M. M. Moore explained several years later. "He was broad-hearted, believing fully in the fatherhood of God and the brotherhood of man."³²

Not until he arrived at Jacksonville did Ross learn from Payne that he was to take on the school. "This somewhat upset me for awhile," he observed, "however I soon recovered from the shock and accepted the position." In order to hold classes that fall, Ross worked round the clock to make necessary preparations, while W. W. Sampson canvassed for money wherever he could. So onerous was Ross's task that he neglected Mt. Zion's needs to some extent. During the year its membership dropped from 500 to 260. In the end, though, he met his goal. The East Florida Divinity High School opened on schedule, using facilities at Mt. Zion. On matriculation day 125 students expressed a desire to attend, 18 of whom were young men desirous of a career in the ministry. Joseph E. Lee assisted Ross in running the theological department. John R. Scott Jr. managed the primary department with Mary E. Miller's support. By year's end, T. C. Denham proudly would declare, "There is a great struggle for intellectual liberty in the conference divinity high school . . . , which bids fair to be made a success if means can be obtained to erect a suitable building to accommodate students."³³

As Professor Ross labored in 1883 to create a divinity high school, the Florida conferences prospered mightily. Especially the St. Johns River region boomed with activity. "In twenty-five years the St. John's river will be built up like the Hudson," T. C. Denham proclaimed. "There are hundreds of little towns along the river side." He continued, "One of the most encouraging things for us is where these booms are found, Ham is there with his orange groves and truck farms." Singleton H. Coleman joined in the excitement. "It is remarkable to say, the mission that I worked alone last year has been divided into four parts with as many ministers," he informed readers of the *Christian Recorder.* "Thus you see the results of one year's hard work." After a "glorious revival" at Maitland in the Fall, he added, "I am glad to say the spirit moved in our midst."[34]

Organizationally, the conference's attempts to till such fertile fields centered on the work of four districts. John R. Robinson acted as presiding elder of the Gainesville District, Primus Gowens for the Enterprise District, T. C. Denham for the Jacksonville District, and R. B. Brookins for the Live Oak District. The Island District no longer existed. Key West rested within the Enterprise District's jurisdiction, which now included missions as far south on the peninsula as Manatee (Bradenton). The Bahama Islands no longer came under the conference's supervision. All told, sixty missions and stations received annual appointments.[35]

The organization worked well, as positive reports flooded into the bishop's hands. Bulley Wiley from Enterprise wrote, "I am glad to say we are having a good time." D. W. Gillislee at Madison observed, "A good feeling still exists." Similar word came from Orlando: "We are not the children of the dead," joked S. D. Williams, "but of the living." Midway's R. W. Chadwick exclaimed, "The Lord has blessed us spiritually, intellectually, and otherwise." Additional "glorious revivals" produced converts at Archer and Bronson. Almost four thousand children attended Sunday schools. Samuel Morgan at St. Augustine completed a chapel; Thomas Higginbotham erected a church at Waycross station; R. B. Brooks began a seventy-by-forty-foot brick structure at LaVilla; Joseph E. Lee repaired Jacksonville's Mt. Olive; and another Jacksonville sanctuary rose at Brooklyn mission under John Roseman. Plenty of good news.[36]

The same was true in West and Middle Florida. In January 1883, W. D. Chipley's railroad finally linked Pensacola with Apalachicola, sparking at least some economic liveliness at a time when crop prices remained low and African Americans continued to leave the region. From the Marianna District, Thomas Moorer would report in the summer, "Our district is in a good, flourishing condition." Church repairs required after hurricane damage proceeded apace, and new parsonages graced Marianna (Benjamin W. Roberts), Springfield Circuit (Milton A. Trapp), and Greenwood Circuit

43. John R. Scott Jr. helped to found the East Florida Divinity High School, the predecessor of Edward Waters College. Courtesy Photographic Collection, Florida State Archives.

(A. J. Kershaw). Fuller White commented at the same time on the Tallahassee District, noting, "We expect to come to the front financially, especially, in dollar money." Pastors were involved in church building at Midway (G. W. T. Wynn), Quincy (Dernard Quarterman), Walker Mission (Henry Starks), and Chattahoochee (Peter Crooms). A new parsonage was rising at Lake Jackson (E. R. Robinson), and Peter Crooms had rented a new home at Chattahoochee for a parsonage. White lamented only that the majority of his district's churches still were constructed of logs.[37]

Bishop Wayman held his final conferences in December 1883 and February 1884, looking forward to the Seventeenth General Conference, to be held in May, when he would receive reassignment. The Florida Conference, which convened first, sat at Apalachicola. The East Florida annual sessions came later at Mt. Zion in Jacksonville. The mood in each place ran happy, especially at Mt. Zion. "The Finance Committee's report shows a great increase in the various amounts raised for the support of the ministry for the past over that of the previous year," the minutes noted. "The other reports were also encouraging and show a large increase in membership, Sunday school scholars and church property." More than a hundred persons attended the meeting, and they claimed for the Florida church a total membership of 13,000 persons (another source gives about 5,500 for the Florida Conference and 6,250 for the East Florida Conference). The tidings grew even better. "There have been donated by a prominent gentleman of this city seven acres of land within forty minutes walk of the city," the Jacksonville newspaper observed, "upon which they propose to erect their Theological Institute, and for the purpose of erecting a temporary building the ministers subscribed $500."[38]

The bishop, if he paused to reflect on his service in Florida, possessed good reason to look with pride on his accomplishments. The state's conferences now contained almost 5 percent of total AME membership, even though Florida remained one of the South's least populated areas. Florida's AME church family numbered at least four times that of Louisiana and almost three times that of Kentucky. Virginia could boast only slightly more than half of Florida's total, while Texas, Arkansas, and North Carolina trailed by several hundred each. Mississippi topped the Sunshine State only by 250 persons. Within four short years Wayman had helped to remold a troubled institution into a dynamic one. Converts crowded many of its churches, while coffers rested comfortably full if not overflowing. New sanctuaries, parsonages, and campgrounds dotted the countryside or else anchored the church in new and growing communities. Wayman had encouraged Florida lads to pursue university educations, and he had made it possible for many local students, male and female, to obtain the basics of secondary schooling. He had put in place a training center for the clergy. The results of his labors spoke for themselves.[39]

In good times, though, we sometimes miss subtle signals of problems lurking on the horizon, and so it was with Florida's AME Church in early 1884. Of critical importance to the future, in October 1883 the U.S. Supreme Court had declared the Civil Rights Act of 1875 unconstitutional, despite the authority of the Thirteenth, Fourteenth, and Fifteenth Amendments. Thirteen years later the same panel would stamp its constitutional approval on state-mandated racial discrimination, allowing the "separate but equal" doctrine and the era of Jim Crow to stand. In between the decisions, Florida and other southern states would grind away at hard-won rights of African Americans, posing a challenge of massive proportions to the AME Church.[40]

Within the church, problems of a different nature lay waiting for the right time to surface. A better-educated clergy and middle class had sought to bring order, symmetry, and quiet respectability to the church and its services. Although not an AME member, Jonathan C. Gibbs's son Thomas V. Gibbs explained objections to shouting and other forms of emotionalism during church services in an article published in August 1883:

> We are an emotional people, I admit, giving expression to our feelings on all occasions with an unction intense to boisterousness. Political, social, and street demonstrations all call these expressions forth, but I have seen and heard but few calculated to win the respect or admiration of a criticizing public. I know that many powerful ministers in our race commend by practice and toleration these rantings in the church, but I have yet to hear or read one convincing, reasonable argument in their favor. My observations, which I have tried to make in kindliness and impartiality, lead me to believe that "shouting" is simply the effect of animal excitement brought about sometime by the personal magnetism of the speaker, but oftener by the volition and actual effort of the devotee.[41]

The "new style" ministers carried the word out into the countryside with mixed results at best. "Our colored churches in town have abandoned the old style of singing and beating time with their feet since the purchase of their handsome new organ and an experienced organist," commented a Tampa newspaper in November 1883, "which is a decided improvement to the old way of doing things."[42]

The changes were not going to come so easy, though. Not too long a time would pass before other voices would be heard. A Palatka man would express the resentments of many "common men" in these words:

> To disapprove of his manner of worshipping God, brings down his utmost contempt, accompanied with the assertion that your religion is "book larnt" and will not do "to die" with. He has no faith in prayer books or any prescribed form of worship. He believes in "moving by the spirit."[43]

How long then would it be before those who "moved by the spirit" decided to step from criticizing the lesson to clashing openly with the teacher?

8

BISHOP PAYNE AND THE DEMOCRATS IN POWER, 1884–1888

A little personal misunderstanding
between preacher and Bishop.

The national and state elections held in late 1884 placed control of government in Florida firmly in the hands of former Confederates. They rewrote the state constitution and began mandating racial discrimination by statute. As events unfolded, the AME Church remained mostly on the sidelines except where politics intersected with particular moral issues. Instead, the institution dealt with other important challenges. They included fulfilling certain commitments already entered into and at the same time coming to grips with internal rifts that would have been considered of little consequence a few years earlier. By 1888 the state's political crisis threatened to explode, and the church found itself divided and drifting. A number of its stalwarts already had sought the comfort of more congenial religious climes. Those who remained did so within the confines of a church that had moved away from its historic roots.

Two events or sets of events occurred in 1884 that prepared the scene for the subsequent four years of the Florida AME Church. The first took place at Baltimore in May, during the Seventeenth General Conference. Bishop Alexander C. Wayman's four-year term soon would expire. As was traditional, a new bishop received appointment to the Seventh Episcopal District, which included the Alabama, North Alabama, Florida, and East Florida Conferences. The man chosen was Senior Bishop Daniel A. Payne.[1]

Unlike his immediate Florida predecessors, Bishop Payne hailed from the South rather than from the Middle Atlantic states. Born February 24,

1811, in Charleston, South Carolina, to London and Martha Payne, Daniel Alexander Payne at age twelve commenced working as a carpenter, a trade at which he spent the next four years. Payne's call to the ministry came at age eighteen. As unfortunately is the case with so many early churchmen, details of Payne's family life are little known. Of his many contributions to African Methodism, the greatest related to education, whether building schools or calling for higher educational standards for the clergy. Having served the church in any number of capacities, Payne received ordination as a bishop on May 13, 1852.[2]

Because of his prominence in church and race affairs, many have sought to describe the appearance and character of Daniel A. Payne. William E. B. Du Bois—a sociologist, historian, educator, and later editor of the National Association for the Advancement of Colored People's *Crisis* magazine—called him "the little bishop." Florida writer, poet, and later NAACP secretary James Weldon Johnson referred to him as "a small shrivelled figure, a deep-lined face and sunken cheeks." According to historian George Singleton, "the overall appearance of Daniel A. Payne was of a chronic invalid; thin almost to the point of emaciation, below the average in height; features sharp; keen, penetrating eyes; voice, sharp and shrill; but with an ample forehead indicating intellectual strength and refinement." As one of the oldest and most experienced of the church's bishops, Payne knew the hills and valleys of the Seventh Episcopal District, including the personalities and ambitions of the elders who presided over Florida's AME churches.[3]

As of the 1884 designation, Bishop Payne had been associated with the church in Florida for two decades. His man Charles H. Pearce had provided much of its leadership during that period. The bishop himself had resided in the state during winter months for several years. Under Bishop Wayman's episcopate, Payne had toured numerous times helping to rejuvenate the conferences. In the process, he had discovered to his chagrin that many ministers, especially in the Florida Conference, did not hew to the moral standards that he expected of the clergy. The bishop believed, for example, in strict adherence to the church's temperance positions. That is to say, he felt that preachers should shun all use of tobacco and alcohol. Additional issues of personal morality ranked high with Payne, as well. Finally, the bishop had revised certain views that earlier had helped to mold the Florida church. As explained by historian Stephen Ward Angell, Payne had "soured on black ministers' involvement in politics during the latter part of Reconstruction, with its widespread corruption and vice."[4]

Thus, word of Payne's appointment did not come as welcome news to many Florida preachers even though they held him, generally speaking, in the highest esteem. This especially proved the case with Florida Conference members, such as Robert Meacham and George W. Witherspoon, who engaged actively in politics and had dealt in their lives with moral dilemmas that involved drinking or questions of intimate relations outside matrimonial bonds. No surprise, then, that the bishop's first Florida Conference meeting (held at Tallahassee in late November 1884) found those present a bit anxious. "Most of the brethren were like scared rats," explained Singleton H. Coleman, "for they thought the great educator would handle them without mercy." For the time being, the bishop chose to go easy on the conference members. He did, though, "teach them lessons of usefulness." Payne arranged the rejection of the eighteen ordination candidates, and he transferred Robert Meacham to East Florida.[5]

The transfer of Robert Meacham, then the most well-known political preacher in the Florida church, highlighted the second of the sets of events that helped to prepare the scene to come. Days before the 1884 Florida Conference met, Democrats had achieved two great goals. In an election marked by charges of corruption and violence, they had captured the presidency for Grover Cleveland, and they had elected a former Confederate general, Pensacola's Edward A. Perry, to the Florida governor's office. The campaign had stirred racial animosities, with Perry's workers insisting that the alternative to a Democratic victory was "negro supremacy." By the time results were announced, the old Rebels and Rebel sympathizers knew that the state was in for a dramatic change from the way things had operated during the previous eight years of relatively moderate Democratic control. Symbolizing this fact, several hundred citizens gathered at Bartow to watch a one-time Confederate officer ride around the Polk County courthouse on horseback "armed with a new broom" and carrying "a great flag on which were painted the names of Cleveland and Perry."[6]

By the time the East Florida Conference met in February 1885, Perry's men had taken over the legislature and the state supreme court. Telegraphing the kinds of changes to come, the lawmakers permitted Perry to seize control of Pensacola from its Republican town government, one that included black officeholders as tax assessor, marshal, and aldermen. The Perry men on the supreme court then upheld the new Pensacola law, although the court had turned down a similar measure four years earlier. The governor quickly appointed his own Pensacola officials. Stunning most politically aware Floridians, the list included George W. Witherspoon's name. The longtime minister and political leader had become so bitter at white Republicans and at what he perceived as political corruption that he had decided the Democrats likely would do no worse. He had urged African Americans "to join the Democrats in all undertakings of reform, particularly in municipal affairs."[7]

Witherspoon's disaffection with the Republicans—when combined with Bishop Payne's antagonism to political preachers, the consolidation of power in Democrats' hands, and the often present possibility of economic and violent intimidation—dramatically undercut black voting power in the state. When Perry's legislative forces called a constitutional convention to revise the Republican charter of 1868, turnout among African Americans ran very low in delegate selection races. Only seven black men won in contests for 108 seats. These victors primarily were professional men such as teachers and lawyers. No AME ministers sat among them. Marion County's Henry W. Chandler, a Baptist, obtained his place by defeating his state senate predecessor, AME elder Thomas W. Long.[8]

In fact, in 1885 an AME minister could gain the bishop's eye and eventual preferment within the church more easily by attacking political preachers than by engaging in politics. The career of Albert Julius Kershaw offers an example. Born in Leon County on July 3, 1852, Kershaw had pursued the ministry in the early 1870s. He received ordination as a deacon in 1876. The freshly minted minister subsequently served quietly in various posts in the Tallahassee and Marianna Districts. When he involved himself in the details of Florida Conference proceedings, he did so on issues involving little local controversy, including education and African missionary work.[9]

Kershaw's modest formative years as a minister ended in 1885 when he took action that commanded the whole church's attention and, given the new conditions then prevalent, set his career on an upward course. Specifically, from his pastorate at Marianna he penned a strong denunciation of political preachers to the *Christian Recorder*. "We shall shoot at random and if you are in the line of our shaft you must expect to fall beneath the stroke," he warned his subjects. "Ministers cannot spare time to enter the political field, because the enemies of the cause of God and goodness are too strong and numerous," Kershaw insisted, "our duty, as ministers, is to capture the world for Christ, and not for political parties." He continued, "The pulpit must occupy an elevation so high that the 'Tweedites' [a term for corrupt politicians] cannot reach it, so steep that the political train, with its load of star-ranters, cannot gain entrance." These sentiments exactly paralleled those of Bishop Payne. As Kershaw persisted in speaking out on church issues thereafter, he rose within three years to become presiding elder of the Monticello District. Not without some irony, his grandson Joe Lang Kershaw would become the first African American in the modern era elected to the Florida legislature.[10]

With the aid of supporters such as A. J. Kershaw, Bishop Payne kept the church from involving itself directly in the political struggles at and following the 1885 constitutional convention, a circumstance that affected the course of ensuing political events. Still, many of Payne's closest associates—men seen by other AME leaders and influential members of the laity as the pride of the church due to their fine educations—refused to believe that most Democratic officials posed much of a threat. This was the case, at least in part, because they associated easily with many of the same men in support of the temperance cause. Joseph E. Lee, for example, endorsed the new constitution. Other black leaders, who formerly might have followed the AME lead, now sought new allies. They aligned themselves especially with a national labor organization called the Knights of Labor. The combination proved a potent one, and election results began to reverse the political tides in some of the state's larger cities. In response, legislators adopted more and more punitive laws. Meanwhile, black representation in the legislative chambers plummeted.[11]

As early as 1886 the political mess had commenced to take a toll within the AME Church. Robert Meacham and other of the church's old warhorses raised alarms about the problems to come. They stood discredited, though, and their warnings went unheeded. When the East Florida Conference met in March, Meacham quit the AME ministry in protest of Payne's leadership. He transferred his membership to the AME Zion Church. Apparently, others soon followed. "I used to delight in reading [the *Christian Recorder*] because they spoke of the improvement of the churches and the increase of the AME connection," wrote W. L. G. Jones from Marianna. "But here of late almost the very first thing our eyes fall upon is something detrimental to the church or injurious to true Christian progress," he continued. "I am sorry to my soul that I can hear of so many of our noble ministers withdrawing from the connection and trying to form a church of their own, tearing asunder and scattering the whole church for a little personal misunderstanding between preacher and Bishop!"[12]

Bishop Payne seems to have responded to the situation with misunder-

44. Pensacola minister Morris Marcellus Moore was fired by Bishop Daniel A. Payne in 1886. Undaunted by the setback, Morris would be elected a bishop in 1900. Courtesy Photographic Collection, Florida State Archives.

standing, anger, and hurt feelings. He let the departing preachers go without serious attempts to shepherd them back into the fold, and yet his temper also flared at the political setbacks. The bishop particularly chafed when he realized that many ministers were standing by, in the face of political disaster, without encouraging their congregations to vote. What Payne failed to see was that those preachers, particularly ones in the Florida Conference, had interpreted his policies as barring politics in their churches, as opposed to barring political preachers from the church. During a speech in midsummer 1886, he blasted ministers in "rural districts" who "dare not say anything about politics or kindred subjects" because they were "under the control of ex-slaveholders." Florida Conference leaders took this badly. As a result, they slowed the pace of fund-raising on the church's behalf.

The possibility of fireworks loomed as the Florida Conference annual sessions convened on November 16, 1886, days after the election at which voters approved the new constitution. Payne arranged early on at the

Pensacola meeting for A. J. Kershaw to be elected conference secretary for the second year in a row, drawing a symbolic line between supporters and others. Matters proceeded according to schedule until the fifth day. Then, the bishop's committee on circuits, stations, and missions brought before the gathering a stunning report. Payne had decided to abolish the Marianna District and to depose its presiding elder, W. L. G. Jones, whose temerity in publishing his views in the *Christian Recorder* had not gone unnoticed. The report "caused quite a sensation." The bishop refused to allow a "no" vote on the proposal, and it took effect. The seventh day, Payne released his appointments list. It disclosed that he had fired Morris M. Moore as pastor at Pensacola and transferred him to East Florida, along with John Speight and C. L. Clary. Others found themselves unexpectedly transferred to less desirable locations. Appeals proved of no avail. "Bishop Payne's motto seems to be 'What I have written, I have written,'" observed John Speight.[13]

Payne's actions at Pensacola brought into high relief a problem that had been simmering in Florida since Bishop Wayman's departure. While beloved for his pioneering service to the church, Bishop Payne evidenced far more than had his predecessor the raw power of episcopal authority and, to some critics, an air of superiority. Where Wayman's "common touch" endeared him as a fellow human being to thousands of church members, Payne's attitudes kept him at a distance. He associated in Florida mostly with the well-educated, prominent, and affluent segments of the African American community and ministry.[14]

Many out-of-favor clergymen and everyday sorts of church members consequently saw Payne as out of touch. Most pastors preached not in the relatively sophisticated urban churches he frequented but in rural or small-town chapels. The experience at Baldwin of one preacher, James Randolph, is illustrative. The community of about four hundred persons survived by timbering and turpentining. A few dirt roads served as streets. At the intersection of two of them stood Campbell's AME Chapel. "The chapel was a small wooden building, with wooden shutters, and lit at night by kerosene lamps and storm lanterns hanging from the rafters," described a biographer of Randolph's son A. Philip Randolph. "The membership was small, about fifty." The family lived in a log cabin two miles from the church. A relation recalled that, in the winter, "old newspapers and rags had to be stuffed into cracks in the siding to keep out the cold wind." He added, "When it rained, water leaked through holes in the roof, and all the family's tubs and buckets had to be used to catch the rain."[15]

Given such conditions among much of the membership and clergy, it would be difficult to understand if there were not resentments of well-paid and distant bishops such as Daniel A. Payne. And there most certainly were, and more as time went on. "I find the reason some of our ministers don't get any more Dollar Money than they do is because they don't tell the people what becomes of the money," N. S. Jenkins wrote from Columbia County's Mt. Tabor in 1885. "I heard them say that the Bishops have got a fine house, and they would not notice them if they would go to their house." In time the bishops commonly would be known as the "black princes." With tougher economic times in future years, greater resistance to paying scarce money into the church would find its justification in resentment of princely maintenance costs. For now, it focused on the costs of what appeared to many to be princely projects, none more so than the East Florida Divinity High School.[16]

Bishop Payne had preached the cause of the Divinity High School since the days of its 1883 origins under Bishop Wayman. Throughout the church his dedication to education had been recognized and applauded for decades, with Wilberforce University standing as the great monument of his service. As bishop for Florida, he intended to repeat that achievement on a smaller scale. When Payne assumed the episcopal authority in the state in late 1884, the school already operated at Jacksonville in a building at Mt. Zion AME Church. "We had last [academic] year in attendance 125 students, 18 of whom were young men preparing for the ministry," reported President William Preston Ross that fall. "Your humble servant has charge of the theological department," he continued. "Revs. J. E. Lee and J. R. Scott [Jr.] have charge of the normal department." Ross added: "The primary department is taught by Mrs. E. Miller and Miss S. Davis. Both of these ladies are refined and accomplished."[17]

That the school operated at all represented a great achievement, but its problems were many. A chronic lack of funding topped the list. When classes commenced in October 1884, Ross found himself forced to open the doors "without one cent" (except tuition payments) to defray costs. Enrollment had dropped to about one hundred. With J. J. Sawyer desperately attempting to raise contributions, H. F. Chisolm appealed in the *Christian Recorder* for emergency assistance. "We must show our anxiety and ardor for education in the South by action, especially by paying what we have promised," he declared. The minister added, "We cannot afford to see this grand effort go to naught." By early 1885 conditions had grown more critical.

"Now is the time to show our love for God and humanity," Ross pled in the church publication, "now is the time to practice what we preach." He warned, "No school can be conducted without faculty, and no faculty can work without pay, or will not, at least."[18]

Payne strove to rescue the school by regularizing its administration and securing dependable sources of funding. He succeeded in the former endeavor. In particular, the bishop sought legislation in early 1885 to revise the old Brown Theological Institute charter to authorize "the Divinity School." In practice the institution came to carry the name Florida Normal and Divinity High School and, subsequently, the Florida Normal, Scientific, Industrial, and Divinity High School. Trustees designated by the law included Payne, Charles H. Pearce, William W. Sampson, Primus G. Gowens, Thomas W. Long, George W. Witherspoon, William A. Bird, E. W. Johnson, and Morris M. Moore.[19]

When it came to sources of funding, though, the bishop faltered. In February 1885, as the legislature was addressing his charter amendments, Payne approached the East Florida Conference annual gathering for monetary assistance. There, he found preachers reluctant to commit sufficient funds to such ambitious purposes. This ambivalence reflected several attitudes. It represented, in part, the beginnings of resentments at Payne's distant eminence and of princely projects at a time when so many ministers and members remained so poor. Perhaps more, it expressed concerns that the school existed mostly to serve Jacksonville-area students, especially those whose families belonged to the affluent and elite Mt. Zion church, then the state's largest AME congregation, with eight hundred members. Finally, the ambivalence hinted at disagreement with the whole idea of a church-funded normal school. Since 1883 the state had operated annual free normal schools at Gainesville and Tallahassee for African American teachers. Why, then, should poor church members pay scarce funds to duplicate at a dear cost what already came free from the state?[20]

The seeming opposition to his episcopal leadership, however subtle, left Payne frustrated and searching for alternatives. As a result, he faced acceptance of a much less agreeable course of action. He capitulated to it in March 1885 when the new board met at Jacksonville to organize and elected the bishop as its chairman. At his insistence, they then opted to sell the school's principal asset. It consisted of a 640-acre tract of rural land.[21]

Payne's lack of success in obtaining adequate funding telegraphed real troubles ahead for the school. His personal popularity among Florida min-

45. The Florida Normal and Divinity High School building erected at Jacksonville in the mid-1880s by Mount Zion AME Church members. This building soon would house Edward Waters College. Courtesy Photographic Collection, Florida State Archives.

isters likely crested at that 1885 Ocala meeting of the East Florida Conference, where members "received [him] with gladness." Even then, he could not move his admirers sufficiently to guarantee the institution's continued existence, much less to furnish President Ross with any of the items on his wish list. "What we need now, right now, is a larger school building right in the spot where the present building stands," Ross argued. "We have not room enough," he continued. "We could have 250 students to-day, if we had the room." Eventually, Ross and Payne fell back on the generosity and resources of Mt. Zion's Jacksonville members. Their church borrowed $4,400 and erected "a fine and commodius building" of brick. As Morris M. Moore recollected, "The school building was built... with tacit understanding that the trustees of the school would rent the building for school purposes at $50 per month, and as soon as possible purchase the said building for the African Methodist Episcopal Connection in the State of Florida."[22]

The agreement with Mt. Zion notwithstanding, the possibility of purchasing the school building during the remainder of Bishop Payne's tenure remained a remote one. Usually, the coffers stood empty or almost so. Matters worsened in the spring of 1887 when the state legislature, taking advantage of federal support for agricultural extension work, created the State Normal College for Colored Students at Tallahassee. The credibility of this forerunner of Florida A&M University rocketed upward in the African American community when it attracted two outstanding individuals as its first president and vice president. Pensacola lawyer Thomas De Saille Tucker, a graduate of the distinguished Oberlin College, accepted the presidency and a professorship. Jonathan C. Gibbs's accomplished son Thomas Van Renssalaer Gibbs—educated at Howard University, the U.S. Military Academy, and Oberlin College—left the state legislature to become Tucker's second. With attention and support redirected to Tallahassee as these events occurred, Ross resigned as president of the AME high school. The action came during the trustees meeting held in June 1887, and circumstances suggest that pressure from the bishop lay behind it. A majority of the board regretted the decision. Payne accepted it. He then took control of the institution himself.[23]

The remaining months of Payne's Florida episcopate saw the school's fortunes ebb further. The bishop had succumbed to a fever in early 1886 that had left him, as he described, "in a state of child-like weakness." Convalescence proved slow. "I was too enfeebled to recover strength rapidly," Payne explained. Still weakened one year later, he found himself simply unable to run the school. Accordingly, the bishop turned to John H. Welch, a young minister he had imported from the Baltimore Conference to replace Ross as pastor of Jacksonville's Mt. Zion. Welch attempted to fill the void created by Ross's departure and Payne's disability, but his combined church and school duties overwhelmed him. School enrollment dropped from 110 to 50. "The falling off in attendance I think was caused by some premature changes in the administration," Ross observed in the *Christian Recorder*. "The question now with us . . . is, what steps can we take to make the school successful?"[24]

To make matters worse, declines in political and social life matched the declines in Payne's health and the high school's fortunes. The critical state elections of 1886 had spurred incidents of racial violence that persisted into the next year. Soon, Florida would bear the ignominious label of one of the nation's most lynch-prone states. Although the alliance of black leaders and

46. Fernandina's Macedonia AME Church. Courtesy Photographic Collection, Florida State Archives.

the Knights of Labor produced a few electoral wins in 1886, such as Thomas V. Gibbs's Duval County legislative victory, the legislature passed into the control of young white Democrats determined to segregate society along racial lines and to drive African Americans from politics. In the spring of 1887 they enacted the state's first law mandating Jim Crow segregation on railroads, as well as new provisions toughening voter registration. "Too late to talk about the 'suppressed vote' now," wrote a Pensacola man. "We are in the hands of the devil." When the Knights of Labor alliance scored more municipal victories in 1888, the state government responded in 1889 by authorizing a poll tax law and additional devices aimed at denying the vote to blacks. It also seized control of local government at Jacksonville and Key West, while drastically altering the nature of municipal governance at other towns. African Americans, for the most part, had been removed from any substantive role in public affairs.[25]

As the era of black political power ended, many of the Florida AME founders also were passing from the scene, depriving the church of a wealth of wisdom drawn from long experience and destabilizing its foundations to some extent. In addition to those such as Robert Meacham, P. L. Cuyler, and Thomas W. Walker who resigned in the late 1880s, others retired or passed away. Death claimed Dernard Quarterman, for example, in May 1887. At Lower Peachtree, Alabama, on July 16, William Bradwell departed life to be mourned by many Florida friends. More significantly, Elder Charles H. Pearce died at Jacksonville three months and nine days later. Since 1886 he had supervised the Enterprise District as its presiding elder, overseeing the church's most dynamic region. His return to prominence under Bishops Wayman and Payne had resuscitated his reputation within the church, but his labors had taxed him beyond his capacity. A. J. Kershaw, echoing the sentiments of many, eulogized the great builder of African Methodism in Florida in these words:

> Jacob Livingston, Fuller White and William Bradwell, Jacksonville's first pastor, these are all gone to rest beyond the river. But, above and beyond all these and the rest, I hear a voice, and see a figure, as it, like a flying meteor sweeps Florida from the muddy banks of the Apalachicola river to the meandering banks of the St. John, and I inquire who is it? and am told, it is the irresistable, the immortal, the triumphant Charles H. Pearce. Taken all things into consideration we doubt very much if African Methodism has ever produced a man superior to Charles H. Pearce. We make no comparison as regards scholarship, but as a zealous worker, a practical theologian, and an expounder of the New Testament, we repeat, Charles H. Pearce had no superiors. The young itinerants always found in him a true friend, a correct guide, and a safe counselor. But woe unto the young itinerant whose coat was not cut according to the Wesleyan rule, or whose collar partook of dudeism. But Charles H. Pearce is gone, for he, hearing a voice, he drop[p]ed his trumpet, and, mounting Heaven's eternal steepness, he there awaits our arrival.[26]

The toll produced by these negative circumstances—political reverses, racial violence, societal change, growing friction in the church, stricter concepts of clerical morality, the bishop's ailing health, and the departure of old hands who could share the wisdom of experience and a sense of stability—came to public view most clearly in the Panhandle limits of the Florida Conference. The already weakened jurisdiction attempted to cope with poor finances and depressed morale as best it could, but resources would stretch only so far. Tensions in the conference rose after the 1886 annual sessions at Pensacola in which Bishop Payne abolished the Marianna District and transferred several influential members against their desires. That the troubles would break into public view seemed only a matter of time.[27]

The flare-up came at Pensacola. A large camp meeting had been planned for the early fall of 1887 to revive spirits and attract badly needed new members. The effort disappointed its planners, to say the least. "The recent AME Church camp meeting was a complete failure spiritually and financially," reported one local resident. Although Pensacola's pastor, J. H. Spears, suffered no loss of popularity at his home church, Bishop Payne apparently blamed him for the fiasco. At the Florida Conference gathering in November, the bishop punished Spears by transferring him to "a little backwoods circuit." Spears promptly resigned, as tempers seethed. Many conference members were left yearning, as A. J. Kershaw put it, for "love and good will."[28]

Any person assessing Florida's worsening conditions for African Americans during the 1885–1888 period and the concurrent intra-AME Church problems might assume that Bishop Payne and other church fathers labored in an environment marked by gloomy foreboding or defeatism, but such was not the case. Instead, they often breathed deeply of optimism and marked what they understood as significant progress. The fact was that their attention was diverted elsewhere much of the time, and where they looked the sun continued to shine brightly. For one thing, church headquarters and the homes of many key figures in the church lay at Jacksonville, a city where thousands of African Americans prospered. As political conditions deteriorated in the state, the Knights of Labor alliance captured control of the city's municipal government, annexed adjacent suburbs that were heavily black, and created a solid African American voting majority. AME minister Joseph E. Lee sat, by 1888, as municipal judge. The situation would not change until 1889.[29]

Meanwhile, the peninsula experienced breathtaking growth as millionaire Henry B. Plant and others pressed rail connections into Central and Southwest Florida, giving birth to new towns and filling old ones with new residents. At this time Henry M. Flagler—John D. Rockefeller's Standard Oil Company partner—pioneered the operation in the state of truly luxurious resorts. His fabulous Ponce de Leon Hotel in St. Augustine first opened its doors to guests on January 10, 1888, generating publicity that, in turn, spurred the growth of the tourism industry. Resort hotels and lesser attractions brought new amenities such as electric power plants, sewerage systems, and mosquito control programs that made urban life more attractive. As the towns and cities grew, thousands of job opportunities for African Americans arose. A black migration southward ensued.[30]

As African American eyes looked yearningly toward peninsular jobs, AME Church fathers gazed in the same direction. This fact, already the case for years, intensified in its importance as the church spread to accommodate the growth. Ormond Beach saw the birth of New Bethel in 1885. Bartowans founded St. James. In the next year, Mt. Nebo organized at Silver Springs in Marion, Mt. Zion at Putnam Hall in Putnam, Grant Chapel at Oviedo in Seminole, Zion at Center Hill in Sumter, and New Bethel at Port Orange in Volusia. In 1887, Allen Temple opened at Brooksville, and in Marion County Mt. Tabor was founded at Kendrick and Orange Lake AME at Orange Lake. Okahumpka's Bethel followed in 1888, as did Younge's Chapel at Ocala, St. Paul's at Apopka, Allen Chapel at Pomona in Putnam, Bethel at Kissimmee, and New St. Paul at St. Augustine. More were to come.[31]

New congregations sparked the excitement of older ones, as the rising economic and population tide swelled membership rolls. "I rejoice to know that the grand old flag of African Methodism, notwithstanding adverse winds, is waving in triumph," exulted Orlando's minister in late 1886. "Our membership continues to increase." He added, "The Dollar Money boom is assuming phenomenal proportions." Orlando's experience found its echoes elsewhere. "The pastor of Tampa is sorry for but one thing," a correspondent declared, "his church is too small for his congregation." The Enterprise District upped the salary of its presiding elder to a lucrative $1,000 per year and found funds to subsidize the labors of numerous missionaries. Out of the district meeting of May 1886, for instance, came instructions for three new missions: R. S. Quarterman, Maitland; G. B. Hill, Pemberton Ferry; and A. B. Collins, Plant City.[32]

Through the region the sounds of hammers and saws resounded. Examples are easy to find. At Orlando, S. H. Coleman oversaw construction of his new and larger sanctuary in 1885. "We now have the frame up and paid for," he reported in August. At Melbourne, members erected Allen Chapel's first building at a site on Lipscomb Street. The next year J. A. Quarterman moved into his new parsonage at Enterprise as he planned other projects. "Soon we shall build a new church here," he proudly commented. The steady pace of improvements quickened somewhat in 1887. From the Crescent City Mission in Putnam County, for instance, J. L. Moore passed on

47. Palatka's Bethel AME Church. Courtesy Photographic Collection, Florida State Archives.

the good news. "We have three churches in this mission—Union Bethel, Crescent City; Mt. Moriah, Welaka; Pleasant Grove, Georgetown," he wrote, "and our efficient pastor, Rev. S. P. Pettis, will soon have another church erected at Pomona, Fla." Similarly, Mandarin's Robert Lewis informed *Christian Recorder* readers, "We have built a new church 22 x 36 at this place, also a new church at Orangedale, and repaired the church at Fruit Cove." He concluded, "African Methodism is in the lead here."[33]

The heady excitement extended into 1888, the final year of Daniel A. Payne's episcopate in Florida. "Revivals in Enterprise District have been going on successfully all over the district this year," J. A. Quarterman recorded in the summer. "Rev. T. W. Long, in Orlando, has increased to one hundred and eighteen," he continued. "He is having one of the grandest revivals ever held in this part of the South." Winter Park had doubled its membership under Quarterman, while the Maitland station—renamed the Eatonville Circuit—shared in the good times. "Our church in South Florida has this year made rapid progress," Quarterman concluded. "Our church, of course, is the leading colored denomination in South Florida, as well as other places."[34]

Greater membership brought with it busier schedules and richer programs for many of the peninsula's AME churches. The 1888 East Florida

48. St. Augustine's newly constructed New St. Paul AME Church as it appeared in 1889. Courtesy Photographic Collection, Florida State Archives.

Conference, Bishop Payne's last, was held at Mt. Zion near the St. Johns River resort town of Palatka. The next month, to provide a sense of the plentitude of activities now common, the church sponsored the birth of an immigration society. In April, "a series of revival services" under R. B. Brookins proved "very successful in securing many converts yet quite so in a pecuniary sense, as far as the pockets of the visitors were concerned." The same month a biracial assembly convened in the church to congratulate "the scholars of the colored high school." And in May, weddings brought joy while "the AME Sunday School gave a picnic excursion out to Interlachen."[35]

The Palatka gathering of the East Florida Conference in February 1888 delighted in the reports presented to it of growth and development. Still, the old problems lingered in the air. Members worried about the health of W. W. Sampson, who lay prostrate at Jacksonville. Likely, news of Allen

Jones Sr.'s last illness circulated, as well. He would die at Quincy on the twenty-eighth. Bishop Payne cited the prosperity of the conference as he opened a discussion of "the feasibility of raising contingent funds." One report notes that "animated discussion" followed, "resulting in the elimination of the compulsory clause adopted at the last conference." The bishop enjoyed more success in encouraging the expulsion of Solomon Sampson from the conference based on morals charges of an unspecified nature. The sessions concluded with memorials to Charles H. Pearce. "From nearly every eye in the conference the cheeks could be seen bathed with tears," commented one onlooker. Without further ado, the bishop issued his appointments for the year, "bade the brethren Godspeed," and adjourned his final conference session in Florida.[36]

Doubtlessly, most, if not all, the ministers of Florida's AME Church wished godspeed to Bishop Payne. An individual of so much accomplishment deserved no less. Yet the same men looked forward to new leadership for a perilous and challenging era, knowing that the general conference to be held at Indianapolis in May would chose Payne's successor. The need for a suitable pilot likely escaped few minds. The church had shaken loose from its historic moorings in rural and agricultural Middle Florida, where a political role for the church often had been taken for granted. Now, it had shifted its direction toward work aimed more at moral purification than political redemption, and its sights were fixed down the peninsula toward Central and South Florida. Dangerous waters lay ahead. The hand on the tiller, the church leaders knew, must be a steady and sure one.

9

A HEALER CREATES A COLLEGE, 1888-1892

*Everything is full of life
at the AME Church.*

The AME Church's 1888 General Conference, held at Indianapolis, witnessed the designation of a new bishop to oversee Florida's conferences for the four years extending to 1892. In ways reminiscent of the 1880 naming of Alexander W. Wayman, the new appointment put the right man at the right time in the right position to meet needs critical to the Sunshine State's church. The process that the new prelate undertook to accomplish his task proved a slow and demanding one, requiring firm leadership and goodly measures of patience and understanding. Still, this remarkable man accomplished much for the church, including a legacy in the form of a college that would survive and endure. In bringing that institution to life, he helped realize a dream that for decades had tantalized and frustrated church fathers, not to mention many of the bishop's senior episcopal colleagues.

The man assigned in 1888 to preside over the reorganized Seventh Episcopal District (now South Carolina and Florida) was newly installed bishop Benjamin W. Arnett Sr. Compared to his immediate predecessor, Bishop Daniel A. Payne, Arnett was a relatively young man. He was born in Brownsville, Fayette County, Pennsylvania, on March 6, 1838. Unlike many other bishops, Arnett was a clean-shaven man with a rather large forehead, sharp nose, and rather straight hair. He married Mary Louisa Gordon of Uniontown, Pennsylvania, on May 25, 1858. To that union were born six children, four boys and two girls. A prolific writer, Arnett started his early career as a schoolteacher in Brownsville. He labored in the vine-

49. Bishop and Mrs. Benjamin W. Arnett Sr. Courtesy Photographic Collection, Florida State Archives.

yards of the school system until 1867, when he actively associated with the AME Church. A very energetic man in politics, he became vice president of Ohio's Republican state convention in 1878, and its first black chaplain in 1880. Like some other energetic men, he moved up in the hierarchy of the AME church to become bishop. His election occurred at Indianapolis in May 1888.[1]

Rising faster than most of his AME colleagues, a bishop at age fifty, Arnett unfortunately possessed little personal experience in matters relating to the Deep South, having spent much of his ministerial career in Kentucky and Ohio. He had traveled widely, though, particularly after 1880 when he assumed the position of financial secretary of the church. Accordingly, many Floridians knew him well. Arnett benefited from a brilliant mind and a talent for statistics and financial matters generally, and as it turned out, he did not allow his elevation to prominence to distance him from those of lesser station. "He is a general favorite of the people," commented one acquaintance soon after his installation.[2]

Arnett had other talents and gifts that were to serve him well in Florida. For one thing, a "popular style" of speaking that was "peculiarly his own" captured attention and endeared him to many. The bishop's love for the AME Church shone brightly and clearly, but he viewed the world around him ecumenically. "As a churchman, he has no narrow, sectarian feeling," explained the acquaintance. This permitted Arnett a broad range of relationships among black and white, greatly enhancing the corps of supporters available to assist the Florida church. Arnett also took immense pride in the accomplishments of African Americans, sharing those achievements with all who would listen. In doing so, he respected the power of history to motivate, to inspire, and to bridge divisions. Finally, unlike Bishop Payne in his later years, Arnett did not disdain politics or politicians. While it was said in 1888 that "the good Bishop has entirely retired from the political arena," the fact was that he had served in the Ohio legislature within a year or two past. According to W. E. B. Du Bois, Arnett would become "[President] William McKinley's favorite advisor on Negro Affairs." As a legislator who proudly wore the Republican party's colors, he had battled fiercely to repeal Ohio's "Black Laws." Arnett felt little hesitation at mixing a good dose of politics with Christianity.[3]

Upon his election as bishop and his appointment to the Seventh District in May, Arnett likely knew that he faced serious problems with his charge. Although conditions in the peninsula were better than those in the Panhandle, dissension bubbled in both the East Florida and the Florida Conferences. During the four years of Bishop Payne's episcopacy, this had resulted in key resignations from the clergy, a slowdown in financial collections, membership stagnation in the old AME Middle Florida heartland, and a chronic refusal by the conferences to support sufficiently the church's Florida Normal and Divinity High School located at Jacksonville.

Statistics help tell the story. State-by-state church membership reports published by AME officials of the situation in 1888 to 1889 seem to reflect inflated totals of adherents everywhere. Still, comparisons of percentage growth based on these reports suggest that once dynamic Florida now stood among the most anemic of the states of the lower South. Where nearby Georgia had witnessed growth since 1884 of almost 2.5 times, Florida claimed an increase by a factor of only 1.8 times. Raw numbers placed nearly thirty-four thousand more new adherents in the Peach State, while the Sunshine State's claims amounted to a ten thousand–member increase. More accurate figures reported for 1890, after a period of growth to be discussed shortly, show that the actual rise in Florida involved a factor of only slightly more than 1.3 times as of that year, about four thousand members. Texas and Arkansas, which had trailed Florida in total membership five or six years earlier, now apparently stood higher in rank, which helped to explain why so many outstanding members of the Florida clergy had accepted transfer to those distant jurisdictions.[4]

Beneath the visible challenges lay other and more fundamental problems. Rural residents groaned beneath the burden of depressed farm commodity prices and the refusal of local and national political leaders to address their needs. Further, the state's social and political climates had soured. White conservatives, hoping to generate support for disenfranchising African Americans and driving them from the halls of government, had paraded far and wide stirring racial hatred and, sometimes, committing terrible acts of racial violence. Meanwhile, the AME Church had waited on the sidelines as disaster ensued. What the church could have accomplished in the face of changing conditions is uncertain, but its refusal to become involved directly represented in many eyes a retreat from—and, for some, a betrayal of—the promise of the church's early activism.

Such disenchantment—added to tensions created by a widening gap in the church between poor members who mostly resided in rural areas and relatively more affluent urban dwellers—fed the alienation of some AME adherents from the church hierarchy. Perceptions of "black princes" and their entourages squandering hard-earned contributions angered everyday members. These were the men and women whom the church existed to serve and upon whom it depended for support. Moreover, ministers aplenty, particularly those without advanced education, believed that only the bishops' favorites would prosper in the church and enjoy its rewards. "Over the years, because of his lack of formal training, the Reverend Mr. [James] Randolph was unable to rise to any position of prominence in the AME ministry," concluded one historian in a discussion of A. Philip Randolph's father. "Nor for the same reason," the writer continued, "was he ever found attractive by the wealthier and more sophisticated middle-class congregations." Randolph's son Asa recalled the situation in slightly different terms. His father, Asa insisted, could never bring himself "to lick the boots of the powerful bishops."[5]

As if these dilemmas posed insufficient concerns, the summer of 1888 introduced new ones for Bishop Arnett's early consideration. At worldly Pensacola, where the church had grappled with problems since its earliest days in Florida, an evangelist named Sherwood appeared on the scene in a manner that fanned intrachurch tensions to a white-hot level. Specifically, Sherwood demanded the ouster of district presiding elder George W. Witherspoon for bad judgment and questionable morals. As to the questionable morals, the visiting preacher declared that his target had been seen "playing croquet, checkers, casino, visiting the opera, the theater, the circus and saloons." Although the venerable presiding elder had suffered from political missteps in recent years, he remained tremendously popular as a preacher among the church's rank and file. The particulars of the clash that followed blazed into newspapers in Florida and as far away as New York City, with Sherwood taking the heavier verbal blows. "Some so-called preachers will resort to any method to gain some trashy and cheap notoriety," a Pensacolan commented. The evangelist soon departed town, but he left in his wake rekindled anger at church attempts to set higher and higher moral standards for clergymen, resentments at high-handed actions by the church elite generally, and heightened concerns about the new bishop's sentiments on such issues.[6]

At virtually the same moment, tragedy struck in northeast Florida when yellow fever beset Fernandina, Jacksonville, St. Augustine, and nearby places. Residents fled if they could, but most African Americans found themselves without any place to go. Within weeks quarantines produced the threat of starvation for those unable to leave. "Hundreds of our people who were living by the day and week are now suffering for want of the necessaries of life," William P. Ross reported in mid-September from Jacksonville. Courageously, numerous AME ministers and lay officials remained to care for those in want, including Ross, William W. Sampson, Joseph E. Lee, John H. Welch, John R. Scott Jr., Thomas Higginbotham, and S. T. Tice. For the AME Zion Church, Robert Meacham joined his old AME colleagues. As weeks of plague passed, Welch fell ill. Higginbotham, Sampson, and Ross perished. The fatal toll mounted well into December.[7]

The 1888 yellow fever epidemic devastated Jacksonville, by then the financial and temporal capital of African Methodism in Florida. Almost five thousand cases of the disease resulted in more than four hundred deaths. Business affairs experienced disruptions for months, with the city's tourist industry suffering a profound blow. Into the new year Jacksonville gasped for breath as it coped with its losses. "How sad and dreary it seems after the dreadful fever!" one winter resident commented. "Many who left the city have not returned." AME families suffered from losses along with the rest, whether of loved ones or of economic security. To a lesser extent, the same conditions blanketed the region. From Columbia County's Mt. Tabor, A. B. Collins expressed by understatement the feelings of many. "We are not having a very pleasant time," he wrote, "owing to the yellow fever."[8]

It thus may be seen that, by late 1888, church morale suffered throughout most of Florida. The principal exception lay in the booming central and southern peninsula, where the Enterprise District's ministers were holding

50. The Reverend S. Timothy Tice, born in Florida's Madison County, stood among those who risked their lives to nurse victims of the 1888 yellow fever epidemic. From the *Philadelphia Christian Recorder*, April 19, 1900.

successful revivals and boosting membership rolls (the glorious times eluded Key West, where a recent fire and the departure of the cigar industry to Tampa had depressed the economy). For the remainder of the state, the prevailing atmosphere was evoked by the report of a member of the Boulogne congregation. "There are a lot of us colored people here who cannot make a good living without going off to work on the public works," he observed with a degree of resignation. "Our church has blown down," the man continued, "but by God's help we hope to rebuild it soon." He added: "At the same time our pastor, Rev. J. D. Bennet, was down in bed sick. It was my privilege to visit him in his affliction and pray with him."[9]

The situation cried out for leadership, and Bishop Arnett arrived just in time to provide it. The advent of his episcopacy came at Monticello on December 19, 1888, when he convened the annual session of the Florida Conference. Anticipating and, in many cases, praying for new directions, over one thousand persons attended. Arnett's presence, thanks to a number of factors, essentially exploded upon the gathering. For one thing, he insisted that so much be accomplished during the few days' meetings that those present found themselves with little time to harbor resentments and grudges. "Never in the history of our conference," declared one minister, "was there so much business transacted in the same amount of time." Further, Arnett brought with him a retinue of high-church officials to lend credibility and weight to his pronouncements. He summed up his intentions with the phrase "you must" and invoked Scripture to provide encouragement. "Be strong in the Lord," he demanded, "and in the power of his might."[10]

The impact of Arnett's iron-fisted leadership was softened by the velvet glove of his personality and outlook. The context for its use was described by an onlooker. "For some cause the brethren had come to look upon a bishop with a degree of fear bordering on abhorrence," he observed, "afraid to preach, sing or pray." Now, the situation quickly turned around, as Arnett "gave us to understand that he, though a bishop, was a natural man, and for us to serve God with all our heart, soul, mind and strength." His words led to a palpable release of tensions. "After this positive declaration," the onlooker recorded, "the brethren broke loose from their accustomed surroundings at conference and we had an animated and enthusiastic session." Arnett also clarified that his administration would vary from what many ministers had perceived to be the unfortunate pattern of his predecessor. Particularly, he promised new standards for advancement in the church. As the meeting's minutes recounted: "Ministers will fall or stand as their merits demand. Favoritism will be relegated to the rear and we will make our own appointment, according to our capacity, resolution and energy."[11]

Beyond making broad policy decisions, Arnett displayed an intimate awareness of the conference and its problems. The situation at Pensacola provides an illustration. Presiding Elder Witherspoon remained furious at evangelist Sherwood's attacks. The bishop assuaged him by convincing the popular preacher to accept transfer to Key West, where opportunities for great service awaited in the state's largest city. For the Pensacola District's new presiding elder, the bishop tapped William A. Bird, a man of impeccable reputation who, like Witherspoon, had engaged actively in politics (as a Republican) and had served as recently as 1885 in the Florida legislature. Arnett also managed to avoid a clash with Bishop Payne's men over reappointment of J. G. Grimes to the Pensacola church. A Payne disciple, Pastor Grimes nonetheless had shown skill in navigating the treacherous waters that swirled within and around Witherspoon and church affairs at the town. Though blamed for some church problems, he counted many supporters. In the circumstances, Arnett delayed any change until a future conference.

This series of actions succeeded. Peace settled on the district. As one Pensacolan noted of Grimes's reappointment, "The congregation of the AME Church was agreeably surprised."[12]

The whirlwind created out of Arnett's bold approach and thoughtful initiatives breathed renewed life into the conference, and Arnett's stock rose accordingly in the hearts and minds of many of his charges. "Under Bishop Arnett's administration," asserted an onlooker, "the status of the Florida Conference will be perceptibly changed." Now was the time for the clergy to respond. "Then brethren," the onlooker charged, "let us bestir ourselves." He concluded, "The Bishop's parting words were affectionate and inspiring."[13]

Arnett followed his Monticello triumph with similar success at Madison, where the East Florida Conference gathered on February 13, 1889. He repeated the patterns he had set two months earlier. Particularly, he let those assembled know that he now was in charge. "In a very forcible manner," described a correspondent, "[he] pointed out to the ministers the best course to pursue to elevate the standard of the profession and insure success as gospel ministers." Given that Bishop Payne's support had centered in the East Florida Conference, Arnett's task as the newcomer must have appeared daunting to him. "One with a scrutinizing eye and a strict sense of discrimination would often detect an expression in their deliberation which would occasionally remind him of a desire to give utterance to some inmost feeling, brought about by severe affliction," commented a visiting churchman. Yet Arnett did not flinch, as another visitor appreciated. "I looked and often wondered at his skill in business," C. L. Lane recalled, "and thought no man could manage better than he."[14]

The bishop understood that, with the assertion of his authority, came a responsibility to uplift spirits in the midst of racial turmoil and yellow fever devastation. As to problems of violence and discrimination, he endeavored in a creative way to help his flock believe that they were not alone in their struggles, that even some whites cared about them and sympathized in their predicaments. He did so by inviting to the session the Reverend Robert L. Wiggins, the white presiding elder of the Live Oak District of the Methodist Episcopal Church South. Wiggins greeted his audience as "coworkers in the vineyard of the Lord." He then related details of his 1866 encounter with Elder Charles H. Pearce on the streets of Jacksonville, a chance meeting that proved key to the AME presence in northeast Florida. "[I] opened to him the Methodist Episcopal Church, South, at Jacksonville," Wiggins boasted, "in which he preached his first sermon in Florida." The presentation achieved its desired goal. "The Conference was highly gratified with the sentiments and friendship expressed by Elder Wiggins," explained a reporter, "which had a very happy effect."[15]

Arnett complemented the "happy effect" of Wiggins's appearance by striving to inspire his listeners through a renewed appreciation of how far they had come—recent setbacks notwithstanding—in the past thirty years. His friend and fellow bishop W. J. Gaines of Georgia assisted. A part of their colloquy is reflected by conference minutes:

Bishop Gaines brought the house down by asking Bishop Arnett:

"Where were you in 1860?"
"A knife shiner in a Pittsburgh hotel in Pennsylvania," responded Bishop Arnett, amid laughter and applause.
"What are you doing now?" asked Bishop Gaines.
"Shining brains," promptly responded Bishop Arnett, amid shouts of applause and roars of laughter.

Using the lessons of his and Bishop Gaines's lives, Arnett urged that today's depression be set aside and that the potential of the future be embraced. "[He exhorted] his people to seize the powers of race elevation," the minutes reflected, "to get money, and not only to organize societies to buy a shroud—but to organize societies to buy homes and lots; not a place in the grave yard, but in the town and that the gospel to be preached is for the body as well as the soul."[16]

For those disciples of Bishop Payne who remained unconvinced, Arnett played a trump card. In several ways, he served notice that the advancement of Jacksonville's Divinity High School rated among the highest of priorities for his episcopate. He encouraged the assembling of a racially mixed audience to hear school president J. H. Welch preach the conference educational sermon. The bishop then arranged for national financial secretary Dr. James A. Handy to make "a strong argument in favor of education." Finally, Arnett closed the conference with a stirring call to arms. Specifically, he charged the ministers "to advance the standard of education" and "to do all in their power to promote the success of Divinity High School at Jacksonville." Delegates reacted by voting to designate each minister as a local agent for the school and to commit each preacher to send at least one student to Jacksonville. They then departed Madison filled, in good part,

51. John H. Welch, minister and president of the Divinity High School at Jacksonville. Courtesy Photographic Collection, Florida State Archives.

with optimism and renewed determination. "Bishop Arnett . . . is doing all in his power to excite a Christian zeal among the members, yes, more—intellectual development of the entire man," summarized one man, "and he is going to succeed."[17]

Wasting little time, the bishop set about capitalizing on his early successes, placing special emphasis on stricken Northeast Florida. To provide tangible evidence of progress, he convinced the Divinity High School trustees to purchase its land and buildings from Jacksonville's Mt. Zion church, effectively carrying out the commitment of years past. The price came to $10,000, all or most of which was paid in church notes. Payments would help defer costs of programs at cash-poor Mt. Zion. The April 1889 purchase also reassured the conference's educational and financial elite of the bishop's good intentions.[18]

Arnett then sought to boost the spirits of area residents more generally. He abetted efforts to invite famed abolitionist and civil rights activist Fred-

52. Annie L. Welch, teacher at Edward Waters College. Courtesy Photographic Collection, Florida State Archives.

erick Douglass to appear in early April at the Sub-Tropical Exposition, a state fair held at Jacksonville. White and black officials, along with a racially integrated crowd of thousands, gathered to honor the former U.S. marshal of the District of Columbia and soon-to-be U.S. minister to Haiti. Joseph E. Lee presided, and Bishop Payne delivered the prayer. Then Arnett rose to introduce the speaker. Audience members repeatedly interrupted his words with applause. When Douglass took the podium, he expressed a theme taken from the bishop's historical argument for the advancement of African Americans. "Look back at our history and think of what it has been!" he exclaimed.

> We see today a new heaven and a new earth in comparison with that of fifty years ago. Why, it really seems to me that the sun rises and sets in a different place from where it used to. The very air seems changed. We breathe freer; we breathe deeper; we have aspirations higher than

we ever dreamed of in those days. The change is so great, so vast, so wonderful, so complete, so sudden that we hardly know what to make of it.[19]

The bishop rode the momentum from the thundering success of Douglass's appearance to push for church renewal and expansion in Northeast Florida. In the fall, 175 new members joined Jacksonville's Mt. Olive, and 140 stepped forth to place their names on the rolls at Mt. Zion. By November, Presiding Elder P. B. Braddock exulted in the progress scored. "My district is in a good condition," he reported, "and the ministers, with myself, are striving to make the best report to the next conference that has ever been made from the Jacksonville district." Braddock added, "There have been the greatest revivals here this year that have been known."[20]

Similar advances evidenced themselves in many areas of the state. From Pensacola came word that Elder Bird "is making it quite interesting" and that "everything is full of life at the AME Church." Thomas W. Long proclaimed that "the AME Church is in better condition now than it ever was at Key West." The Enterprise District laid out new missions and saw churches erected at Bartow and Fort Myers. At least nine new congregations blossomed into life. Those tracing their origins to 1889 include Bethel at Punta Gorda (then DeSoto, now Charlotte County); Macedonia at Fort White, Columbia County; Mt. Moriah in south Jacksonville; New Bethel at White Springs in Hamilton County; Jackson County's Post Oak, near Bascom; New Zion at Raleigh, Levy County; Mt. Zion at Dade City, Pasco County; Mt. Pisgah at Federal Point, Putnam County; and Mt. Pisgah at Webster, Sumter County.[21]

When Florida Conference clergymen gathered for their annual sessions on December 20, 1889, at Quincy, many stood amazed at the year's advances. "If you but read the 'signs of the times' and are unable to reduce doubting to a trade," commented A. J. Kershaw, "you will be convinced that the Florida conference under the leadership of Bishop B. W. Arnett is making strong strides and steady steps to reach the vanguard of the African Methodist army." Kershaw continued, "The Florida Conference is in a better condition now than it has been these fifteen years we have been a member of it."[22]

The bishop followed his now customary practices once the gathering opened. Typically, he laid out an ambitious agenda for each session, and he made sure that numerous church dignitaries would be present to support him. Especially, he relied upon James A. Handy's oratorical gifts to buttress the enhanced confidence and esteem that had arisen out of Arnett's earlier efforts at renewing appreciation of Florida AME accomplishments. Handy reminisced about the church's earliest days in the state and drew attention to the almost forgotten role played by the still popular William G. Stewart. "Elder Stewart was the founder," he insisted. Handy also helped Arnett address the prickly question of why badly needed local funds were being drained off for national church purposes, an issue that aroused resentment on the part of ministers and members. Discussions that followed covered this and other important concerns, with the bishop and financial secretary attempting to coax rather than to command.[23]

Good news proved a valuable ally for Arnett. For the first time in years, local financial reports reflected major advances, producing happy acceptance and good-natured joshing. Applause swelled when counters revealed more than one thousand new members added to the conference rolls during the previous year. Tangible evidence of the progress came with the dedication of Quincy's new Arnett Chapel amid suitable ceremonies. The sixty-by-forty-foot structure could hold 350 worshippers in fine style. "It is nicely ceiled with pine, tastily painted, has a walnut stained pulpit," an account described, "and a gallery at the end of the church, constructed with a view to extending it along the sides." Overall, a minister remembered, "Nothing but love and good will reigned supreme." The fact that Arnett had backed off harsh enforcement of moral strictures against clergymen helped, as well. "There was not even a mark against a single minister," A. J. Kershaw added.[24]

During the year 1890 the advances of the Arnett episcopate were consolidated and pressed forward. By February, membership figures for the state had rebounded from the slump associated with Bishop Payne's administration to levels greater than those of the peak mid-1870s years. In the state, a total of 15,806 members worshipped in 230 churches or chapels. While the Florida Conference enjoyed health not experienced since the 1870s, the East Florida Conference had taken the lead with 8,019 members, 113 ministers, 171 churches or chapels, and 192 Sunday schools. The Divinity High School under President Welch hosted 147 pupils in facilities worth $12,000. Although $8,500 in school debt remained to be satisfied, collections during the past year had amounted to a respectable $2,475.[25]

As the months passed, new congregations and maturing missions combined their successes with the fruits of camp meetings and revivals to push totals higher, especially in the peninsula. Pensacola's Houser Chapel and St.

Philips at Wacissa in Jefferson County added their names to Florida Conference rolls. Marion County's Pleasant View (Fairfield) and Bethel (Orange Springs), Plant City's Allen Chapel, Ocoee in Orange County, Mt. Moriah at Tarpon Springs, Crescent City's Union Bethel, Suwannee County's Mt. Pleasant, and Macedonia at Oak Hill in Volusia County formally joined the East Florida Conference. That conference's reach now extended down the still sparsely inhabited Atlantic coast to today's Martin County, where St. Peter's Chapel at Tick Ridge (or Jensen) had begun serving the community.[26]

The 1890 conference meetings pulsed with the kind of excitement to be expected, given the church's change in circumstances. At Gainesville in February, according to G. B. Hill, "Bishop Arnett announced that the East Florida conference is the banner conference of all the conferences in the Seventh Episcopal District." Delegates beamed. Over $1,800 poured forth for the Divinity High School, with funds left over for expanded missionary efforts. At Pensacola ten months later, a similar—if somewhat less exuberant—situation prevailed. Returns for Florida Conference districts, one participant recorded, "were in advance of the previous session." The growth, in turn, permitted Arnett to rectify one of Bishop Payne's unpopular actions. Where the senior bishop had abolished the Marianna District, seemingly in reaction to mild criticism from its presiding elder, Arnett now permitted its reestablishment, to general approval. The growth also permitted the conference to increase its support for the divinity school.[27]

Thus, by the time of the 1890 Florida Conference annual sessions the state's AME Church bloomed with optimism; yet the sunny reports masked certain current and future problems that would find their own days of reckoning in the months and years ahead. As far as Bishop Arnett's leadership was concerned, a thorny situation arose out of an unexpected intersection of two important issues, his advocacy for meritocracy within the church and the appointment of a new president for the Divinity High School. The result would inhibit the momentum for progress that the bishop had established and diminish his reputation in the eyes of some Florida pastors.

The seeds of the controversy were planted prior to the December 1890 sessions of the Florida Conference when the bishop tapped his son Benjamin W. Arnett Jr. as the Divinity High School's president to replace John H. Welch. The young man possessed credentials as a Wilberforce University graduate, but the appointment's inherent nepotism alarmed churchmen anxious about a return to favoritism. The situation also concerned Bishop

Payne's supporters as they assessed Arnett Sr.'s attitudes toward the high school. The new president insisted that "he intends by hard work, with the assistance of the people, to make this one of the best schools in the country," but doubts persisted.[28]

It may have been that Bishop Arnett planned all along to upgrade the status of the Florida Normal and Divinity High School, but the less than enthusiastic reception of his son's placement also may have weighed as a factor in his subsequent actions. In any event, on May 23, 1891, the bishop joined trustees Morris M. Moore, A. J. Kershaw, Thomas W. Long, Singleton H. Coleman, William A. Bird, and E. W. Johnson in approving a new name and expanded mission for the school. In honor of the church's deceased third bishop, the institution thereafter would be called Edward Waters College. Charles Sumner Long believed that President Arnett contributed greatly to enhancing the quality of the school's faculty. Others agreed. "This college is becoming more popular with the people every day, and the members of the AME church can congratulate themselves on having such an excellent place for the education of their youth," commented a Jacksonville resident in February 1892. He added, "The discipline is first-class, and everything goes on like clockwork."[29]

Whatever gains could be credited to President Arnett, critics of his tenure declined to accept silence. When graduation exercises were held on May 24, 1891, Reverend Welch, rather than the school president, took center stage. In June a published report would note, "Rev. John R. Scott, pastor of St. Paul's AME church, is one of the most scholarly ministers in the AME connection, and the ministers of this state are thinking of making him president of the Edward Waters College of this city." Arnett persisted in his role at the school through graduation exercises in May 1892. That month, the church's general conference reassigned his father to the Ninth Episcopal District, which included Mississippi, Indian Territory, and Arkansas. Apparently, the bishop then arranged for his son to be offered the presidency of Shorter University (previously Bethel Institute) at North Little Rock, Arkansas. John R. Scott Jr., son of one of the Florida church's renowned founders and himself a graduate of Wilberforce University, acceded to the vacancy at Edward Waters College.[30]

Rosy reports and distractions such as the college presidency controversy may have diverted Bishop Arnett and other church leaders from appreciating properly the church's true condition in Florida, as well as the critical importance of negative developments then under way in the state. In the

53. Benjamin W. Arnett, Jr., president of Edward Waters College. Courtesy Photographic Collection, Florida State Archives.

former case, had growing membership totals been viewed in the context of demographic changes, a less happy atmosphere might have prevailed. In 1870, Florida's population had amounted to about 188,000 persons, 92,000 of whom were black. The AME Church then claimed 7,874 members, almost 12 percent of African Americans. By mid-decade, the church figure had risen roughly to 11,000 out of an estimated black population of 109,000 (10.1 percent). Fifteen years later, the state contained 391,422 residents, among whom were 166,178 blacks. The church's 1890 membership of 15,806 amounted to just 9.5 percent of the race's total. As the coverage of African Methodism slipped, the predominance of African Baptists increased. Baptist statistics for 1890 are not available, but an 1893 estimate tallied three hundred churches and 47,000 members. A second estimate two years later set the figure at more than 40,000. In either case, African Methodism's influence continued to slip in the face of Baptist strength.[31]

54. Edward Waters College's board of trustees in 1892. On the front row are, *left to right*, Singleton H. Coleman, Bishop Benjamin W. Arnett Sr., Thomas W. Long, and Marcellus M. Moore. Those on the back row are, *left to right*, unidentified, Albert J. Kershaw, Benjamin W. Arnett Jr., Reuben Brooks, and William A. Bird. Courtesy Photographic Collection, Florida State Archives.

As relative AME strength waned, the onset of Jim Crow racial discrimination plowed ahead at an enhanced pace. In 1889, the Florida legislature signaled the death knell of black political strength by adopting a poll tax and other mechanisms designed to eject African Americans from voting booths. The lawmakers also seized control of government at Key West and Jacksonville, while restricting black access to public office in other municipalities. Not surprisingly, Florida's last two African American legislators of the post–Civil War era—Duval County's John R. Scott Jr. and George A. Lewis, one a minister and the other an AME member—served in 1889. A few individuals remained or were elected thereafter to local political office, but they could exercise little influence. AME minister Joseph E. Lee retained power in the state's Republican party into the twentieth century through his control of key appointive federal offices, but the party had long since ceased to matter in the state.[32]

Public office and protections of the law denied them, black Floridians also found themselves beset with waves of racial violence. Of course, violence in Florida often represented the status quo, but now it took on ever more cruel racial overtones. By the century's end and on a per capita basis, the state would lead the nation in lynchings. From 1900 to 1930 the rate ran twice as high as that for Mississippi, Georgia, and Louisiana, three times as high as Alabama's, and six times as high as South Carolina's. The front pages of white-owned newspapers featured tales of the horrible deaths. While the Florida Conference was meeting at Tallahassee in December 1891, to cite one example, Alfred Jones and Brady Young were taken from the Live Oak jail by a mob of two hundred men, dragged to nearby woods, and "riddled with bullets." When the same conference convened at Quincy in January 1893, vigilantes hung Pat Wells at a spot five miles from town. Typically, a news account declared, "No clue to the lynchers has yet been found."[33]

Even though Bishop Arnett understood the need for organized resistance to Jim Crow and to the violence, the time had passed when the church could offer real resistance on its own. Though it could organize voters, the fact was that after 1889, their numbers dwindled to such an extent that little could be done. The coalition of the Knights of Labor and black Republicans had offered some hope, but the Knights' power collapsed by 1890. The Colored Farmers' Alliance also strove to assert black strength, and Arnett may have encouraged AME minister Joseph Leandria Moore to assume its presidency. When the People's Party attempted after May 1891 to combine blacks and whites to contest the Bourbon Democrats, Moore served on its executive committee. Sadly, the party failed to achieve significant power in Florida.[34]

All the while, many Floridians looked to the church for leadership and instead found disappointment. "I beg the church to pray God to put an end to the murdering of men in Florida," the Reverend I. D. Coffee pled. Instead of the activist response of earlier years, some church leaders counseled accommodation. A. J. Kershaw perhaps stood out most in this regard, even taking to task northern newspapers for criticizing the South. "If the South ascends," he contended in words similar to those soon to be voiced by Booker T. Washington, "the Southern negro will ascend." Bishop Arnett found himself forced by the circumstances to a position that veered dangerously close to Kershaw's, one that avoided temporal action and stressed only spiritual care. "The welfare of the race depends on the rectitude of its people," he announced. "Honesty, sobriety, intelligence, morality, and religion will elevate a race," Arnett continued, "and the ministers of the Lord Jesus Christ must take their position in advocacy of these virtues."[35]

55. Ocala's brick Mt. Zion AME Church, erected in 1891. Courtesy Photographic Collection, Florida State Archives.

For the remainder of Bishop Arnett's tenure in Florida, the church grappled with the tension that grew out of a desire to expand an institution that had so limited its own appeal. The results were mixed. The Florida Conference experienced the greatest difficulty as farm economy doldrums and racial violence inhibited growth while encouraging outmigration. The year 1891 saw organization of only two new churches there: Palace at Havana and St. Joseph at DeFuniak Springs. Prospects for the region's future dimmed.[36]

In East Florida signs of progress were easier to find. Ocala church members erected a beautiful brick church for Mt. Zion in 1891, and at Fernandina members dedicated "one of the finest churches in the state." Fund-raising drives anticipated new structures at Midway and in Jacksonville for New Hope. One thousand persons attended ceremonies for the opening of Mt. Zion's new lecture room in Jacksonville. Camp meetings at Orlando and Sweetwater attracted more thousands. Congregations coalesced at Arcadia (Mt. Zion), at New Smyrna Beach (Allen Chapel), and at Lawtey in Bradford County (Mt. Zion). Yet the excited tone of recent reports grew more sober, and the volume of reports decreased dramatically. The steam seemed to have run out in many places, as Floridians began to anticipate 1892, when a new bishop again would arrive to fuel the AME engine.[37]

One glorious moment remained for the church before Bishop Arnett departed Florida. In February 1891, the council of African Methodist bishops met at Mt. Zion Church in Jacksonville, the first such gathering on Florida soil. Virtually the entire church hierarchy arrived to wait upon the prelates and to view the achievements of the Florida church. Bishop Payne's eightieth birthday gave rise to celebrations, and huge crowds gathered to hear sermons preached by the grand men. "The visiting ministers have been handsomely entertained by the African Methodists here," noted a Jacksonville reporter, "who seem to be proud of their prelates, and whose impressions appear to be deepened by the inspirations quickened." The reporter added, "The bishops have made their power felt in the city, as representative men and pulpit orators."[38]

The Georgian Henry McNeal Turner stood out among the great churchmen during their Florida sojourn. When speakers raised the issues of the times, he, almost alone, stood forth boldly, "reiterating his convictions that the hope of the negro race was in the successful conduct of a black nationality." A Jacksonville resident took down his words.

> He spoke of what the negro had done in the South and for its development, he said that he had been here nearly three hundred years; that he had been the pioneer in the great agricultural fields, and had enriched them with his sweat and his blood, and that it is a shame upon this ungodly nation that it has not fully [recognized] in fact the rights of the people of African descent guaranteed in the constitution and by the God of nature; that the action of congress is against us; that every decision from the supreme court of the United States is against us; and that the negro interests seem to have been betrayed.[39]

There was little else that Turner or the church could offer his anxious listeners. Most needed more.

10

TUMULT AND TRAGEDY, 1892–1895

A crisis is more than probable.

As the nineteenth century's final decade unfolded, most Floridians overlooked the portents of trouble that soon would shake the AME church to its core. Bishop Benjamin W. Arnett Sr. seemed preoccupied with personal criticisms and a future beyond the state as he served out the final days of his episcopacy in the district in late 1891 and early 1892. His successor, having resided elsewhere than Florida during recent times, likewise concerned himself with matters of an altogether different substance as he prepared to relocate to the state in which he had labored decades previously. Nonetheless, a series of human-initiated events and what some have called acts of God were about to batter, blast, and bedevil the new prelate and his flock, resulting by mid-decade in devastation and widespread despair. Thereafter, as AME leaders and members assessed the new Florida in which they suddenly found themselves attempting to survive, only the return of a gentle native son offered a balm for their afflictions. In him they found a shepherd to lighten the burden of their losses and to inspire them to rebuild their church on renewed foundations.

While underappreciated at the time, hints of a troubled passage ahead were apparent. Some rested in plain sight, although many church fathers took little notice because they involved the sordid world of politics. As discussed previously, white lawmakers had acted in early 1889 to drive African American men from voting booths and public office at a time of worsening economic conditions for farmers and those who depended on farmers. The prevailing climate, which encouraged racial violence, was earning Florida a reputation for lynchings and other acts of mob rule. The problem loomed so large that some prominent whites questioned whether "law or anarchy" would prevail. Passage of the first statutes and ordinances that would come to be called "Jim Crow" laws were beginning to usher in the era of legal enforcement of racial segregation. Efforts to separate the races on rail cars led the movement. Expectations by African Americans of good service—not to mention basic civil treatment—deteriorated with implementation of the Jim Crow restrictions. The future seemed certain to bring more of the same.[1]

The kinds of external tensions that beset the church paralleled problems within the institution. Rank-and-file clergymen and members felt distanced, if not alienated, from a leadership headed by "black princes" and staffed by well-compensated college graduates. Many wondered why the church had retreated from its activist political stance into one that seemed more to advocate puritanical morality. Bishop Arnett had undertaken a serious effort to bridge this gap, but charges of favoritism and nepotism had marred his image and damaged his credibility. Meanwhile, the Panhandle's Florida Conference stagnated, as outmigration and hard times sapped its strength.

Given all these circumstances, it is easy to understand why a riot might symbolize church affairs by 1892 and 1893. The incident occurred at the annual Alachua County camp meeting held in November 1891. At first, success seemed assured when the gathering drew seven thousand persons for its opening day. Unfortunately, as one report had it, "the rough element was conspicuously in the ascendant and the influences were more spirituous than spiritual." When a drunken man fired a pistol into the crowd, sheriff's deputies took him into custody. Outraged at the white lawmen's interference, the crowd demanded the man's release. Deputies placed their prisoner on a train, but "a mob of several thousand followed, swearing to kill any officer who should carry the prisoner to Gainesville." The sheriff asked the governor to call out the state militia. He refused. Subsequently, tempers eased. Still, the incident telegraphed a message: Hot lava boiled beneath the landscape's surface. AME leaders should have comprehended that important circumstance, but for the most part, they do not appear to have done so.[2]

Then, the church—reeling from wounds caused by charges of elitism and remoteness on the part of some of its leaders—suffered a blow that exacerbated the problem. Particularly, it lost its greatest "people preacher." State newspapers reported the details. In December 1891 a yellow fever outbreak beset Florida's largest city, Key West, claiming as one of its victims

George Washington Witherspoon. He died there following a prolonged struggle on January 2, 1892, leaving a biracial community to mourn him. The funeral procession trailed for a full quarter mile. Three white ministers joined three black colleagues as pallbearers. The deceased, it was said, stood out as "the most popular colored man in the country districts of the state." An obituary noted, "The roads would be full of women, children, horses and wagons . . . whenever it was announced that Witherspoon would preach anywhere in the state." At Jacksonville large numbers of mourners attended a memorial service "as a mark of respect and honor to this Christian brother and co-worker, who is sadly missed from the ranks." A white Pensacola editor reflected on Witherspoon's impact on Florida. Acknowledging that the deceased was "naturally smart," he added, "Despite the political school in which he was reared, he possessed to a marked degree the esteem of his political opponents, many of whom will hear of his death with regret."[3]

The next month additional events occurred that would carry profound implications. A series of incidents, for instance, added more fuel to the fires of the elitism controversy. Ministers attending the East Florida Conference sessions from the Jacksonville area evidenced their education, sophistication, and prosperity to such an extent that newspapers detailed their appearance and apparel. As one commentator recorded, "They are all fine looking and splendidly dressed."[4] Presumably, poorer ministers and laymen looked on the parade with less than universal enthusiasm. It was also in February 1892 that Bishop Arnett officially oversaw the birth of Edward Waters College out of the Florida Normal and Divinity High School, with his own son as its first president. Nepotism had joined elitism as a subject for discussion. A birthday party added tinder to the growing pile. Bishop Daniel A. Payne, under whose previous administration the elitism charges had begun to flourish, celebrated his eighty-first birthday at Jacksonville on February 24. Churchmen and educators close to the bishop presented him with a gift apparently so expensive that its nature was not disclosed in news reports. The action helped little to narrow the widening chasm within the church.

Of greater significance in an immediate sense, the East Florida Conference decided in February 1892 to split itself. In doing so, it recognized that dynamism in church affairs now lay distant from Jacksonville and adjacent areas of Northeast Florida. As if to emphasize the point, the state's largest congregation, Jacksonville's Mt. Zion, was torn with internal feuding. Surviving records fail to disclose a full account of the matter, but the congregation seems to have divided over actions of its minister, D. W. Gillislee.

56. The Reverend John Walter Dukes. Courtesy Photographic Collection, Florida State Archives.

Bishop Arnett attempted to mediate the conflict. At the February 1892 East Florida Conference meeting he elevated Gillislee to presiding elder of the Live Oak District and named J. H. Welch to replace him at Mt. Zion. "It is hoped that the good people of Mt. Zion church will heal all differences and now work to the interest of the church," exclaimed one frustrated onlooker. Passions took time to cool, though, and the divisions had undermined conference strength just as its most promising territories were stripped away.[5]

And promising those territories were. The new and growing towns of the central and southern peninsula—recently opened to easy access by new railroads—offered the principal fields for missionary work and church growth in the state. Fittingly, the decision as to the South Florida Conference's creation was taken at one of those towns, Orlando. The occasion permitted Bishop Arnett and other dignitaries to dedicate the community's newly constructed AME sanctuary with appropriate pomp and circumstance. Within months similar ceremonies followed for the dedication of Tampa's Allen Temple.[6]

The new South Florida Conference, which received national church approval at the Nineteenth General Conference at Philadelphia in May 1892, stretched virtually the length of the peninsula on its western side. Conference limits were defined, with some ambiguity, as "all that part of the peninsula of Florida, south of the line running due east and west, leaving Palatka on the north and Starke on the south." Three districts comprised its subdivisions. Bishop Arnett named venerable churchman Thomas W. Long to lead the Gainesville District and future bishop M. M. Moore to head the Enterprise District. The huge new Key West District, to be supervised by J. W. Dukes of Ocala, reached up the southwest Gulf coast as far north as Cedar Key and into the peninsula as far northeast as Kissimmee.[7]

The creation of a new conference, leaders believed in 1892, confirmed what they perceived as the church's solid standing. "Surely this shows a wonderful growth of the AME church in this state," declared an observer. On the other hand, AME historian Charles Spencer Smith, considering the fact that the Nineteenth General Conference approved more new conferences than any of its predecessors, tellingly questioned "whether the creation of so many new Conferences at this time was a necessity." Smith's point was that, as he put it, "the division of an Annual Conference is not necessarily a token of expansion." He added, "Attenuation is to thin out; expansion is to increase." The South Florida Conference's creation effectively permitted church expansion in theretofore sparsely settled areas but "thinned out" what remained of the East Florida Conference. Now, East Florida meetings would begin to take on more of the tone that was returning to Florida Conference sessions, that is, an atmosphere ridden with dour recitations of disappointing reports. By 1894, the bishop would decline even to make appointments at the East Florida Conference's conclusion, waiting instead to gauge the needs of the South Florida Conference before acting. Church morale in Northeast Florida ebbed accordingly.[8]

The same general conference took a separate action that also would dampen church morale in subsequent years. It reacted enthusiastically to an overture from the African Methodist Episcopal Zion Church for organic union. Commissioners agreed that the new church would carry the name African and Zion Methodist Episcopal Church, a fact that irritated some AME bishops. Although a large majority of the members of both churches appear to have embraced the merger with delight as reinforcing the cause and strength of African Methodism, the proposed jointure foundered as opposing AME bishops made their power felt. High hopes crashed. Disenchantment resulted among both churches' rank and file. AMEZ Bishop William J. Walls explained, "Neither group could present *bona fide* or justifiable reasons for the actual failure." From this and other causes, including a national economic depression, in 1896 the AME general conference would spend precious time and energy not on organic union but on "the need of retrenchment."[9]

The 1892 general conference also carried out its responsibility to assign a new bishop to Florida for the ensuing four years. Having already exercised episcopal authority in the state from 1872 to 1876, Thomas M. D. Ward was well known to many senior churchmen. The state had changed dramatically since the mid-1870s, however, as had Ward. Now almost seventy years of age, he likely looked to Florida for the comforts of its climate more than for the challenges of its church. A man who loved poetry and eloquent discourse, his capacity for healing wounds borne by the common man while simultaneously spurring expansion remained open to question. Unfortunately, his baggage weighed even more heavily. More than a few Floridians recalled that the controversy of Dr. R. O. Sidney's theft of Brown's Theological University funds had centered on Ward's support for the man and that the bishop had initiated the church's movement away from political activism.[10]

While Bishop Ward's appointment to Florida entailed certain drawbacks, he brought with him an asset of tremendous importance. Among his protégés was Bishop Abram Grant, a one-time Florida slave and political leader whom Ward had ordained a deacon in 1872 and an elder in 1874. Grant had been elevated to the episcopacy in 1888 (Ward had consecrated him) and four years afterward had been assigned to the Sixth District, which included Georgia and Alabama. Where Ward's age limited his range, Grant fairly brimmed with energy for God's cause.[11]

Details of Grant's life before 1892 may shed light on his special talents and sensitivities. Born in an ox cart on a small farm near Lake City, Florida, on August 25, 1848, Grant held bitter memories of slavery. He remembered clearly, for example, the day just before the Civil War's outbreak when his younger brother Isaac was sold to "Slave Traders." Abram, not yet a teenager, cried "at his going." It would require four decades before the brothers could reunite. Besides Isaac, Abram had three other brothers and a sister. Grant married first a woman from Columbia County named Florida. They had at least one son. After Florida's passing, Grant would marry her sister, the widow of his friend Josiah Armstrong. Described in his maturity as a

57. Bishop and Mrs. Abram Grant. Courtesy Photographic Collection, Florida State Archives.

240-pound mulatto with a rather large build, slightly balding, with a full beard, large nose, and recessed eyes, Grant seemed at times overpowering.[12]

While Grant's appearance implied power and strength, he was a kind man who loved saving people for Christ. "Bishop Grant was an evangelist," explained Charles Sumner Long. "He had a passion for souls." Further, Grant benefited from an impeccable reputation. "He stood upon high moral ground," a colleague recorded. As a man who did not forget his humble beginnings, Bishop Grant never lost the common touch. "He is a man whom all delight to honor, because he pays due honor to all men," the colleague added. "His influence is very great, and his friends numerous."[13]

With Grant as his strong right arm, Florida's new prelate set about addressing the church's business by early 1893. At Quincy in late January, Ward presided over the Florida Conference annual sessions, but it was his protégé who grabbed attention. "Bishop Grant preached a powerful sermon there," a Jacksonville newspaper reported, "and fifty-six people were taken into the church." A total of 106 persons answered a call during the extended meeting. A few weeks later the two men repeated their initiative at Fernandina, where the East Florida Conference had convened. And on March 2 they organized the South Florida Conference at Tampa. Charles Sumner Long recalled, "In St. Paul Church, Tampa, [Bishop Grant] preached and thirty souls joined the church." Such successes compelled Long to describe Ward's second tenure as "an era of soul saving."[14]

Though it may have been an era of soul saving, Ward's term saw few new churches established, especially in areas outside the South Florida Conference. In 1892, revivals in Gadsden County had resulted in the formation of three new churches: St. Peter's, near Midway; New Bethel, near Quincy; and Sinai, six miles south of Quincy. An additional congregation at Concord (St. John's) resulted the following year. Otherwise, the year found new churches only at Watertown in Columbia County (Mt. Zion), Evinston in Marion County (Jones Chapel Zion), Satsuma in Putman (Disney), at or near Bushnell in Sumter (Mt. Olive and Oaklawn), and Chipley in Washington (Grant's Tabernacle).[15]

Aside from St. John's in Gadsden County, Ward oversaw the official establishment of but four new churches in 1893, all in the peninsula. They included Mt. Olive near Williston in Levy County, Allen Temple at Tampa (actually opened in 1892), St. Andrews at Palmetto in Manatee County, and Payne Chapel in the new railroad town of West Palm Beach. In the next year came seven additional houses of worship, all in the peninsula except Mt. Sinai at Columbia City in Columbia County. They were Bethel at Newberry in Alachua County, Mt. Carmel at Tampa, Bethel in St. Petersburg, Mt. Olive in Clearwater, Allen Chapel at Sanford, and Ward's Chapel at Seville in Volusia County.[16]

Why did the fields tilled by Bishops Ward and Grant not prove more productive? Part of the answer involved old disputes that died hard. The elitism issue numbered high among those that refused to go away, particularly after Ward decided that the church should purchase an official "Episcopal mansion" at Jacksonville. Few would have denied the aged prelate a comfortable home, but the timing of the decison set a poor tone for his episcopate. The tone grew harsher when Jacksonville area AME clergymen gathered on February 7, 1893, to welcome the bishop to his new residence. On that occasion, "Rev. Dr." C. A. A. Taylor declared, "The hope of the negroes as a race is in their ability to appreciate the labors of those who have led them, and the Episcopal residence manifests such appreciation on the part of the race in Florida." This, of course, came at a time when many were questioning just such leadership.[17]

Under the circumstances, the need for healing within the church stood out as a paramount concern. Unfortunately, Bishop Grant could spend little time in Florida to act as healer, and Bishop Ward's weakened stamina kept

188 Laborers in the Vineyard of the Lord

58. The Reverend Caesar A. A. Taylor. Courtesy Photographic Collection, Florida State Archives.

him from circulating as he might have liked to do. Even at Jacksonville where Ward resided, old feuds simmered, to burst on occasion into the open. Thus, a local newspaper could report in April 1893, "The colored people are making preparations to erect a Congregational church in this city." The item continued, "The promoters of the idea are a portion of the members of Mt. Zion AME church."[18]

Not that attempts were not made. The church managed to turn out three thousand persons at Mt. Zion to witness St. John's River baptism for fifty-five persons in late April 1893. "It is no doubt the greatest service of the kind ever held by this church," boasted a member. The event brought three church stalwarts together "for the first time in twenty years" in an attempt to pull in more and more listeners. William G. Stewart, Thomas W. Long, and Major Johnson proclaimed the word of God as they reminded area residents of the rich and longstanding AME presence in Florida. Three months later, Presiding Elder Singleton Coleman staged "a good, old-fashioned and religious camp meeting" at Sweetwater, south of Jacksonville on the St. Augustine road. Although attendance figures are not available, backers had entertained hopes that it would result in the "biggest camp meeting of the age."[19]

Such events certainly did no harm, but circumstances had added by mid-1893 a new element to the equation, one that dwarfed the church's other problems and when combined with them staggered its leadership. May 4, 1893, marked the beginning of one of the worse economic depressions the nation had been called upon to endure. Southern rural areas, as has been mentioned, already were suffering from depressed conditions. Now, thanks to the Panic of 1893, misery flowed throughout the country. Businesses failed, bankruptcies soared, and labor strikes resulted, as one historian noted, "in bitterness, bloodshed, and property damage." Through 1894 and into 1895 conditions worsened. As the historian added, "For the poor the effects of the depression kept mounting." In the South, desperation spread from the countryside into urban centers. "The panic . . . ," explained a student of its results, "[brought] home to the cities and industrial towns of the South as never before the distress that had gripped the surrounding countryside for years."[20]

Although developer Henry Flagler's railroad and resort construction along the Atlantic coast offered some relief to embattled Floridians, residents of most areas felt the depression's sting in the same manner as did those in other southern regions. So profound were the panic's consequences that Governor Henry L. Mitchell's tenure in office has been labeled "a hard times administration." Making matters worse, the world market for phosphate plummeted just as the depression deepened. Many Southwest Florida mines closed and others cut back on output, with the result that one of the state's major cash-producing and wage-paying industries teetered on the brink of collapse. The crisis undercut land values and threatened the ruin of workers and dependent businessmen.[21]

The AME Church bent beneath the weight of events, as did others. In most districts, collections understandably dropped. Bishop Grant summed up the situation still prevailing in February 1895 when he informed delegates to the East Florida Conference that "the scarcity of money in all parts of the country shows itself in the shortage of the church's finances." The national church's financial secretary, Josiah H. Armstrong, formerly of Florida where he had served in the state legislature, made clear that financially speaking, the state's conferences were on their own. "This time he came in to give the conference some sound practical views on the financial system of the church," conference minutes reported. "It is safe to say that his hearers had a clearer idea of the vast amount of money needed by the church in order that its work may be done."[22]

Edward Waters College, chronically short of funds, faced dire possibilities. Resentments about paying for a college when the state provided normal schools for teachers, coupled with continuing conflicts at Jacksonville's Mt. Zion Church, had undercut the institution's ability to survive, much less thrive. Already in late May 1893, trustees were seeking routes of escape from the financial dilemma they faced. Gordon G. Rogers of Maitland and Orlando's J. A. Groover had offered five acres of land and other assistance toward building an AME college at Eatonville, and this looked to some to be a welcome life preserver for Edward Waters. Preliminary negotiations proved inconclusive. President John R. Scott Jr. endeavored to preserve the campus for Jacksonville, managing to add a "new kitchen, dining hall, bathroom and printing office" by year's end. Still, after the college opened for the fall term of 1894, Scott was compelled to report that "the number of boarding students is about one-half as large as it was last year." The president added: "The college's receipts for the present year have been altogether inadequate to meet the most necessary demands. Unless provision is made for these demands, a crisis is more than probable."[23]

Complications extending from the Panic of 1893 carried personal disaster with them and, often, unforeseen consequences. To cite one example, Orlando District Presiding Elder M. M. Moore lost $1,200 in August 1893 when his local bank closed its doors. "He has thousands of friends who sympathize with him in his loss," commented a Jacksonville admirer. A few months later Moore and business manager G. C. Henderson of Winter Park launched from Orlando a newspaper called the *Florida Christian Recorder* "in the interest of the African Methodist Episcopal Church and good government." It proved short-lived, possibly providing the impetus for Moore to seek the position of national church financial secretary in 1896. Four years afterward he achieved election as bishop, but he died suddenly on November 23, 1900.[24]

One unanticipated consequence of the trials of 1893 was the emergence of women in greater roles of leadership and service within the church. Since the immediate post–Civil War period, women had labored selflessly on behalf of African Methodism. "We are glad to say that the AME Church has ever given prominence to her females, and woman throughout her borders

59. The Edward Waters College faculty in 1892. President Benjamin W. Arnett Jr. sits center front. Courtesy Photographic Collection, Florida State Archives.

she hath delighted to honor when honor was due her," Mrs. M. E. C. Smith proudly declared as the decade of the 1890s commenced. She continued:

> We refer with pride to the names of such illustrious, self sacrificing, Christian hearted women as sisters: Mary Still and G. G. Waterman, Sisters, [Mary] E. Miller, and [Susan L. Waterman] Raif, [Martha D. Sickles] Greenwood, [Josephine] Jones, [M. A.] Comer, and others, all of whom were zealous workers in the cause of Christ. They are the ones whom we regard as our Deborahs, Phoebes, Lydias, and Dorcases. They went about doing good. They held up the missionary's hands when they were weak. They bore the heat and burden of the day.[25]

Traditionally, women had helped to educate the young people, whether to read and write or to understand Bible lessons and church beliefs, while performing numerous other church-related duties. Such an individual was G. G. Waterman, who arrived in Florida from New Jersey in 1873. "Two years later she commenced teaching, and has been ever since then actively engaged in the work," Smith related. "She is founder of Finley High School in Lake City, founded June 10, 1889, and still operating successfully," the church historian continued. "She has filled every office in the Sabbath School of Lake City, and is the present Superintendent. She has been for years in the employment of the publication Department." Smith concluded, "Manager [Theodore] Gould remarked thus of her on introducing her to Dr. [B. T.] Tanner, now Bishop: 'Dr.' said he, 'If all our preachers worked for the publishing department as Sister Waterman has done, I would feel like standing upon a steeple and proclaiming our consequent success to the world.'"[26]

With the economic doldrums of 1893 and subsequent years, women's roles expanded to encompass leadership for greater church programs for relief of the needy and afflicted. As had been true over time in many African American churches, women's "societies" offered an organizational framework for translating AME beliefs into practical, daily action. Thus, Mariah Grant could be remembered on her passing in August 1893 as having "organized and established the society known as the Mary and Martha social band of New Hope AME church [of Jacksonville]." As was true of so many others, it was said that she died "in full triumph of faith."[27]

Sometimes women took over the reins of leadership from men who were stymied in the search for solutions to dire problems. "The ladies of the official board of Mt. Zion AME church met pursuant to the call of Mrs. M. E. [Miller] and formed an organization to be known as the Daughters of Mt. Zion; object, the financial advancement of the church," reported the *Jacksonville Evening Telegram* on September 25, 1893. Officers of the organization included Mrs. M. E. C. Smith, president; Mrs. Eliza Myers, vice president; Mrs. Adaline Broadie, secretary; Mrs. Gertrude Alexander, assistant secretary; and Mrs. Jane Taylor, treasurer. Having thus acted, the women opened the doors of their organization to interested persons without regard to sex. "All members as well as friends of this church are cordially invited to become members of this association," they proclaimed.[28]

By this time also women began to step into the pulpits of Florida's AME churches. Until the last half of the 1880s, they had been relegated entirely to auxiliary status. As historian William E. Montgomery explained, "As a rule women exercised their considerable power in the church from the pew and from their auxiliary organizations." The issue of women's ordination nonetheless had commanded church attention. In 1884, the general conference had authorized licenses for women evangelists but had barred them from ordination as regular ministers. When Bishop Henry McNeal Turner defied the conference and ordained Sarah Ann Hughes as a deacon in 1885, the act sparked widespread controversy. Perhaps as a result, Turner declined to assign Hughes a pastorate. His stand-in at the 1887 North Carolina annual meeting, Bishop Jabez Campbell, removed her name from the deacons' list. The 1888 general conference thereafter declared the ordination of a woman "contrary to the usage of our Church."[29]

The first woman evangelist known to have been licensed in Florida by an AME church was Amanda Brantley. She accepted the call as a member of Pensacola's Allen Chapel, possibly as early as the mid-1880s. In any event, during 1893 she emerged as a force to be reckoned with in the war to save souls. During the summer and fall of that year Brantley toured Northeast Florida. When she appeared in Jacksonville at Mt. Zion in July, it was reported that "so many went that hundreds went away for want of room." At Macedonia later the same month, the evangelist preached "to an overflowing congregation." An account noted, "Her congregations at this place were such as were never before congregated under similar circumstances."[30]

At least a few others soon followed in Brantley's footsteps. In September 1893, "two lady applicants to preach" appeared before the quarterly conference at Mt. Zion in Jacksonville. One report suggested that "they will doubtless be licensed." One of the women, Mary Jane Taylor, subsequently distinguished herself for effective preaching and found the same kind of ready acceptance that Sister Brantley had enjoyed. When Taylor first spoke at Mt. Zion in November, a member of the congregation insisted that "her language was splendid for a new preacher, and she explained her subject, in an excellent manner, and was congratulated by all."[31]

Even with the enormous assistance provided by lay women and evangelists, Florida's AME church groaned beneath the burden of its collective problems by 1894. The principal light of those days came from Bishop Grant. "At all the conferences in Fla., the veteran hero, Rt. Rev. T. M. D. Ward, D.D., is ably associated by the jovial, erudite, and eloquent prelate, Rt. Rev. Abram Grant, D.D.," recorded C. A. A. Taylor in March. Grant's popularity and importance during trying times prompted Bishop Ward to offer him a token of the church's appreciation. In February he directed the renaming of Jacksonville's St. Mark's church. Henceforth, it would be known by the name Grant's Chapel.[32]

Bishop Ward depended more and more on his protégé as 1894 evolved and the stress and challenges took their toll upon the prelate's health. By midyear, it all proved too much. The end came suddenly. In early June, Ward had traveled to DeLand for one of M. M. Moore's Sunday school

60. As did thousands of other women, Mary Alice LaRoche Certain, wife of the Reverend W. D. Certain, strove in countless ways to support and further the AME Church's work in Florida. She taught public and Sunday school, organized missionary activities, and raised money, among many other worthwhile projects. Courtesy Photographic Collection, Florida State Archives.

conventions. He returned home on the ninth. "Next morning he was found a corpse in his room at the Episcopal Residence at 1468 Florida Avenue, Jacksonville," recalled Charles Sumner Long. "All Florida mourned the passing of this good man," he added. "Bishop T. M. D. Ward never ceased, not day or night, to preach a living gospel," declared Ward's fellow Florida clergy. "The church has lost a great man, a gentleman, and a preacher of power." Among other memorials, Ward's Campground at Lakeland recalled for many years the lamented bishop's service to the state.[33]

The sad news of the bishop's death fell upon a church yearning for better days. In an eloquent funeral sermon at Mt. Zion church, Bishop Grant offered reassurances, but news of a more felicitous nature took some additional time to arrive. When it did, Floridians finally felt that they could exult. The Council of Bishops had transferred Grant to their state to serve out Ward's episcopal term. Better times surely were on the way.[34]

61. The Reverend W. D. Certain was licensed to preach at Jacksonville's Mount Zion AME Church in May 1888. Courtesy Photographic Collection, Florida State Archives.

Most in the church suddenly were able to look forward eagerly to the AME district sessions scheduled for early 1895, and they did so. But nature held in store another cruel lesson.

The Great Freeze of 1895 came unexpectedly. In the closing days of 1894 a hard freeze lasting three days had reached its icy tentacles as far south as Fort Myers, damaging citrus trees and killing most vegetables growing north of the Manatee River. Surely, Floridians believed, the winter would not produce another such phenomenon. In fact, six weeks of balmy weather followed. On February 1, the soft winter temperatures helped to make even more pleasant Bishop Grant's dedication of St. James Church at Bartow. Six days later, a killer cold front blanketed the peninsula. For four days it smothered the landscape, destroying citrus groves and whatever farm crops remained from the December storm. Devastation lay at every hand except on the sparsely populated lower Atlantic coast.[35]

Although some residents assessed the freeze's impact optimistically in the days following, most realized the truth. From as far south on the Atlantic coast as Jensen, one man reported that "the last cold snap was the worst in the section in 500 years as evidenced by the rubber trees being killed which he is satisfied are that old, also killed mango and mastic plum trees." In Central and Southwest Florida, conditions fared worse. "It is well to look things squarely in the face," declared one farmer. "It is at best a serious disaster, to many it means ruin; to all it means a time of care, anxiety and doubt as to the future." Another bemoaned, "The (1894–1895) freezes did the work for us all, sweeping away a lifetime's labor, leaving us poor, which seems to be the inevitable doom of all pioneers in all countries."[36]

Eight days after the freeze lifted, the East Florida Conference annual sessions drew most state AME leaders to St. Augustine to assess what actions the church should take at the dawning of such a difficult new era. Little wonder that one of the early sermons was titled "The Privilege of Suffering." Then, no sooner had the gathering gotten well under way than more news arrived to confirm that the old era indeed had ended. Telegraph wires brought word of the death at Washington, D.C., of Frederick Douglass. This newest blow was received, conference minutes indicate, "with many manifestations of sorrow." Members desired that they be recorded in their expressions of grief. "We feel that the death of the Hon. Frederick Douglass removes from the earth," their memorial intoned, "one of the strongest advocates of our doctrine of 'the fatherhood in God and the brotherhood in man,' the most distinguished layman in our church, the great friend of our schools and a mighty helper in extending the kingdom of God."[37]

Too many problems confronted the churchmen, and too few answers came to hand. Despite Bishop Grant's efforts to keep conference business flowing in proper order, delegates soon adjourned without clear direction. The prelate and other dignitaries then headed for Ocala where the South Florida Conference was scheduled to convene February 27. Visitors crowded sanctuaries there to listen eagerly as the church's luminaries attempted to revive spirits with impassioned oratory and congregational singing. M. M. Moore stood out in the effort, crying out for "renewed energy." Particular attention also was paid to the presentation of M. M. Lewey, the "chief commissioner of the negro department of industrial exhibits" for Atlanta's upcoming Cotton States Exhibition, indicating some surviving hope that the future somehow would bring greater comfort. Electricity—

anxious though it may have been—at times filled the air, but real solutions remained elusive.[38]

Events soon set firmly the church's tone for the following months and years. It evidenced itself as early as July 1895 when the trustees of Edward Waters College, frustrated by funding problems and a sense that Jacksonville "no longer fully appreciated the college," voted to relocate to Eatonville. Bishop Grant endeavored with all of his might to rekindle church spirits, but in 1896 the general conference removed him from Florida and appointed in his place the ailing former director of the church's book concern, Bishop J. C. Embry. The same year, the U.S. Supreme Court's *Plessy v. Ferguson* decision gave constitutional approval to enforced racial segregation and the now infamous "separate but equal" doctrine. Meanwhile, Bishop Embry's health delayed his arrival in Florida. Once in the state, he lived only a short while, and he died at Philadelphia in early 1897.[39]

By the time of that sad occurrence, a tendency to look back had replaced for many any idea of looking to the future for comfort. Nostalgia gripped imaginations. At the 1897 Florida Conference annual sessions, "the old plantation melodies were rehearsed and the old-fashioned way of seeking religion was resorted to." Tensions festered by then to such an extent that the East Florida Conference "for some cause not yet fully understood" erupted in "much bitterness." According to a church historian, "The result was a slight break resulting in what is known as the 'Independent Church.'" And so it went.[40]

Although it was not well appreciated at the time, the direction of the new era for African Americans in the South and for Florida's AME church had been set. Gone were the heady days of the late 1860s and early 1870s when possibilities for the race seemed unlimited, when thoughts that African Methodism might rule Florida were more than plausible. Now, practicality ruled the day. The art of the possible supplanted the dreams of men such as William G. Stewart, Robert Meacham, Charles H. Pearce, William Bradwell, and George Washington Witherspoon.

Booker T. Washington, who had emerged in the wake of Frederick Douglass's death as the leading spokesman for African Americans in the South, first sounded the theme seven months following the Great Freeze of 1895. Speaking at Atlanta's Cotton States Exposition, he introduced what would come to be known as the Atlanta Compromise. To southern blacks, he entreated, "Cast down your buckets where you are." He argued—however reluctantly—that, given the times, economic progress for the race must be bought at the price of political and social inequality. The price to be paid truly was a heavy one.[41]

Such pragmatism, if indeed it was, carried the day for the Florida church, as well. Survival as an institution meant compromise elsewhere. A large portion of available resources now were allocated to missionary efforts that followed the newly constructed railways. Thus, in 1896 it meant the organization of Greater Bethel Church in the tiny village and nascent resort community of Miami. Funds to support other projects such as Edward Waters College, on the other hand, remained extremely hard to come by (although the school managed to cling to its Jacksonville home).

Great symbolic meaning, then, attached to two events that occurred around the century's end. At Miami, a new church arose near the center of what would become Florida's greatest city and its gateway to the twentieth-century world. At Jacksonville, where much of the old era had centered, flames swept away the relics of a bygone day when fire destroyed much of the city. "Beloved in Jesus...," Bishop W. B. Derrick would lament in May 1901, "our beautiful Mt. Zion Church, Edward Waters' College, Grants' Chapel and perhaps other church buildings are things of the past." He added, "Many of our most worthy ministers who had secured for themselves and families comfortable homes are today without shelter to protect them from the ware of the elements." Bishop Derrick closed, "I am yours, dearly beloved, in the bonds of Christian affliction."[42]

The Florida AME Church and its members felt the chilling winds of political and social change, along with most black Floridians and other African Americans throughout the country. And the conditions would not improve anytime soon. As historian Rayford Logan has noted, the period from the late 1890s until around 1910 marked the "nadir" in black/white relations in America. The economic problems that faced Florida's AME Church and its members were reflected in the circumstances of many, if not most, African Americans at the century's turn. Millions would toil long in the vineyard, but better times would arrive, for black Floridians generally and the AME Church in particular.[43]

NOTES

Introduction

1. *Bartow Courier-Informant*, February 6, 1895.
2. Kealing, *History of African Methodism in Texas*, 199–203; "Bishop A. Grant"; *NYA*, January 26, 1911.
3. Brown, *Florida's Black Public Officials*, 55–66; Brown, "Bishop Payne," 23–39; Brown, "Prelude to the Poll Tax," 69–81.
4. See, for example, Rivers, "Baptist Minister James Page"; McKinney and McKinney, *History of Black Baptists*, 37–40; Brown, *Florida's Black Public Officials*, 3, 7–8, 37; *JFU*, November 23, 1867; *Salisbury (N.C.) Star of Zion*, February 28, May 16, 1895, October 17, November 19, 1903; *JFT-U*, March 3, 1895.
5. Covington, *Story of Southwestern Florida*, I, 171–89; Brown, *Florida's Peace River Frontier*, 266–91, 317–21; Brown, *Henry Bradley Plant*, 13–17.
6. St. James AME Church, Bartow, folder: Polk County, CH-RECs; St. James AME Church, "Souvenir of the Dedicatory Services"; St. James AME Church, "4th Annual Homecoming Program"; Brown, *Florida's Peace River Frontier*, 282–83.
7. Mayo, *Sixth Census*, 90; Brown, *Florida's Black Public Officials*, 43–48; T. Davis, *History of Jacksonville*, 219–27.
8. C. Smith, *History of the African Methodist Episcopal Church*, 172, 190; Brown, *Florida's Black Public Officials*, 76, 115, 123, 141.
9. Covington, *Story of Southwestern Florida*, 1:195–96; Brown, *Florida's Peace River Frontier*, 321–23; U.S. Department of Agriculture, *Yearbook, 1900*, 756–59, 798–800, 809–11.
10. Akin, *Flagler*, 160–67; McCarthy, *Black Florida*, 192; Rivers and Brown, "African Americans in South Florida," 11–12.

Chapter 1

1. Rivers, *Slavery in Florida*; Temple, *Florida Flame*, 32–33; Brooks, *From Saddlebags to Satellites*, 23–24.
2. *Southern Christian Advocate*, March 4, 1874.
3. E. Martin, *Florida During the Territorial Days*, 36, 108–12; Rivers, *Slavery in Florida*; J. F. Smith, *Slavery and Plantation Growth*, 9–52.
4. Groene, *Ante-Bellum Tallahassee*, 3–22; Temple, *Florida Flame*, 40–41, 52.

5. Shofner, *Jackson County*, 178.
6. *Southern Christian Advocate*, September 13, 1850, May 23, 1851; Temple, *Florida Flame*, 120–21, 127.
7. Shofner, *Jefferson County*, 133; *TFP*, January 2, 1858; *Tallahassee Floridian and Journal*, January 14, 1860.
8. Nichols, "Six Weeks in Florida," 663; Rawick, *American Slave*, 17:35; Rivers, *Slavery in Florida*; Brown, "Race Relations in Territorial Florida," 293–94.
9. *Southern Christian Advocate*, May 23, 1851; Temple, *Florida Flame*, 127–28.
10. Frey and Wood, *Come Shouting to Zion*, 118–19. See also Mathews, *Slavery and Methodism*, 6–7; Quarles, *Negro in the American Revolution*, 33–50, Jefferson, *Notes on the State of Virginia*, 138, 162–63.
11. Frey and Wood, *Come Shouting to Zion*, 179; Mathews, *Slavery and Methodism*, 3–29; Lock, *Anti-Slavery in America*, 9–15.
12. Frey and Wood, *Come Shouting to Zion*, 111–12; J. Wesley, *Thoughts upon Slavery*, 35; Mathews, *Slavery and Methodism*, 5, 10–13, 21; Goen, *Broken Churches*, 79–80.
13. Frey and Wood, *Come Shouting to Zion*, 136; Mathews, *Slavery and Methodism*, 21; Aptheker, *American Negro Slave Revolts*, 101–3; Heyrman, *Southern Cross*, 92–94.
14. Heyrman, *Southern Cross*, 92–94; *Tallahassee Florida Sentinel*, October 15, 29, 1850; Mathews, *Slavery and Methodism*, 25–26.
15. Mathews, *Slavery and Methodism*, 245–82; Goen, *Broken Churches*, 81–83.
16. Cartwright, *Autobiography of Peter Cartwright*, 276; Mathews, *Slavery and Methodism*, 246–82; Goen, *Broken Churches*, 82; Temple, *Florida Flame*, 59; Thrift, *Trail of the Circuit Rider*, 62–64; Rifwer, *Constitutional History*, 371; Chandler, "Formation of the Methodist Protestant Church," 1:646.
17. Mathews, *Slavery and Methodism*, 246–47; Goen, *Broken Churches*, 83–88; Thrift, *Trail of the Circuit Rider*, 62–63; Temple, *Florida Flame*, 93–108.
18. Ossian B. Hart to Josiah Walls, January 16, 1874, vol. 8 (January–April 1874), Florida Governor's Office, Letterbooks, vol. 8.
19. S. Richardson, *Lights and Shadows of Itinerant Life*, 70–71.
20. Rivers, "Baptist Minister James Page," 43–47; Rivers, *Slavery in Florida*; McKinney and McKinney, *History of the Black Baptists*, 16–19; *TS*, May 18, 1872.
21. Joiner, *History of Florida Baptists*, 46–47.
22. McKinney and McKinney, *History of the Black Baptists*, 16–17.
23. Rivers, *Slavery in Florida*; Rivers, "Troublesome Property," 107; Rawick, *American Slave*, 17:35, 97–98, 252.
24. Rivers, *Slavery in Florida*.
25. Dodd, "Florida in 1845," 3–4; Temple, *Florida Flame*, 100; *Negro Population 1790–1915*, 57; Thrift, *Trail of the Circuit Rider*, 95.
26. Rivers, *Slavery in Florida*; Berlin, "Slaves' Changing World," 58; Oliver O. Howard to Lizzie Howard, July 22, 1857, Howard Papers; Walker, *Rock in a Weary Land*, 23.

27. S. Richardson, *Lights and Shadows of Itinerant Life*, 71.
28. Temple, *Florida Flame*, 134–35; Hart to Walls, January 16, 1874.
29. Temple, *Florida Flame*, 136–38; *Southern Christian Advocate*, August 14, 1862.
30. Montgomery, *Under Their Own Vine and Fig Tree*, 49–54; Thrift, *Trail of the Circuit Rider*, 95–96; Temple, *Florida Flame*, 138–42.
31. *Guide to Supplementary Vital Statistics*, 2:434, 442, 580; Mt. Moriah AME Church, Marion County, and Bethlehem and Mt. Olive AME Churches, Jackson County, CH-RECs; Long, *History of the AME Church in Florida*, 57.
32. *Guide to Supplementary Vital Statistics*, 1:137, 241, II, 498, 553; Concord and Bethel AME Churches, Leon County; Jeslam AME Church, Madison County; Hope Henry AME Church, Columbia County; and Midway AME Church, Duval County, CH-RECs.
33. 1870 Jackson County census; Bethlehem and Mt. Olive AME Churches, Jackson County; Arnett, *Proceedings of the Quarto-Centennial*, CH-RECs, 165, 177; *PCR*, October 14, 1875, March 1, 1877.
34. Brown, *Florida's Black Public Officials*, 100–101; Wayman, *Cyclopaedia of African Methodism*, 90; *PCR*, April 29, 1880; *JET*, April 21, 25, 1893; McCarthy, *Black Florida*, 251.
35. Brown, *Florida's Black Public Officials*, 141; Dowda, *History of Palatka and Putnam County*, 33–34; *JET*, April 20, 1893.
36. Brown, "Where Are Now the Hopes," 1–36; Muse, "From Slavery to State Senate."
37. Brown, *Florida's Black Public Officials*, 131; Arnett, *Proceedings of the Quarto-Centennial*, 170; Ferrell, "History of St. Paul AME Church," 179.
38. Brown, *Florida's Black Public Officials*, 79; Long, *History of the AME Church in Florida*, 56; Call, *History of Allen Chapel*, 2.
39. The paragraphing of this quotation has been changed for clarity. Long, *History of the AME Church in Florida*, 56–57.
40. Brown, *Florida's Black Public Officials*, 79; Call, *History of Allen Chapel*, 1–3.
41. Mathews, *Slavery and Methodism*, 64; Aptheker, *Documentary History*, 37–38; Woodson, *History of the Negro Church*, 78–85; Angell, *Bishop Henry McNeal Turner*, 25–26. See also George, *Segregated Sabbaths*, 21–55; Allen, *Life, Experience, and Gospel Labors*, 15–26; Frey and Wood, *Come Shouting to Zion*, 167, 179.
42. Angell, *Bishop Henry McNeal Turner*, 25–26; Payne, *History of the African Methodist Episcopal Church*, 3–4; Montgomery, *Under Their Own Vine and Fig Tree*, 7–9; Walker, *Rock in a Weary Land*, 4–11.
43. Walker, *Rock in a Weary Land*, 4–5; C. Wesley, *Richard Allen*, 71–72. For general history of the founding of the AME church, see Payne, *History of the African Methodist Episcopal Church*, and C. Smith, *History of the African Methodist Episcopal Church*.
44. Walker, *Rock in a Weary Land*, 8–9; C. Wesley, *Richard Allen*, 77; Hood, *One Hundred Years*, 56–57; Walls, *African Methodist Episcopal Zion Church*, 51–69.

45. C. Smith, *History of the African Methodist Episcopal Church*, 14–15; Payne, *History of the African Methodist Episcopal Church*, 45.
46. Arnett, *Budget* (1883), 5–10.
47. Payne, *History of the African Methodist Episcopal Church*, 34; C. Smith, *History of the African Methodist Episcopal Church*, 16, 19; Walker, *Rock in a Weary Land*, 19.
48. Walker, *Rock in a Weary Land*, 46–75; C. Smith, *History of the African Methodist Episcopal Church*, 51–59; Payne, *History of the African Methodist Episcopal Church*, 469.

Chapter 2

1. Du Bois, *Autobiography*, 187; Pfeffer, *A. Philip Randolph*, 7.
2. McPherson, *Battle Cry of Freedom*, 848–62; Du Bois, *Black Reconstruction*, 124.
3. Payne, *History of the African Methodist Episcopal Church*, 469–70.
4. Handy, *Scraps of African Methodist Episcopal History*, 409.
5. *NYF*, March 27, 1886; *Tallahassee Weekly True Democrat*, June 16, 1911; Long, *History of the AME Church in Florida*, 55.
6. Long, *History of the AME Church in Florida*, 153.
7. Ibid., 73.
8. Brown, "Civil War," 231–46.
9. Rivers, *Slavery in Florida*; Kennedy, *Population in 1860*, 54.
10. *Jacksonville Tri-Weekly Florida Sun*, January 29, 1876; Reid, *After the War*, 162.
11. *American Missionary*, September 1865, 209–10; J. Richardson, *Christian Reconstruction*, 62; Kennedy, *Population in 1860*, 54; Brown, *Ossian Bingley Hart*, 163–65.
12. Temple, *Florida Flame*, 140–41.
13. Foster and Foster, *Beechers, Stowes, and Yankee Strangers*, 1–31.
14. Long, *History of the AME Church in Florida*, 73; Arnett, *Proceedings of the Quarto-Centennial*, 170.
15. Long, *History of the AME Church in Florida*, 57.
16. Ibid., 73; *JFU*, July 2, 1865; Bethlehem, Mt. Olive, Springfield, and St. James AME Churches, Jackson County, CH-RECs.
17. Long, *History of the AME Church in Florida*, 73; Arnett, *Proceedings of the Quarto-Centennial*, 164; *Guide to Supplementary Vital Statistics*, 1:137, 241, 2:434, 442, 498, 552, 580; Brown, "Where Are Now the Hopes," 4.
18. The principal sources for Florida's Reconstruction-era history are Wallace, *Carpetbag Rule*; W. Davis, *Civil War and Reconstruction in Florida*; Shofner, *Nor Is It Over Yet*; and Brown, *Ossian Bingley Hart*.
19. Brown, *Ossian Bingley Hart*, 167–68; *New York Herald*, November 19, 1865.
20. Klingman, "Rascal or Representative?" 52–57; *Pensacola Daily News*, October 12, 1906; Wallace, *Carpetbag Rule*, 38–39; Brown, *Florida's Black Public Officials*, 2, 113.
21. Walker, *A Rock in a Weary Land*, 21; Handy, *Scraps of African Methodist Episcopal History*, 350–51.

22. Charles Pearce to George G. Meade, April 2, 1868, U.S. War Department, Incoming Correspondence, box 8, entry 5738.
23. Arnett, *Proceedings of the Quarto-Centennial*, 175.
24. Angell, *Bishop Henry McNeal Turner*, 85–88; Anderson, *A. Philip Randolph*, 30.
25. *JFU*, June 1, 1867; Florida Annual Conference of the AME Church, *Minutes*, 18.
26. Walker, *Rock in a Weary Land*, 52; Dodd, "'Bishop' Pearce," 5–6.
27. Arnett, *Proceedings of the Quarto-Centennial*, 166, 173.
28. Ibid., 166; *JFT-U*, February 19, 1889; Thrift, *Trail of the Circuit Rider*, 108; Temple, *Florida Flame*, 378, 394. For an excellent recent study on the links between black and white Methodists in the South during the immediate post–Civil War era, see Owen, *Sacred Flame of Love*.
29. Arnett, *Proceedings of the Quarto-Centennial*, 166, 182; McCarthy, *Black Florida*, 131; Jones and McCarthy, *African Americans in Florida*, 160.
30. *American Missionary*, January 1866, 9; Foster and Foster, *Beechers, Stowes, and Yankee Strangers*, 40–41; *PCR*, June 10, 1871, April 22, 1875; *JT-WFU*, March 26, 1874.
31. Arnett, *Proceedings of the Quarto-Centennial*, 166; Dodd, "'Bishop' Pearce," 6; Brown, "Where Are Now the Hopes," 4; *Tallahassee Semi-Weekly Floridian*, February 20, 1866.
32. Arnett, *Proceedings of the Quarto-Centennial*, 166.
33. Long, *History of the AME Church in Florida*, 73.
34. Call, *History of Allen Chapel*, 3.
35. C. Smith, *History of the African Methodist Episcopal Church*, 507–8; *PCR*, June 9, 1866.
36. *TS*, March 16, 1872; 1870 Jackson County census; Arnett, *Proceedings of the Quarto-Centennial*, 167; C. Smith, *History of the African Methodist Episcopal Church*, 508; *PCR*, June 9, 1866; Wayman, *Cyclopaedia of African Methodism*, 155; St. Paul's AME Church, Franklin County, CH-RECs.
37. Brown, *Florida's Black Public Officials*, 76; Brown, *Ossian Bingley Hart*, 187; *TWF*, November 26, 1867; *New York Tribune*, February 5, 1868; Long, *History of the AME Church in Florida*, 196.
38. Long, *History of the AME Church in Florida*, 59–60; C. Smith, *History of the African Methodist Episcopal Church*, 508–9; 1870 Bradford County census (Washington, D.C.: Government Printing Office); 1885 Bradford County census.
39. *PCR*, September 8, 1866; Arnett, *Proceedings of the Quarto-Centennial*, 185, 440.
40. *Savannah Daily News and Herald*, September 8, 1866.
41. *PCR*, November 10, 1866.
42. Brown, *Ossian B. Hart*, 168–71, 177–84; *Savannah Daily News and Herald*, June 28, 1866.
43. Foner, *Reconstruction*, 261–71.
44. *New York Times*, July 23, 1866.

Chapter 3

1. Shofner, *Nor Is It Over Yet*, 157–59.
2. *Savannah Daily News and Herald*, April 22, 1867; *Washington (D.C.) Daily Morning Chronicle*, March 28, 1867; *Tallahassee Semi-Weekly Floridian*, March 26, 1867; Brown, *Ossian Bingley Hart*, 187–88.
3. Brown, *Ossian Bingley Hart*, 188–89.
4. C. Smith, *History of the African Methodist Episcopal Church*, 509–14; Wayman, *My Recollections*, 144.
5. C. Smith, *History of the African Methodist Episcopal Church*, 512, 517–19.
6. Ibid., 520–21.
7. Brown, *Florida's Black Public Officials*, 6–7; *Savannah Daily News and Herald*, May 8, 28, 1867; Brown, "Where Are Now the Hopes," 6.
8. *PCR*, July 13, 1867.
9. Womack, *Gadsden*, 136; *PCR*, July 6, 13, August 10, 1867, May 16, 1868.
10. *PCR*, July 6, 1867; *Tallahassee Semi-Weekly Floridian*, June 14, 1867; Arnett, *Proceedings of the Quarto-Centennial*, 163–64.
11. Arnett, *Proceedings of the Quarto-Centennial*, 164–65; *Tallahassee Semi-Weekly Floridian*, June 14, 1867; *PCR*, July 6, 1867.
12. Arnett, *Proceedings of the Quarto-Centennial*, 164–65; *Tallahassee Semi-Weekly Floridian*, June 14, 1867; *PCR*, July 6, 1867; Walls, *African Methodist Episcopal Zion Church*, 200.
13. Brown, *Florida's Black Public Officials*, 3–7; *PCR*, August 10, 1867.
14. *PCR*, August 10, 1867; Walker, *Rock in a Weary Land*, 103.
15. J. Richardson, *Negro in the Reconstruction of Florida*, 141; Brown, *Florida's Black Public Officials*, 7–8; *Pensacola Daily News*, November 18, 1906.
16. Brown, *Ossian Bingley Hart*, 190–98; *New York Daily Tribune*, July 27, 1867.
17. *JFU*, November 9, 1867; *New York Daily Tribune*, February 5, 1868; *TWF*, February 11, 1868; Brown, *Florida's Black Public Officials*, 8–9.
18. J. Richardson, *Negro in the Reconstruction of Florida*, 152–60; Brown, *Florida's Black Public Officials*, 9–10.
19. Brown, *Ossian Bingley Hart*, 206–14; Brown, *Florida's Black Public Officials*, 10–11; Wallace, *Carpetbag Rule*, 420–21.
20. *PCR*, April 4, 1868; Wayman, *My Recollections*, 150.
21. *PCR*, April 4, 1868; Long, *History of the AME Church in Florida*, 66; Wayman, *My Recollections*, 150.
22. Long, *History of the AME Church in Florida*, 66–68; *PCR*, April 4, 1868.
23. Long, *History of the AME Church in Florida*, 68–69; *PCR*, April 4, 1868.
24. *Washington (D.C.) Daily Morning Chronicle*, March 16, 1868.
25. Ibid., April 6, 1868; *TS*, April 9, 1868.
26. Osborn, "Letters of a Carpetbagger," 269, 271–72.
27. Daniel Richards to Elihu B. Washburn, May 7, 1868, Washburn Papers; Richards to Thaddeus Stevens, March 18, 1868, Stevens Papers.
28. Brown, *Florida's Black Public Officials*, 13.

29. Shofner, *Nor Is It Over Yet*, 187–202; Brown, *Ossian Bingley Hart*, 215–22, 231–32.
30. Brown, *Ossian Bingley Hart*, 231–32; Brown, "Where Are Now the Hopes," 11; *TFP*, August 22, 1868.
31. Brown, *Florida's Black Public Officials*, 105–6, 109–10, 115; *JFU*, August 6, 1868; Robert Meacham to Harrison Reed, February 11, 1869, Florida Governor's Office, Incoming Correspondence, box 2, folder 5. For an interesting look at Jefferson County's school situation, see Blair, "Education of Blacks in Jefferson County."
32. Wallace, *Carpetbag Rule*, 88; Brown, "Where Are Now the Hopes," 12–13; *JFU*, February 11, 1869.
33. *Laws of Florida* (1869), 7–19; Brown, "Where Are Now the Hopes," 12–13; Brown, *Ossian Bingley Hart*, 233–34; *Washington (D.C.) Daily National Intelligencer*, January 11, 1869.
34. *PCR*, May 16, July 18, 1868, April 17, July 31, 1869.
35. Montgomery, *Under Their Own Vine and Fig Tree*, 114; C. Smith, *History of the African Methodist Episcopal Church*, 77–81.
36. *PCR*, May 16, 1868.
37. *JFU*, December 24, 1868.
38. Arnett, *Budget* (1883), 19–23.
39. Ibid.; *PCR*, April 17, 1869.
40. *PCR*, April 17, 1869; Long, *History of the AME Church in Florida*, 70.

Chapter 4

1. Dodd, "'Bishop' Pearce," 7–9; Brown, *Florida's Black Public Officials*, 15–19, 115; *PCR*, April 17, 1869, April 17, 1873.
2. *PCR*, July 31, 1869.
3. *JFU*, February 18, 1869; *PCR*, July 31, 1869.
4. Wayman, *My Recollections*, 144, 151.
5. Menard, *Lays in Summer Lands*, 27–28.
6. *PCR*, July 31, 1869.
7. *JFU*, July 22, 1869; *PCR*, July 31, 1869.
8. Walls, *African Methodist Episcopal Zion Church*, 202.
9. Walker, *Rock in a Weary Land*, 103–6; Montgomery, *Under Their Own Fig and Vine Tree*, 120–25; *TWF*, October 14, 1873.
10. C. Smith, *History of the African Methodist Episcopal Church*, 522.
11. Walker, *Rock in a Weary Land*, 21; Long, *History of the AME Church in Florida*, 70.
12. *PCR*, January 15, 1870, June 10, 1871.
13. Ibid., January 22, 1870.
14. Ibid.
15. *TS*, January 15, 1870; *PCR*, January 15, 22, 1870, April 17, 1873; Long, *History of the AME Church in Florida*, 82.
16. *PCR*, January 22, 1870; *TS*, January 15, 1870.

17. *TS*, January 15, 1870.
18. Brown, *Florida's Black Public Officials*, 20.
19. Brown, *Ossian Bingley Hart*, 238–42; Wallace, *Carpetbag Rule*, 113–26.
20. Long, *History of the AME Church in Florida*, 77–78.
21. Ibid., 77–79; *Guide to Supplementary Vital Statistics*, 2:370, 412, 519, 521, 527, 530, 3:865; Brown, *African Americans on the Tampa Bay Frontier*, 55; Ferrell, "History of St. Paul AME Church," 179; Maloney, *Sketch*, 35–36.
22. *Guide to Supplementary Vital Statistics*, 1:5, 13, 29, 35, 111, 205, 245, 2:596, 3:885–86; *TS*, December 2, 1871; *PCR*, October 1, 1870; May 29, 1873; Talbert, *Sons of Allen*, 68; Nassau County Deed Records, book L, 492.
23. *Savannah Daily Republican*, May 1, 1870; Bragg, *Men of Maryland*, 64–78.
24. *PCR*, April 17, 1873; *JET*, February 11, 1892, August 15, 1893; *Jacksonville Evening Times-Union*, May 19, 1894.
25. *TS*, July 16, 1870; Brown, *Florida's Black Public Officials*, 20–22; Brown, "Where Are Now the Hopes," 15–16; Klingman, *Josiah Walls*, 32–37.
26. Wallace, *Carpetbag Rule*, 106–8; Brown, *Florida's Black Public Officials*, 22; J. Richardson, *Negro in the Reconstruction of Florida*, 191.
27. Brown, *Florida's Black Public Officials*, 22–23; Rivers, "Baptist Minister James Page," 50; *PCR*, July 29, 1871.
28. *TS*, January 7, 1871; Angell, *Bishop Henry McNeal Turner*, 83. See also Walker, *Rock in a Weary Land*, 24; Du Bois, *Black Reconstruction*, 497–511; Nathans, *Losing the Peace*, 15–25; E. Martin, "Life of Henry McNeal Turner"; Coulter, "Henry M. Turner."
29. *TS*, March 4, July 8, 1871; *TFP*, March 15, 1871.
30. *PCR*, April 15, 29, May 27, June 10, July 29, 1871; *TS*, August 26, December 2, 1871; *SMN*, August 31, 1871.
31. *TS*, July 8, 1871.
32. *PCR*, February 10, 1872; *TS*, March 16, 1872.
33. *TS*, December 23, 1871.
34. Long, *History of the AME Church in Florida*, 82; Scott, *Education of Black People in Florida*, 50; Arnett, *Proceedings of the Quarto-Centennial*, 437; *TS*, March 16, 1872; McKinney and McKinney, *History of the Black Baptists*, 47–48.
35. Brown, *Florida's Black Public Officials*, 24–25; Brown, *Ossian Bingley Hart*, 253–56; *Laws of Florida* (1872), 68–69; *TS*, March 16, 1872.
36. C. Smith, *History of the African Methodist Episcopal Church*, 95–104; *PCR*, May 23, 1872; *TS*, June 22, 1872; *JT-WFU*, June 25, 1872.
37. *JT-WFU*, July 9, 1872; *TS*, July 6, 1872.
38. Brown, *Ossian Bingley Hart*, 259–60; *Philadelphia Times*, December 1, 1883; *TS*, July 6, 1872; *JT-WFU*, July 6, 9, 1872.

Chapter 5

1. Brown, *Florida's Black Public Officials*, 15–25; Brown, "Where Are Now the Hopes," 4–20; Dodd, "'Bishop' Pearce," 6–11.

2. Brown, *Ossian Bingley Hart*, 260–63; Brown, *Florida's Black Public Officials*, 24–25; *TWF*, August 13, 1872.
3. Brown, *Ossian Bingley Hart*, 263–68; *PCR*, December 28, 1872.
4. Dodd, "'Bishop' Pearce," 10–12; Warner, *Free Men*, 103–5; *TWF*, November 5, 12, 1872.
5. Brown, *Florida's Black Public Officials*, 26–27; *Savannah Daily Advertiser*, October 20, 1872; *PCR*, December 28, 1872.
6. Arnett, *Budget* (1883), 19, 49.
7. *JT-WFU*, January 2, 1873.
8. Ibid.; Long, *History of the AME Church in Florida*, 102.
9. *PCR*, January 30, April 17, 1873; *JT-WFU*, January 9, 1873.
10. Brown, *Ossian Bingley Hart*, 270–76.
11. Ibid., 273–81; *Laws of Florida* (1873), 26. On Gibbs, see J. Richardson, "Jonathan C. Gibbs."
12. Brown, *Ossian Bingley Hart*, 229, 286; Brown, *Florida's Black Public Officials*, 79, 88, 109–10, 133, 138.
13. Brown, *Ossian Bingley Hart*, 283–84; *Newark (N.J.) Sentinel of Freedom*, March 25, 1873; *New York Times*, October 20, 1873.
14. *SMN*, October 11, 1872; Brown, *Ossian Bingley Hart*, 266–70; *PCR*, November 6, 1873.
15. *JT-WFU*, January 9, 1873; *Philadelphia Times*, December 1, 1883; *New York Evening Post*, April 3, 1873; Long, *History of the AME Church in Florida*, 180–81; Arnett, *Proceedings of the Quarto-Centennial*, 438–39.
16. R. Hall, "Gospel According to Radicalism," 76; *TWF*, April 7, 15, July 15, 1873, February 23, 1875; Arnett, *Proceedings of the Quarto-Centennial*, 438.
17. *TWF*, April 29, 1873; Arnett, *Proceedings of the Quarto-Centennial*, 438; *PCR*, June 12, 1873.
18. *PCR*, June 12, October 30, 1873.
19. Ibid., June 5, 12, 1873, July 8, 1875.
20. Ibid., June 5, 12, 1873; R. Hall, "Gospel According to Radicalism," 80.
21. R. Hall, "Gospel According to Radicalism," 80; *TWF*, September 16, 1873.
22. Foner, *Reconstruction*, 512; Brown, *Ossian Bingley Hart*, 289–90; *TWF*, September 30, 1873; *Philadelphia Times*, December 1, 1883.
23. *TWF*, September 30, 1873; *PCR*, December 18, 1873; Arnett, *Proceedings of the Quarto-Centennial*, 438.
24. *PCR*, December 18, 1873; *JDFU*, March 7, 1876.
25. *JFU*, quoted in *TWF*, December 16, 1873.
26. Brown, *Ossian Bingley Hart*, 287–90.
27. *PCR*, November 27, 1873.
28. Ibid., January 15, 1874.
29. Arnett, *Budget* (1883), 19; Long, *History of the AME Church in Florida*, 102–3.
30. *SMN*, January 7, 1874; *PCR*, January 8, 15, 1874.

31. Brown, *Ossian Bingley Hart*, 289–93; *Savannah Advertiser-Republican*, February 10, 22, 1874.
32. Brown, *Ossian Bingley Hart*, 293–98; Brown, *Florida's Black Public Officials*, 29–31, 92; Shofner, *Nor Is It Over Yet*, 270, 288–94; T. Davis, *History of Jacksonville*, 141; R. Martin, *City Makers*, 100–102.
33. *Savannah Advertiser-Republican*, May 20, 1874; Long, *History of the AME Church in Florida*, 181.
34. *PCR*, July 23, 1874.
35. Ibid.
36. Ibid., May 7, August 20, 1874, September 26, 1878.
37. *TWF*, January 7, 1879; *JDFU*, March 7, 1876; *PCR*, January 21, April 15, 1875, September 26, 1878.
38. Brown, *Florida's Black Public Officials*, 30–31; Brown, "Where Are Now the Hopes," 23–29; *PCR*, January 21, April 15, 1875.
39. *PCR*, April 15, 1875, March 30, 1876.
40. *JDFU*, March 7, 1876; *PCR*, April 22, June 17, July 1, September 30, 1875.
41. *Congressional Globe*, 43rd. Cong., 1st sess., vol. 2, pt. 1, p. 88; Klingman, *Josiah Walls*, 63–70; Long, *History of the AME Church in Florida*, 181; Tucker, *Phoenix from the Ashes*, 10–11.
42. *PCR*, July 1, 8, September 30, 1875.
43. *JDFU*, February 29, March 1, 3, 7, 1876; *PCR*, March 30, 1876.

Chapter 6

1. Brown, *Florida's Black Public Officials*, 31, 72, 103–4, 123–24.
2. J. Richardson, *Negro in the Reconstruction of Florida*, 161–76; Du Bois, *Black Reconstruction*, 670–708; Franklin, *Reconstruction After the Civil War*, 152–73; J. D. Smith, *Black Voices*, 128–29; K. Hall, *Magic Mirror*, 145–46.
3. Dodd, "'Bishop' Pearce," 12; *PCR*, April 13, 1876. On Henry McNeal Turner, see Angell, *Bishop Henry McNeal Turner*.
4. Brown, *Florida's Black Public Officials*, 32–33, 128–29; Brown, "Where Are Now the Hopes," 28–29; Brown, "George Washington Witherspoon," 9.
5. *PCR*, January 22, 1870.
6. *TS*, July 8, 1871.
7. *JDFU*, February 29, 1876; *PCR*, April 13, 1876.
8. Fahey, *Temperance and Racism*, 5–31; *TS*, October 28, 1876; *PCR*, June 13, 1878; *Birmingham (Eng.) Good Templars Watchword*, January 8, 1879.
9. *PCR*, October 3, 10, 1878.
10. Fahey, *Temperance and Racism*, 106–8.
11. *Birmingham (Eng.) Good Templars' Watchword*, January 8, 1879.
12. Brown, "Where Are Now the Hopes," 31–32; *TWF*, October 1, 1878.
13. *PCR*, March 30, April 13, 1876, February 24, 1881, July 9, 1885.
14. *JDFU*, March 3, 1876.
15. de Czege, *History of Astor*, 23–26; *Sanford South Florida Argus*, February 17,

1887; *Louisville (Ky.) Courier-Journal,* October 21, 1883; *TWF,* July 12, 1881; *JET,* November 7, 1892; Bentley, *Georgetown,* 6–7; Otey, *Eatonville,* 2–3; McRae, *Fourth Census,* 16–19.
16. *JDFU,* March 7, 1876.
17. C. Smith, *History of the African Methodist Episcopal Church,* 114–19; Long, *History of the AME Church in Florida,* 199–200.
18. Arnett, *Budget* (1883), 16.
19. Brown, *Florida's Black Public Officials,* 36–39; Brown, "Where Are Now the Hopes," 29–31.
20. *PCR,* April 13, 1876, January 27, 1877; *TS,* July 29, 1876; *Guide to Supplementary Vital Statistics,* 1:278, 2:511, 597.
21. *PCR,* November 2, 1876, January 18, 1877.
22. Arnett, *Proceedings of the Quarto-Centennial,* 178; Arnett, *Budget* (1883), 16; Long, *History of the AME Church in Florida,* 199–200; *PCR,* March 1, 1877.
23. *TWF,* January 1, 1878; *PCR,* March 1, 1877; Long, *History of the AME Church in Florida,* 103; Arnett, *Proceedings of the Quarto-Centennial,* 171.
24. *PCR,* April 11, 1878, April 8, 1880; *TWF,* November 20, 1877; Angell, *Bishop Henry McNeal Turner,* 134–41; *DeLand Volusia County Herald,* February 28, 1878.
25. *PCR,* August 19, 1880.
26. *Pensacola Advance,* December 28, 1878, quoted in *TWF,* January 7, 1879; *SMN,* January 1, 1879; Brown, *Florida's Black Public Officials,* 142; *PCR,* August 19, 1880.
27. *PCR,* July 29, August 19, 1880.
28. Ibid., July 4, 1878; *TWF,* April 8, July 8, 1879.
29. *PCR,* July 4, 1878.
30. *Guide to Supplementary Vital Statistics,* 1:22, 116, 137, 144, 243, 294, 312, 316, 326, 2:477, 512, 520, 579, 597, III, 787, 859, 894, 918, 922, 959, 962.
31. *PCR,* April 11, 1878; Wright, *Centennial Encyclopaedia,* 309.
32. Wright, *Centennial Encyclopaedia,* 309; *PCR,* May 20, 1880; Brown, *Florida's Black Public Officials,* 123; *Fernandina Florida Mirror,* March 15, 1879; Kealing, *History of African Methodism in Texas,* 199–203, 207–9; Long, *History of the AME Church in Florida,* 103.
33. *PCR,* May 23, November 28, 1878.
34. Ibid., March 29, April 18, November 28, 1878.
35. Brown, "Where Are Now the Hopes," 31; Brown, *Florida's Black Public Officials,* 40–41.
36. Brown, "George Washington Witherspoon," 10–11.

Chapter 7

1. Long, *History of the AME Church in Florida,* 75–79; Brown, *Florida's Black Public Officials,* 105–6.
2. *Fernandina Florida Mirror,* April 17, 24, 1880; Drake, *Florida Legislature,* 55;

"Hon. Henry Wilkins Chandler, A.B., A.M.," box 1, folder 4, Florida Negro Papers; *Tallahassee Semi-Weekly Floridian,* September 3, 1880; Brown, *Florida's Black Public Officials,* 80.
3. Mayo, *Sixth Census,* 90.
4. Johnson, "Henry Bradley Plant," 120–24; Pettengill, *Story of the Florida Railroads,* 63–72; Brown, *Henry Bradley Plant,* 13–15; *JFT-U,* September 20, 1885; *Pensacola Commercial,* January 30, 1884.
5. Brown, *Florida's Black Public Officials,* 43–54, 79, 81, 93, 123, 132, 137. See also B. Richardson, "History of Blacks in Jacksonville," and Kenney, "LaVilla."
6. *Key West News,* quoted in *NYG,* March 29, 1884; *NYG,* August 18, 1883, October 18, 1884; *PCR,* May 3, 1883.
7. Rivers, "Baptist Minister James Page," 52–53; *TWF,* April 30, 1882.
8. McKinney and McKinney, *History of the Black Baptists,* 47–56; McKinney, "American Baptists," 309–13.
9. Talbert, *Sons of Allen,* 130, 154–55; *PCR,* November 24, 1881, June 29, 1882.
10. Arnett, *Proceedings of the Quarto-Centennial,* 439; *PCR,* May 20, 1880.
11. Arnett, *Budget* (1883), 15–16.
12. *PCR,* February 24, August 4, 1881; *JDFU,* December 6, 1881.
13. Bragg, *Men of Maryland,* 111–13; Arnett, *Budget* (1883), 15; *Indianapolis Freeman,* December 7, 1895.
14. Long, *History of the AME Church in Florida,* 104; *PCR,* April 13, 1882.
15. *PCR,* April 13, 1882.
16. Ibid., April 7, 1881.
17. *Guide to Supplementary Vital Statistics,* 1:19, 247, 319, 2:445, 477, 484, 576, 604, 3:665, 686, 784, 922, 931, 954.
18. *PCR,* April 21, July 7, August 11, 18, November 17, 1881; *Tampa Sunland Tribune,* June 11, 1881.
19. *PCR,* June 9, 23, July 14, November 24, 1881.
20. Ibid., July 13, 20, September 7, 21, October 26, 1882.
21. Ibid., May 11, August 3, August 31, September 14, October 12, November 9, 1882.
22. Brown, "Bishop Payne," 23–33; *JDFU,* April 6, 1882.
23. Brown, "Bishop Payne," 33–39; Payne, *Recollections,* 288; *PCR,* April 27, August 3, 1882.
24. Skinner, *Reminiscences,* 156, 167–68; Florida Annual Conference of the AME Church, *Minutes,* 13; *Pensacola Semi-Weekly Commercial,* December 1, 1882.
25. *TWF,* September 12, 19, 1882; *Jacksonville Florida Daily Times,* September 10, 1882; *PCR,* August 2, 1883.
26. Florida Annual Conference of the AME Church, *Minutes,* 3, 11–12, 25.
27. Ibid., 4, 6–8, 11.
28. Ibid., 3; *JDFU,* December 6, 1881.
29. Florida Annual Conference of the AME Church, *Minutes,* 15–16.
30. Ibid., 16–18.

31. *PCR*, January 10, October 30, December 18, 1884.
32. *JFT-U*, March 8, 1883; *PCR*, May 3, 1883, January 10, 1884, January 24, 1889.
33. *PCR*, January 10, October 30, 1884.
34. Ibid., May 14, November 1, 1883, January 10, 1884.
35. *JFT-U*, March 8, 1883.
36. Arnett, *Budget* (1884), 120; *PCR*, August 9, September 13, November 1, 1883, January 10, 1884.
37. *PCR*, August 2, 1883.
38. Arnett, *Budget* (1883), 148; Arnett, *Budget* (1884), 221; *JFT-U*, February 28, 29, 1884.
39. Arnett, *Budget* (1884), 221.
40. Woodward, *Origins of the New South*, 216; K. Hall, *Magic Mirror*, 147, 219, 233, 330.
41. *NYG*, August 18, 1883.
42. *Tampa Guardian* quoted in *NYG*, December 8, 1883.
43. *NYA*, July 14, 1888.

Chapter 8

1. C. Smith, *History of the African Methodist Episcopal Church*, 146; Rogers, *Thomas County*, 182–86.
2. Arnett, *Budget* (1883), 9–15.
3. Du Bois, *Darkwater*, 18; Singleton, *Romance of African Methodism*, 123.
4. Angell, *Bishop Henry McNeal Turner*, 137–38, 146–47.
5. *PCR*, January 1, 1885; Payne, *Recollections*, 306–9.
6. Williamson, *Florida Politics in the Gilded Age*, 101–27; Brown, *Florida's Black Public Officials*, 57–58; *JFT-U*, November 11, 18, 1884.
7. Brown, *Florida's Black Public Officials*, 58–59; Manley, Brown, and Rise, *Supreme Court of Florida*, 267, 273–78; *JFT-U*, January 5, December 24, 30, 1884, February 19, 18, 1885; *TWF*, February 19, 1885.
8. Brown, *Florida's Black Public Officials*, 59; *TWF*, June 4, 1885.
9. Joe Lang Kershaw interview; Kershaw Family Genealogical and Family Materials; *PCR*, March 30, April 13, 1876, July 4, 1878; *Minutes of the Seventeenth Session of the Florida Annual Conference*, 11.
10. *PCR*, June 4, 1885, January 16, 23, 1890; Shofner, *History of Jefferson County*, 351, 421; Kershaw interview.
11. Brown, "Prelude to the Poll Tax," 69–79; Brown, *Florida's Black Public Officials*, 59–63.
12. *JFT-U*, March 6, 1886; *NYF*, February 19, 1887; *PCR*, June 10, 1886.
13. *PCR*, January 21, June 10, 1886, January 13, 1887.
14. Ibid., May 14, 1885, June 10, 1886; Payne, *Recollections*, 306–22; Stevenson, *Journals of Charlotte Forten Grimke*, 515–25.
15. Anderson, *A. Philip Randolph*, 31.
16. *PCR*, May 14, 1885; *JFT-U*, February 23, 1891.

17. *PCR*, October 30, 1884.
18. Ibid., December 18, 1884, February 26, 1885.
19. Long, *History of the AME Church in Florida*, 85, 89, 107.
20. *PCR*, March 19, 1885, August 16, 1888; Neyland and Riley, *History of Florida Agricultural and Mechanical University*, 3–4.
21. Arnett, *Proceedings of the Quarto-Centennial*, 439–40; Payne, *Recollections*, 313–14; Wright, *Centennial Encyclopaedia*, 306; *PCR*, January 13, 1887.
22. *PCR*, February 26, 1885, January 13, 1887; Arnett, *Proceedings of the Quarto-Centennial*, 439.
23. Neyland and Riley, *History of Florida Agricultural and Mechanical University*, 7–14; *PCR*, June 9, 30, 1887.
24. Payne, *Recollections*, 322–23; *PCR*, April 14, June 9, 1887, March 1, August 16, 1888.
25. Brown, *Florida's Black Public Officials*, 60–63; Brown, "Prelude to the Poll Tax," 74–81; Brown, "Bishop Payne," 38–39; *NYF*, June 25, 1887.
26. *PCR*, April 29, 1886, July 14, October 13, 1887, March 15, 1888; Brown, *Florida's Black Public Officials*, 76, 115; Arnett, *Proceedings of the Quarto-Centennial*, 167.
27. *PCR*, June 10, 1886, January 13, July 14, 1887.
28. *NYF*, October 8, 1887; *NYA*, December 3, 1887; *PCR*, January 23, 1890.
29. Akin, "When a Minority Becomes the Majority," 127–28; Brown, "Prelude to the Poll Tax," 77; Brown, *Florida's Black Public Officials*, 62, 103. See also C. Richardson, "History of Blacks in Jacksonville," and Kinney, "LaVilla."
30. Brown, *Florida's Peace River Frontier*, 272–91; Akin, *Flagler*, 113–23; Proctor, "Prelude to the New Florida," 266–71.
31. *Guide to Supplementary Vital Statistics*, 2:370, 482, 586, 599, 602, 3:649, 794, 850, 865, 933, 936; St. James AME Church, Bartow, CH-RECs; McCarthy, *Black Florida*, 155.
32. *PCR*, July 1, 1886, January 6, 1887; *Tampa Guardian*, June 2, 1886.
33. *PCR*, October 1, 1885, April 29, 1886, October 6, December 8, 1887; Keuchel and Sellers, *Family, Community, Business Enterprise*, 34–35; McCarthy, *Black Florida*, 178.
34. *PCR*, August 23, 1888.
35. *NYA*, February 11, 25, March 31, April 7, 21, May 19, 1888.
36. *PCR*, March 1, 15, 1888; *NYA*, February 25, March 3, 1888; *JFT-U*, March 8, 1888.

Chapter 9

1. "Rt. Reverend Benjamin W. Arnett," 197–98; Arnett, *Budget* (1884), 14–15.
2. "Rt. Rev. Benjamin W. Arnett," 197.
3. C. Smith, *History of the African Methodist Episcopal Church*, 257; "Rt. Rev. Benjamin W. Arnett," 197–98; Lewis, *W. E. B. Du Bois*, 177.

4. Arnett, *Proceedings of the Quarto-Centennial*, 471–73; Arnett, *Budget* (1884), 221. Other statistical comparisons may be gleaned from *Eleventh Census, 1890*.
5. Anderson, *A. Philip Randolph*, 32–33.
6. *NYA*, August 25, 1888; *Pensacola Daily Commercial*, August 25, 1888.
7. T. Davis, *History of Jacksonville*, 180–86; *PCR*, September 20, November 8, 22, 1888; *Jacksonville Florida Weekly Times-Union*, October 18, 1888; *Journal of United Labor*, October 11, December 27, 1888.
8. T. Davis, *History of Jacksonville*, 185; Stevenson, *Journals of Charlotte Forten Grimke*, 537; *PCR*, October 18, 1888.
9. *PCR*, August 23, October 11, 1888.
10. Wright, *Centennial Encyclopaedia*, 310; *PCR*, April 4, 1889; *TWF*, January 8, 1889.
11. *PCR*, April 4, 1889.
12. *NYA*, November 24, 1888, January 19, April 13, 1889; Brown, *Florida's Black Public Officials*, 75.
13. *PCR*, April 4, 1889.
14. *JFT-U*, February 14, 1889; *PCR*, February 28, March 21, 1889.
15. *JFT-U*, February 19, 1889.
16. Ibid., February 16, 1889.
17. *PCR*, February 28, May 16, 1889; *JFT-U*, February 19, 22, 1889.
18. Long, *History of the AME Church in Florida*, 85; Wright, *Centennial Encyclopaedia*, 306; Tucker, *Phoenix from the Ashes*, 12; C. Smith, *History of the African Methodist Episcopal Church*, 359.
19. *JFT-U*, April 5, 1889, February 21, 1895; *NYA*, April 20, 1889.
20. *PCR*, October 24, November 7, 28, 1889; *JFT-U*, June 2, 1889.
21. *NYA*, April 13, 1889; *PCR*, May 16, 1889; *Fort Myers Press*, May 9, June 27, 1889; "St. James AME Church, Bartow," CH-RECs; *Guide to Supplementary Vital Statistics*, 1:103, 128, 241, 2:348, 433, 530, 721, 785, 870.
22. *PCR*, January 23, 1890.
23. *JFT-U*, December 21, 1889, *PCR*, January 16, 23, 1890; Handy, *Scraps of African Methodist Episcopal History*, 407–10.
24. *JFT-U*, December 21, 1889, *PCR*, January 16, 23, 1890; *Quincy Herald*, December 14, 1889.
25. Arnett, *Proceedings of the Quarto-Centennial*, 166–67, 171, 418.
26. *Guide to Supplementary Vital Statistics*, 1:295, 2:392, 457, 584, 599, 608, 3:655, 757, 782, 886, 930; Keuchel and Sellers, *Family, Community, Business Enterprise*, 34–35.
27. *PCR*, March 13, 1890; *Pensacola Daily News*, December 19, 20, 21, 23, 1890.
28. *Washington (D.C.) Colored American*, June 25, 1898; *JET*, October 13, 1891; *Pensacola Daily News*, December 21, 1889.
29. Long, *History of the AME Church in Florida*, 91; Tucker, *Phoenix from the Ashes*, 12–13; *JET*, October 13, 1891, February 5, 1892.
30. *JET*, May 25, June 20, 1891, February 5, May 31, 1892; C. Smith, *History of the*

African Methodist Episcopal Church, 173, 363; Talbert, *Sons of Allen*, 154–55; *JFT-U*, February 6, 1889.
31. McRae, *Fourth Census*, 18–19; *JDFU*, March 7, 1876; *TS*, July 16, 1870; *TWF*, December 19, 1891; *JET*, December 16, 1893; McKinney and McKinney, *History of the Black Baptists*, 125.
32. Brown, *Florida's Black Public Officials*, 63–65.
33. Raper, *Tragedy of Lynching*, 28; *JFT-U*, December 19, 1891, January 28, 1893.
34. Brown, "Prelude to the Poll Tax," 80–81; Williamson, *Florida Politics in the Gilded Age*, 183–85.
35. *PCR*, November 14, 1889, January 23, 1890; *TWF*, September 3, 1888.
36. *Guide to Supplementary Vital Statistics*, 1:316, 3:952.
37. *JET*, February 17, May 1, July 30, October 10, 16, November 18, 1891, January 14, 1892; *JFT-U*, September 23, 1891; *Struggle for Survival*, 25; *Arcadia DeSoto Leader*, December 1, 1984; *Guide to Supplementary Vital Statistics From Church Records in Florida*, I, 65, 193, 316, III, 928.
38. *JFT-U*, February 26, 27, 1891; *JET*, March 2, 1891.
39. *JFT-U*, February 26, 1891.

Chapter 10

1. Williamson, *Florida Politics in the Gilded Age*, 85–88; Brown, *Florida's Black Public Officials*, 59–63; Brown, "Bishop Payne," 37–39. On Jim Crow laws generally, see Woodward, *Strange Career of Jim Crow*. For an interesting study of racial violence and lynch law in Florida, see Ingalls, *Urban Vigilantes*.
2. *Bradenton Manatee River Journal*, November 26, 1891.
3. Brown, "George Washington Witherspoon," 15; *JFT-U*, January 7, 1892; *JET*, January 6, 30, 1892; *Pensacola Daily News*, January 5, 1892; Long, *History of the AME Church in Florida*, 108.
4. *JET*, February 25, March 2, 17, 1892.
5. Long, *History of the AME Church in Florida*, 108; *JET*, February 4, March 1, 1892.
6. Long, *History of the AME Church in Florida*, 108; *JET*, February 4, 1892; *Tampa Daily Tribune*, September 1, 1892.
7. C. Smith, *History of the African Methodist Episcopal Church*, 170; Wright, *Centennial Encyclopaedia*, 383; *JET*, March 3, 1892.
8. C. Smith, *History of the African Methodist Episcopal Church*, 170–71; *JET*, March 1, 1892, February 22, 1894.
9. C. Smith, *History of the African Methodism Episcopal Church*, 169, 200, 383–87; Walls, *African Methodist Episcopal Zion Church*, 468–70; *JFT-U*, May 26, 1892.
10. C. Smith, *History of the African Methodist Episcopal Church*, 173; Bragg, *Men of Maryland*, 108.
11. "Bishop A. Grant," *AME Church Review* 5 (April 1889), 325–26; Kealing, *History of African Methodism in Texas*, 199–203; Long, *History of the AME Church in Florida*, 108; C. Smith, *History of the African Methodist Episcopal Church*, 173.

12. *JFT-U*, February 27, 1896; *Tampa Morning Tribune*, March 3, 1896, January 5, 1901; Long, *History of the AME Church in Florida*, 110–11; Kealing, *History of African Methodism in Texas*, 199–203; *NYA*, January 26, February 2, 1911; "Bishop A. Grant."
13. "Bishop A. Grant,"; Kealing, *History of African Methodism in Texas*, 199–203; Long, *History of the AME Church in Florida*, 108; C. Smith, *History of the African Methodist Episcopal Church*, 173.
14. *JET*, January 19, 24, February 9, 13, 28, March 9, 1893; Long, *History of the AME Church in Florida*, 108; Wright, *Centennial Encyclopaedia*, 311.
15. *Guide to Supplementary Vital Statistics*, 1:144, 310, 319, 2:328, 583, 3:795, 864, 962.
16. Ibid., 1:25, 108, 125, 310, 2:411, 533, 568, 3:715, 749, 858, 938; Bethel AME and Mt. Olive AME church clippings files, Church Clippings Files, Pinellas County Historical Museum and Heritage Village, Largo.
17. *JET*, February 8, 1893.
18. *JFT-U*, April 2, 1893.
19. *JET*, May 1, August 7, 9, 1893.
20. Ayers, *Promise of the New South*, 283–84; Woodward, *Origins of the New South*, 264–65.
21. Tebeau, *History of Florida*, 301; Covington, *Story of Southwestern Florida*, 194–95; Brown, *Fort Meade*, 132–33.
22. *JFT-U*, February 22, 25, 1895; Wright, *Centennial Encyclopaedia*, 25.
23. *JET*, April 5, May 20, October 7, 1893; *JFT-U*, February 23, 1895.
24. *JET*, September 1, December 5, 1893; Wright, *Centennial Encyclopaedia*, 161.
25. Long, *History of the AME Church in Florida*, 185.
26. Ibid., 189–90.
27. *JET*, November 15, 1893; Montgomery, *Under Their Own Vine and Fig Tree*, 114–15.
28. *JET*, September 25, 1893. On women as church fund-raisers generally, see Montgomery, *Under Their Own Vine and Fig Tree*, 95–96.
29. Montgomery, *Under Their Own Vine and Fig Tree*, 321–22; Angell, *Bishop Henry McNeal Turner*, 181–84. See also Collier-Thomas, *Daughters of Thunder*, part 1, "Pursuing a Ministry Ordained by God, 1850–1900."
30. *JET*, July 10, August 3, October 25, 1893.
31. Ibid., September 23, November 27, 1893.
32. *Indianapolis Freeman*, March 17, 1894; *JET*, February 9, 1894.
33. Wright, *Centennial Encyclopaedia*, 85, 606; Long, *History of the AME Church in Florida*, 110; *JFT-U*, February 26, 1895.
34. Wright, *Centennial Encyclopaedia*, 309; Long, *History of the AME Church in Florida*, 110.
35. Covington, *Story of Southwestern Florida*, 194–95; Brown, *Florida's Peace River Frontier*, 321–22; *Bartow Courier-Informant*, February 6, 1895.

36. *Ocala Banner*, February 22, 1895; *Bartow Courier-Informant*, February 13, 1895; Brown, *Florida's Peace River Frontier*, 322.
37. *JFT-U*, February 21–26, 1895.
38. Ibid., March 3–5, 1895.
39. Ibid., July 13, 1895; Long, *History of the AME Church in Florida*, 112–13; Escott, *Major Problems*, 176–79.
40. *JFT-U*, January 30, 1897; Wright, *Centennial Encyclopaedia*, 310.
41. Ayers, *Promise of the New South*, 322–25; Escott, *Major Problems*, 173–76.
42. McCarthy, *Black Florida*, 192; *PCR*, May 16, 1901.
43. Logan, *Negro in the United States*, 39–58.

BIBLIOGRAPHY

Manuscripts and Collections

Church Records. Questionnaires of the Historical Records Survey of the Florida Writers' Program, WPA. Florida Collection, SLF.
Florida Negro Papers. University of South Florida Special Collections, Tampa.
Howard, Oliver O. Papers. Bowdoin College Library, Brunswick, Maine
Kershaw Family. Genealogical and family papers. Collection of Ed Norwood, Tallahassee.
Stevens, Thaddeus. Papers. LC.
Washburn, Elihu B. Papers. LC.

Public Documents and Public Records

Eleventh Census, 1890: Churches. Washington, D.C.: Government Printing Office, 1890.
Florida Governor's Office. Governors' Letterbooks. RG 101, series 32, FSA.
———. Incoming Correspondence. RG 101, series 577, FSA.
Florida State Census, 1895. Available on microfilm at FSA.
Gadsden County Deed Records. Gadsden County Courthouse, Quincy, Fla.
Guide to Supplementary Vital Statistics from Church Records in Florida. 3 vols. Jacksonville: Florida Historical Records Survey, 1942.
Kennedy, Joseph C. G. *Population of the United States in 1860; Compiled from the Original Returns of the Eighth Census.* Washington, D.C.: Government Printing Office, 1864.
Laws of Florida, 1869–1895. Tallahassee: State of Florida.
Mayo, Nathan. *The Sixth Census of the State of Florida 1935.* Tallahassee: Florida Department of Agriculture, 1935.
McRae, W. A. *The Fourth Census of the State of Florida Taken in the Year 1915.* Tallahassee: T. J. Appleyard, 1915.
Nassau County Deed Records. Available at County Courthouse, Fernandina, Fla.
Negro Population 1790–1915. Washington, D.C.: Government Printing Office, 1918.
U.S. Decennial Census, 1870. Manuscript returns. Available on microfilm at FSA.
U.S. Department of Agriculture. *Yearbook of the United States Department of Agriculture, 1900.* Washington, D.C.: Government Printing Office, 1901.
U.S. War Department. Incoming Correspondence, Third Military District. RG 393, Part 1, NA.

Newspapers and Periodicals

A.M.E Church Review, 1889–1910
American Missionary, 1865–1866
Arcadia DeSoto Leader, 1984
Bartow Courier-Informant, 1895
Birmingham (Eng.) Good Templars' Watchword, 1879
Bradenton Manatee River Journal, 1891
Congressional Globe, 1873–1874
DeLand Volusia County Herald, 1878
Fernandina Florida Mirror, 1879, 1880
Fort Myers Press, 1889
Harper's New Monthly Magazine, 1870
Indianapolis Freeman, 1894–1895
Jacksonville Daily Florida Union, 1876, 1881
Jacksonville Evening Telegram, 1891–1895
Jacksonville Evening Times-Union, 1894
Jacksonville Florida Daily Times, 1882
Jacksonville Florida Times-Union, 1883–1900
Jacksonville Florida Union, 1865–1869
Jacksonville Florida Weekly Times-Union, 1888
Jacksonville Tri-Weekly Florida Sun, 1876
Jacksonville Tri-Weekly Florida Union, 1872–1874
Journal of United Labor, 1888
Louisville (Ky.) Courier-Journal, 1883
Newark (N.J.) Sentinel of Freedom, 1873
New York Age, 1887–1911
New York Daily Tribune, 1867
New York Evening Post, 1873
New York Freeman, 1886–1887
New York Globe, 1883–1884
New York Herald, 1865
New York Times, 1873
New York Tribune, 1868
Ocala Banner, 1895
Pensacola Commercial, 1884
Pensacola Daily Commercial, 1888
Pensacola Daily News, 1890–1906
Pensacola Semi-Weekly Commercial, 1882
Philadelphia Christian Recorder, 1865–1896
Philadelphia Times, 1883
Quincy Herald, 1889
Salisbury (N.C.) Star of Zion, 1895–1903
Sanford South Florida Argus, 1887

Savannah Advertiser-Republican, 1874
Savannah Daily Advertiser, 1872
Savannah Daily News and Herald, 1866–1867
Savannah Daily Republican, 1870
Savannah Morning News, 1871–1879
Southern Christian Advocate, 1850–1874
Tallahassee Florida Sentinel, 1850
Tallahassee Floridian and Journal, 1860
Tallahassee Semi-Weekly Floridian, 1866–1867, 1880
Tallahassee Sentinel, 1867–1876
Tallahassee Weekly Floridian, 1867–1889
Tallahassee Weekly True Democrat, 1911
Tampa Daily Tribune, 1892
Tampa Florida Peninsular, 1858–1871
Tampa Guardian, 1886
Tampa Morning Tribune, 1896, 1901
Tampa Sunland Tribune, 1881
Washington (D.C.) Colored American, 1898
Washington (D.C.) Daily Morning Chronicle, 1867, 1868
Washington (D.C.) Daily National Intelligencer, 1869

Secondary Sources

Akin, Edward N. *Flagler: Rockefeller Partner and Florida Baron*. Kent, Ohio: Kent State University Press, 1988.

———. "When a Minority Becomes the Majority: Blacks in Jacksonville Politics, 1887–1907." *Florida Historical Quarterly* 53 (October 1974): 123–45.

Allen, Richard. *The Life, Experience, and Gospel Labors of the Right Reverend Richard Allen*. Reprint. Nashville: Abingdon, 1983.

Anderson, Jervis. *A. Philip Randolph: A Biographical Portrait*. New York: Harcourt Brace Jovanovich, 1972.

Angell, Stephen Ward. *Bishop Henry McNeal Turner and African-American Religion in the South*. Knoxville: University of Tennessee Press, 1992.

Aptheker, Herbert. *American Negro Slave Revolts*. New York: International, 1943.

———. *Documentary History of the Negro People in the United States*. New York: International, 1951.

Arnett, Benjamin W., ed. *The Budget: Containing Biographical Sketches, Quadrennial and Annual Reports of the General Officers of the African Methodist Episcopal Church of the United States of America*. Dayton, Ohio: Christian Publishing House, 1884.

———. *The Budget: Containing the Annual Reports of the General Officers of the African Methodist Episcopal Church of the United States of America*. Dayton, Ohio: Christian Publishing House, 1883.

———. *Proceedings of the Quarto-Centennial Conference of the African M. E. Church, of South Carolina, at Charleston, S. C., May 15, 16 and 17, 1889*. Charleston: South Carolina AME Conference, 1890.

Bentley, Altermese. *Georgetown: The History of a Black Neighborhood.* Georgetown, Fla.: Privately published, 1989.

Berlin, Ira. "The Slaves' Changing World." In *A History of the African American People: The History, Traditions and Culture of African Americans,* edited by James Oliver Horton and Lois E. Horton. Detroit: Wayne State University Press, 1997.

Bethel AME Church. *100th Anniversary Program, Bethel AME Church, 115 North Eighth Street, Palatka, Florida 32077.* Palatka: Bethel AME Church, 1975.

Blair, Donald I. "The Education of Blacks in Jefferson County, Florida: 1866–1900." Seminar paper, Florida A&M University, 1993.

"Bishop A. Grant." *AME Church Review* 5 (April 1889): 325–26;

Boles, John B., ed. *Masters and Slaves in the House of the Lord: Race and Religion in the American South, 1740–1870.* Lexington: University of Kentucky Press, 1988.

Brady, Rowena Ferrell. *Things Remembered: An Album of African Americans in Tampa.* Tampa: University of Tampa Press, 1997.

Bragg, George F. *Men of Maryland.* Baltimore: Church Advocate Press, 1914.

Brooks, William E., ed. *From Saddlebags to Satellites: A History of Florida Methodism.* Nashville: Parthenon, 1969.

Brown, Canter, Jr. "African Americans and the Tampa Bay Area to World War I." In *Things Remembered: An Album of African Americans in Tampa,* by Rowena Ferrell Brady. Tampa: University of Tampa Press, 1997.

———. *African Americans on the Tampa Bay Frontier.* Tampa: Tampa Bay History Center, 1997.

———. "Bishop Payne and Resistance to Jim Crow in Florida During the 1880s." *Northeast Florida History* 2 (1994): 23–40.

———. "Carpetbagger Intrigues, Black Leadership, and a Southern Loyalist Triumph: Florida's Gubernatorial Election of 1872." *Florida Historical Quarterly* 72 (January 1994): 275–301.

———. "The Civil War, 1861–1865." In *The New History of Florida,* edited by Michael Gannon. Gainesville: University Press of Florida, 1996.

———. *Florida's Black Public Officials, 1867–1924.* Tuscaloosa: University of Alabama Press, 1998.

———. *Florida's Peace River Frontier.* Orlando: University of Central Florida Press, 1991.

———. *Fort Meade, 1849–1900.* Tuscaloosa: University of Alabama Press, 1995.

———. *Genealogical Records of the African American Pioneers of Tampa and Hillsborough County.* Tampa: Tampa Bay History Center, 1999.

———. "George Washington Witherspoon: Florida's Second Generation Black Political Leadership." Unpublished paper presented at the Florida Historical Society Annual Meeting, Fort Myers, May 20, 1994.

———. *Henry Bradley Plant: The Nineteenth Century "King of Florida."* Tampa: Henry B. Plant Museum, 1999.

———. *Ossian Bingley Hart, Florida's Loyalist Reconstruction Governor.* Baton Rouge: Louisiana State University Press, 1997.

———. "Prelude to the Poll Tax: Black Republicans and the Knights of Labor in 1880s Florida." In *Florida's Heritage of Diversity: Essays in Honor of Samuel Proctor*, edited by Mark I. Greenberg, William Warren Rogers, and Canter Brown, Jr. Tallahassee: Sentry, 1997.

———. "Race Relations in Territorial Florida, 1821–1845." *Florida Historical Quarterly* 73 (January 1995): 287–307.

———. "'Where Are Now the Hopes I Cherished?' The Life and Times of Robert Meacham." *Florida Historical Quarterly* 69 (July 1990): 1–36.

Call, C. F. *History of Allen Chapel AME Church, Pensacola, Florida*. Pensacola: Allen Chapel AME Church, 1939.

Cartwright, Peter. *The Autobiography of Peter Cartwright, the Backwoods Preacher*. New York: Carlton and Porter, 1856.

Chandler, Douglas R. "The Formation of the Methodist Protestant Church." In *The History of American Methodism*, edited by Emory S. Bucke. 3 vols. Knoxville: University of Tennessee Press, 1964.

Clarke, Erskine. *Wrestlin' Jacob: A Portrait of Religion in Antebellum Georgia and the Carolina Low Country*. Tuscaloosa: University of Alabama Press, 1979.

Colburn, David R., and Jane L. Landers. *The African American Heritage of Florida*. Gainesville: University Press of Florida: 1995.

Collier-Thomas, Bettye. *Daughters of Thunder: Black Women Preachers and Their Sermons, 1850–1979*. San Francisco: Jossey-Bass, 1998.

Coulter, E. Merton. "Henry M. Turner: Georgia Negro Preacher-Politician During the Reconstruction Era." *Georgia Historical Quarterly* 48 (December 1964): 374–403.

Covington, James W. *The Story of Southwestern Florida*. 2 vols. New York: Lewis Historical Publishing, 1957.

Davis, Thomas Frederick. *History of Jacksonville, Florida, and Vicinity, 1513 to 1924*. Jacksonville: Florida Historical Society, 1925. Reprint, Jacksonville: San Marco Bookstore, 1990.

Davis, William Watson. *Civil War and Reconstruction in Florida*. New York: Columbia University Press, 1913. Reprint, Gainesville: University of Florida Press, 1964.

de Czege, A. Wass, comp. *The History of Astor on the St. Johns, Astor Park, and the Surrounding Area*. Youngstown, Ohio: Catholic Publishing, 1982.

Denham, James M. *"A Rogue's Paradise": Crime and Punishment in Antebellum Florida, 1821–1861*. Tuscaloosa: University of Alabama Press, 1997.

Denham, James M., and Canter Brown Jr. "Black Sheriffs of Post–Civil War Florida." *Sheriff's Star* 42 (September/October 1998): 12–15.

Dodd, Dorothy. "'Bishop' Pearce and the Reconstruction of Leon County." *Apalachee* (1946): 5–12.

———. "Florida in 1845." *Florida Historical Quarterly* 24 (July 1945): 3–29.

Dowda, Robert B. *The History of Palatka and Putnam County*. Palatka: Privately published, 1938–1939.

Drake, J. V. *The Florida Legislature (Twelfth Session), The Official Directory of the State Government*. Jacksonville: Times-Union Book and Job Office, 1883.
Du Bois, W. E. B. *Autobiography of W. E. B. Du Bois*. New York: International, 1968.
———. *Black Reconstruction in America, 1860–1880*. New York: Atheneum, 1992.
———. *Darkwater: Voices from Within the Veil*. Millwood, N.Y.: Kraus-Thomas Organization, 1921.
Dumon, Donald L. *Anti-Slavery: The Crusade for Freedom in America*. Ann Arbor: University of Michigan Press, 1961.
Escott, Paul D., ed. *Major Problems in the History of the American South*. Vol. 2: *The New South*. Lexington, Mass.: Heath, 1990.
Fahey, David M. *Temperance and Racism: John Bull, Johnny Reb, and the Good Templars*. Lexington: University of Kentucky Press, 1996.
Federal Writers' Project. *Negro History in Florida*. Jacksonville: Federal Writers' Project, 1936.
Ferrell, Andrew Jackson, Sr. "History of St. Paul AME Church." In *Things Remembered: An Album of African Americans in Tampa*, edited by Rowena Ferrell Brady. Tampa: University of Tampa Press, 1997.
Florida Annual Conference of the African Methodist Episcopal Church. *Minutes of the Seventeenth Session of the Florida Annual Conference of the African Methodist Episcopal Church*. Marianna: Marianna Courier, 1882.
Foner, Eric. *Reconstruction: America's Unfinished Business, 1863–1877*. New York: Harper and Row, 1988.
Foster, John T., Jr., and Sarah Whitmer Foster. *Beechers, Stowes, and Yankee Strangers: The Transformation of Florida*. Gainesville: University Press of Florida, 1999.
Franklin, John Hope. *Reconstruction After the Civil War*. Chicago: University of Chicago Press, 1961.
Frey, Sylvia, and Betty Wood. *Come Shouting to Zion: African American Protestantism in the American South and British Caribbean to 1830*. Chapel Hill: University of North Carolina Press, 1998.
Gannon, Michael, ed. *The New History of Florida*. Gainesville: University Press of Florida, 1996.
George, Carol V. R. *Segregated Sabbaths: Richard Allen and the Emergence of Black Independent Churches, 1760–1840*. New York: Oxford University Press, 1973.
Goen, C. C. *Broken Churches, Broken Nation: Denominational Schisms and the Coming of the American Civil War*. Macon, Ga.: Mercer University Press, 1985.
Groene, Bertram H. *Ante-Bellum Tallahassee*. Tallahassee: Florida Heritage Foundation, 1981.
Hall, Kermit L. *The Magic Mirror: Law in American History*. New York: Oxford University Press, 1989.
Hall, Robert L. "'Do Lord, Remember Me': Religion and Cultural Change Among Blacks in Florida, 1565–1906." Ph.D. diss., Florida State University, 1984.
———. "The Gospel According to Radicalism: African Methodism Comes to Tallahassee After the Civil War." *Apalachee* 8 (1971–1979): 69–81.

———. "Tallahassee's Black Churches, 1865–1885." *Florida Historical Quarterly* 58 (October 1979): 185–96.
Handy, James A. *Scraps of African Methodist Episcopal History*. Philadelphia: AME Book Concern, n.d.
Heyrman, Christine Leigh. *Southern Cross: The Beginnings of the Bible Belt*. New York: Knopf, 1997.
Hood, J. W. *One Hundred Years of the African Methodist Episcopal Zion Church*. New York: AME Zion Book Concern, 1895.
Ingalls, Robert P. *Urban Vigilantes in the New South: Tampa, 1882–1936*. Knoxville: University of Tennessee Press, 1988.
Jefferson, Thomas. *Notes on the State of Virginia*, edited by William Peden. Chapel Hill: University of North Carolina Press, 1955.
Johnson, Alonzo, and Paul Jersild. *"Ain't Gonna Lay My 'Ligion Down": African American Religion in the South*. Columbia: University of South Carolina Press, 1996.
Johnson, Dudley S. "Henry Bradley Plant and Florida." *Florida Historical Quarterly* 45 (October 1966): 118–31.
Johnson, James Weldon. *Along This Way: The Autobiography of James Weldon Johnson*. New York: Penguin, 1990.
Joiner, Edward Earl. *A History of Florida Baptists*. Jacksonville: Convention, 1972.
Jones, Maxine D., and Kevin M. McCarthy. *African Americans in Florida*. Sarasota: Pineapple, 1993.
Kealing, H. T. *History of African Methodism in Texas*. Waco: C. F. Blanks, 1885.
Kenney, Patricia L. "LaVilla, Florida, 1866–1887: Reconstruction Dreams and the Formation of a Black Community." In *The African American Heritage of Florida*, edited by David L. Colburn and Jane L. Landers. Gainesville: University Press of Florida, 1995.
Kershaw, Joe Lang. Telephone interview, June 10, 1999. Notes in collections of the authors.
Keuchel, Edward F., and Robin J. Sellers. *Family, Community, Business Enterprise: The Millers of Crescent City, Florida*. Tallahassee: Sentry, n.d.
Klingman, Peter D. *Josiah Walls: Florida's Black Congressman of Reconstruction*. Gainesville: University Press of Florida, 1976.
———. "Rascal or Representative? Joe Oats of Tallahassee and the 'Election' of 1866." *Florida Historical Quarterly* 51 (July 1972): 52–57.
Landers, Jane. *Black Society in Spanish Florida*. Urbana: University of Illinois Press, 1999.
Lewis, David Levering. *W. E. B. Du Bois: Biography of a Race, 1868–1919*. New York: Holt, 1993.
Lock, Mary Stoughton. *Anti-Slavery in America from the Introduction of African Slaves to the Prohibition of the Slave Trade, 1619–1808*. Boston: n.p., 1901.
Logan, Rayford W. *The Negro in the United States, A Brief History*. Princeton: Van Nostrand, 1957.

Long, Charles Sumner. *History of the AME Church in Florida*. Philadelphia: AME Book Concern, 1939.
Maloney, Walter C. *A Sketch of the History of Key West, Florida*. Reprint. Gainesville: University of Florida Press, 1968.
Manley, Walter W., Canter Brown Jr., and Eric W. Rise. *The Supreme Court of Florida and Its Predecessor Courts, 1821–1917*. Gainesville: University Press of Florida, 1997.
Martin, Elmer. "The Life of Henry McNeal Turner, 1834 to 1870." M.A. thesis, Florida State University, 1975.
Martin, Richard A. *The City Makers*. Jacksonville: Convention, 1972.
Martin, Sidney Walter. *Florida During the Territorial Days*. Athens: University of Georgia Press, 1944.
Mathews, Donald. *Slavery and Methodism: A Chapter in American Morality, 1780–1845*. Princeton: Princeton University Press, 1965.
McCarthy, Kevin M. *Black Florida*. New York: Hippocrene, 1995.
McFeeley, William S. *Frederick Douglass*. New York: Norton, 1991.
McKinney, George Patterson, Sr., and Richard I. McKinney. *History of the Black Baptists of Florida, 1850–1985*. Miami: Florida Memorial College Press, 1987.
McKinney, Richard I. "American Baptists and Black Education in Florida." *American Baptist Quarterly* 11 (December 1992): 309–26.
McPherson, James. *Battle Cry of Freedom: The Civil War Era*. New York: Oxford University Press, 1988.
Menard, J. Willis. *Lays in Summer Lands*. Washington, D.C.: Enterprise, 1879.
Montgomery, William E. *Under Their Own Vine and Fig Tree: The African-American Church in the South, 1865–1900*. Baton Rouge: Louisiana State University Press, 1993.
Muse, Violet B. "From Slavery to State Senate." In *Negro History in Florida*. Jacksonville: Federal Writers' Project, 1936.
Nathans, Elizabeth S. *Losing the Peace: Georgia Republicans and Reconstruction, 1865–1871*. Baton Rouge: Louisiana State University Press, 1968.
Neyland, Leedell W., and John W. Riley. *The History of Florida Agricultural and Mechanical University*. Gainesville: University of Florida Press, 1963.
Nichols, George Ward. "Six Weeks in Florida." *Harper's New Monthly Magazine* 41 (October 1870): 655–67.
Osborn, George E. "Letters of a Carpetbagger in Florida, 1866–1869." *Florida Historical Quarterly* 36 (January 1958): 239–85.
Otey, Frank M. *Eatonville, Florida: A Brief History*. Winter Park, Fla.: Four-G Publishers, 1989.
Owen, Christopher H. *The Sacred Flame of Love: Methodism and Society in Nineteenth-Century Georgia*. Athens: University of Georgia Press, 1998.
Payne, Daniel Alexander. *History of the African Methodist Episcopal Church*. Nashville: AME Sunday-School Union, 1891.

―――. *Recollections of Seventy Years.* New York: Arno Press and the *New York Times*, 1969.
Pettengill, George W., Jr. *The Story of the Florida Railroads, 1834–1903.* Boston: Railway and Locomotive Historical Society and Baker Library, Harvard Business School, 1952.
Pfeffer, Paula F. *A. Philip Randolph, Pioneer of the Civil Rights Movement.* Baton Rouge: Louisiana State University Press, 1990.
Proctor, Samuel. "Prelude to the New Florida, 1877–1919." In *The New History of Florida*, edited by Michael Gannon. Gainesville: University Press of Florida, 1996.
Quarles, Benjamin. *The Negro in the American Revolution.* Chapel Hill: University of North Carolina Press, 1961.
Raper, Arthur F. *The Tragedy of Lynching.* Chapel Hill: University of North Carolina Press, 1933.
Rawick, George P., ed. *The American Slave: A Composite Autobiography.* 19 vols. Westport, Conn.: Greenwood, 1972–1979.
Reid, Whitelaw. *After the War: A Tour of the Southern States, 1865–1866.* New York: Harper, 1965.
Richardson, Barbara Ann. "A History of Blacks in Jacksonville, Florida, 1860–1895: A Socio-Economic and Political Study." D.A. diss., Carnegie-Mellon University, 1975.
Richardson, Joe M. *Christian Reconstruction: The American Missionary Association and Southern Blacks, 1861–1890.* Athens: University of Georgia Press, 1986.
―――. "Jonathan C. Gibbs: Florida's Only Negro Cabinet Member." *Florida Historical Quarterly* 42 (April 1964): 363–68.
―――. *The Negro in the Reconstruction of Florida, 1865–1877.* Tallahassee: Florida State University Press, 1965. Reprint, Tampa: Trend House, 1973.
―――. "'We are truly doing missionary work': Letters from American Missionary Association Teachers in Florida, 1864–1874." *Florida Historical Quarterly* 54 (October 1975): 178–95.
Richardson, Simon Peter. *The Lights and Shadows of Itinerant Life.* Nashville: Methodist Episcopal Church, South, 1900.
Rifwer, John J. *A Constitutional History of American Episcopal Methodism.* Knoxville: University of Tennessee Press, 1894.
Rivers, Larry E. "Baptist Minister James Page: Alternatives for African American Leadership in Post–Civil War Florida." In *Florida's Heritage of Diversity: Essays in Honor of Samuel Proctor*, edited by Mark I. Greenberg, William Warren Rogers, and Canter Brown Jr. Tallahassee: Sentry, 1997.
―――. "'He Treats His Fellow Man Properly': Building Community in Multi-Cultural Florida." In *Amid Political, Cultural, and Civic Diversity: Building a Sense of Statewide Community in Florida*, edited by Lance deHaven-Smith and David Colburn. Dubuque, Iowa: Kendall/Hunt, 1998.

———. *Slavery in Florida, 1821–1865*. Gainesville: University Press of Florida, 2000.

———. "A Troublesome Property: Master-Slave Relations in Florida, 1821–1865." In *The African American Heritage of Florida*, edited by David R. Colburn and Jane L. Landers. Gainesville: University Press of Florida, 1995.

Rivers, Larry E., and Canter Brown Jr. "African Americans in South Florida: A Home and a Haven for Reconstruction-Era Leaders." *Tequesta* 56 (1996): 5–23.

———. "'The Indispensable Man': John Horse and Florida's Second Seminole War." *Journal of the Georgia Association of Historians* 18 (1997): 1–23.

Rogers, William W. *Thomas County, 1865–1900*. Tallahassee: Florida State University Press, 1973.

Rosser, John Leonidas. *A History of Florida Baptists*. Nashville: Broadman, 1949.

"Rt. Rev. Benjamin W. Arnett, D.D." *AME Church Review* 5 (January 1889): 197–98.

Schafer, Daniel L. "Freedom Was as Close as the River: The Blacks of Northeast Florida and the Civil War." *El Escribano* 23 (1986): 91–116.

Scott, J. Irving E. *The Education of Black People in Florida*. Philadelphia: Dorrance, 1974.

Shofner, Jerrell H. "Florida." In *The Black Press in the South, 1865–1979*, edited by Henry Lewis Suggs. Westport, Conn.: Greenwood, 1983.

———. *History of Jefferson County*. Tallahassee: Sentry, 1976.

———. *Jackson County, Florida—A History*. Marianna: Jackson County Heritage Association, 1985.

———. *Nor Is It Over Yet: Florida in the Era of Reconstruction 1863–1877*. Gainesville: University of Florida Press, 1974.

Shuften, John T. *A Colored Man's Exposition of the Acts and Doings of the Radical Party South, from 1865 to 1876*. Jacksonville: Gibson and Dennis, Steam Book and Job Printers, 1877.

Singleton, George A. *Romance of African Methodism*. New York: Exposition, 1952.

Skinner, Emory Fiske. *Reminiscences*. Chicago: Vestal, 1908.

Smith, Charles Spencer. *A History of the African Methodist Episcopal Church*. Philadelphia: Book Concern of the AME Church, 1922. Reprint, New York: Johnson Reprints, 1968.

Smith, John David. *Black Voices from Reconstruction, 1865–1877*. Gainesville: University Press of Florida, 1997.

Smith, Julia Floyd. *Slavery and Plantation Growth in Antebellum Florida, 1821–1860*. Gainesville: University of Florida Press, 1973.

Stevenson, Brenda, ed. *The Journals of Charlotte Forten Grimké*. New York: Oxford University Press, 1988.

St. James AME Church. "4th Annual Homecoming Program, Sunday, July 14, 1985, Saint James AME Church, Bartow, Florida." Bartow: St. James AME Church, 1985.

———. "Souvenir of the Dedicatory Services, Dedication of St. James AME

Church, Rev. T. S. Johnson, Pastor, June 10, 1956." Bartow: St. James AME Church, 1956.
Stowell, Daniel W. *Rebuilding Zion: The Religious Reconstruction of the South, 1863–1877*. New York: Oxford University Press, 1998.
The Struggle for Survival: A Partial History of the Negroes of Marion County, 1865 to 1976. Ocala: Black Historical Organization of Marion County, 1977.
Talbert, Horace. *The Sons of Allen*. Xenia, Ohio: Aldine, 1906.
Tebeau, Charlton W. *A History of Florida*. Coral Gables: University of Miami Press, 1971.
Temple, Robert M., Jr. *Florida Flame: A History of the Florida Conference of the United Methodist Church*. Nashville: Parthenon, 1987.
Thrift, Charles Tinsley, Jr. *The Trail of the Florida Circuit Rider*. Lakeland: Florida Southern College Press, 1944.
Tucker, Samuel J. *Phoenix from the Ashes: EWC's Past, Present, and Future*. Jacksonville: Convention, 1976.
Walker, Clarence E. *A Rock in a Weary Land: The African Methodist Episcopal Church During the Civil War and Reconstruction*. Baton Rouge: Louisiana State University Press, 1982.
Wallace, John. *Carpetbag Rule in Florida: The Inside Workings of the Reconstruction of Civil Government in Florida After the Close of the Civil War*. Jacksonville: Da Costa, 1888. Reprint, Kennesaw, Ga.: Continental, 1959.
Walls, William J. *The African Methodist Episcopal Zion Church: Reality of the Black Church*. Charlotte, N.C.: AME Zion Publishing, 1974.
Warner, Lee H. *Free Men in an Age of Servitude: Three Generations of a Black Family*. Lexington: University of Kentucky Press, 1992.
Wayman, Alexander W. *Cyclopaedia of African Methodism*. Baltimore: Methodist Episcopal Book Depository, 1882.
———. *My Recollections of African M. E. Ministers, or Forty Years' Experience in the African Methodist Episcopal Church*. Philadelphia: AME Book Rooms, 1881.
Wesley, Charles H. *Richard Allen: Apostle of Freedom*. Washington, D.C.: Associated Publishers, 1935.
Wesley, John. *Thoughts upon Slavery*. London: n.p., 1774.
Williamson, Edward C. *Florida Politics in the Gilded Age, 1877–1893*. Gainesville: University of Florida Press, 1976.
Womack, Miles Kenan, Jr. *Gadsden: A Florida County in Word and Picture*. Quincy: n.p., 1976.
Woodson, Carter G. *The History of the Negro Church*. Reprint. Washington, D.C.: Associated Publishers, 1985.
Woodward, C. Vann. *Origins of the New South, 1877–1913*. Baton Rouge: Louisiana State University Press, 1951.
———. *The Strange Career of Jim Crow*. 3d rev. ed. New York: Oxford University Press, 1974.

Wright, Richard Robert, Jr. *The Bishops of the AME Church*. Nashville: AME Sunday School Union, 1963.
———. *Centennial Encyclopaedia of the African Methodist Episcopal Church*. Philadelphia: Book Concern of the AME Church, 1916.
———. *The Encyclopaedia of the African Methodist Episcopal Church*. Philadelphia: Book Concern of the AME Church, 1947.

INDEX

abolitionism, 6–8
Adamsville, 72
African Methodist Episcopal Church: origins of, in Florida, 16–17, 19, 23–42; origins of, 19–21; early southern ministry of, 21–22; membership of, 21–22; post–Civil War commitment of, to southern freedmen, 24–25; religious, educational, and political policies of, 35, 45–46, 58–59; general conferences of, 54, 58, 80, 112, 117–18, 139, 142, 159–60, 184–85, 192–93; divisions in, based upon charges of elitism, 148–49, 163, 182, 187; meeting at Jacksonville of council of bishops of, 179; proposed union of, with AMEZ church, 184–85
African Methodist Episcopal Zion Church: origins of, 20–21; postwar growth of, in Florida, 49, 72; organization of Florida Conference of, 66; proposed union of, with AME church, 184; mentioned, 67, 164
African missions, 128
Africanization of Florida campaign, 121
Alabama (state), 80, 135, 154, 177, 185
Alabama Conference (AME), 118, 142
Alachua County, 3, 41, 71–72, 87, 119, 130, 181, 187
alcohol consumption. *See* temperance
Alexander, Gertrude, 192
Alexander, Joseph, 54
Allen, L. W., 135
Allen, Richard, 19–21
Allen, Sarah (teacher), 60
Allen Chapel AME Church: High Springs, 130; Melbourne, 156; New Smyrna, 179; Pensacola, 37, 98–99, 131–32, 135, 193; Plant City, 173; Pomona, 156; Sanford, 187

Allen Temple AME Church: Brooksville, 156; Tampa, 183, 187
Anders, L. A., 72
Anders, Walter, 111
Anderson, George, 60, 79, 109
Anderson, T. B., 110
Andrew, James Osgood, 6–7
Angell, Stephen Ward, 143
Anthony, 130
Antioch AME Church, Jackson County, 45, 49, 110
Apalachicola, 9, 37–38, 45, 49, 77, 110, 116, 123, 132, 138–39
Apalachicola River, 2, 69, 154
Apopka, 156
Arcadia, 179
Archer, 72, 110, 132, 138
Arkansas (state), 74, 140, 162, 174
Armstrong, Josiah H.: as Florida churchman, 60, 69, 85–86, 89, 91, 109, 119; likeness of, 61; as political activist, 75, 83, 101; transfer of, to Texas, 119; remarriage of widow of, to Abram Grant, 185; as national financial secretary, 189–90
Armstrong, Owen B., 52
Arnett, Benjamin W., Sr.: as church historian, xviii; early life of, 160–62; as bishop of Florida, 160–80
Arnett, Benjamin W., Jr., 173–76, 191
Arnett, Mary Louisa Gordon, 160–61
Arnett Chapel, Quincy, 14–15, 30, 172
Ashville, 130
Aspalaga, 110
Astor, William, 108
Atlanta, 196–97
Atlanta Compromise, 197
Attaway, A. Henry, 135
Aucilla, 30, 109

Aucilla Circuit, 70
Aucilla Mission, 3, 30, 45, 48

Back to Africa movement, 116
Bahama Islands, 89, 110, 138
Baker, C., 49
Bainbridge, Ga., 48
Baldwin, 105, 111, 129, 148
Baltimore, Md., 20, 127
Baltimore Conference (AME), 17, 22, 53, 63, 152
Baptist Church: attitudes of, toward slaves and slave ministers, 8–10; activism by black members of, following Civil War and during Reconstruction, 31, 43, 56, 75, 83–84; conservative attitudes displayed by some black churchmen and members of, 51; and higher education for blacks, 79; emerging influence of, in post-Reconstruction era, 125–26, 145, 175; African American membership totals in, 175. *See also* Florida Institute
Barnes, S., 108
Barton, Frederick, 54, 60
Bartow, xv–xvii, 144, 156, 171, 195
Bascomb, 171
Bates College, 123
Beaufort, S.C., 24–25, 34
Bel Air, 9
Bellville, 69, 109
Bennet, J. D., 165
Berlin, Ira, 11
Bethel AME Church: DeLand, 118; Gainesville, 72, 76, 130; Key West, 72, 76, 133; Kissimmee, 156; La Crosse, 119; Monticello, 30, 36–37, 40–41, 76; Newberry, 187; Okahumpka, 156; Orange Springs, 173; Palatka, 76–77, 157; Philadelphia, 20; Punta Gorda, 171; San Mateo, 130; St. Petersburg, 187; Tallahassee, 14–16, 30–31, 36–37, 47, 55, 62–63, 69, 71, 73, 77, 115–16, 118, 124
Bethel Institute. *See* Shorter University
Bethlehem Baptist Association, 79
Bethlehem Baptist Church, Bel Air, 9

Bethlehem Church, Cottondale, 13, 16, 30, 45, 48, 110
Billings, Liberty, 51–52
Bird, Mr., 41
Bird, John, 72
Bird, William A., 111–12, 150, 166, 171, 174, 176
black code, 30
"black princes," 149, 163, 180
Bloxham, William D., 116
Boggs, Simon, 54, 108–9, 119
Boulogne, 165
Bowen, J. W., 119
Bradenton. *See* Manatee
Braddock, P. B., 171
Bradford County, 109, 179
Bradwell, Charles L., 38
Bradwell, William S.: early life and career of, 38; as AME churchman, 44–46, 48, 54–55, 58–59, 66, 68–70, 73, 76–77, 79, 85, 92, 99, 103–4; as political activist, 50, 52, 56, 58, 73, 106; death of, 154; mentioned, xvii, 197
Branch, Franklin A., 35
Brantley, Amanda, 193
Brigadier, Richard, 39, 45, 48, 54, 93, 110, 119, 129
Brise, W. A., 108
Broadie, Adaline, 192
Broadinax, Joseph, 68
Bronson, 119, 124, 138
Brookens, E. J., 119
Brookins, R. B., 119, 126–27, 138, 158
Brooklyn Mission, 138
Brooks, Reuben B., 129–30, 138, 176
Brooksville, 69, 71–72, 156
Broome, James E., 9
Brown, Alfred, 78, 108, 110, 119
Brown, Henry, 60
Brown, John Mifflin: death of, xvii; as founder of New Orleans AME congregation, 21; early life of, 59–60; as bishop of Florida, 59–61, 63, 66–71, 76–80; mentioned, 84–85, 90, 126
Brown, Morris, 21, 59, 113
Brown Theological Institute, 68–69, 79–81,

86–89, 91–92, 96, 99–100, 107–8, 115, 125, 150, 185
Brown's Theological and Classical Institute. *See* Brown Theological Institute
Brown's University of the State of Florida. *See* Brown Theological Institute
Bryant, H. E., 48, 54
Buggs, Isaac, 135
Buggs, William, 119
Burch, W. A., 135
Bushnell, 187
Byrd, William A. *See* Bird, William A.

Calhoun Mission, 49
Call, C. F., 19, 37
Call, Henry W., 16–17, 19, 22, 28, 30, 36–37, 39, 68, 79, 87, 99, 111, 116–17
Callahan, 119, 130
Campbell, E., 108
Campbell, Jabez P.: death of, xvii; early life of, 112–13; as bishop of Florida, 112–22; mentioned, 126, 135, 136, 193
Campbell's Chapel AME Church (Baldwin), 148
Campbellton, 3, 30, 45, 49, 111
Campbellton Circuit, 134
camp meetings, 63–64, 66, 73–74, 92, 114, 155, 172, 179, 181, 188–89
Carolina, Francis B., 72, 74, 76, 87, 109, 119, 124
Cedar Key(s), 72, 129, 184
Center Hill, 156
Centerville, 3, 131
Centerville Mission, 54
Certain, Mary Alice, 194
Certain, W. D., 194–95
Chadwick, Richard W., 119, 138
Chambers, Alexander, 119
Chandler, Annie O., 125
Chandler, Henry Wilkins, 122–23, 125–26, 145
Charleston, S.C., 21–23, 25, 143
Charlotte County, 171
Chattahoochee, 134, 139
Chattahoochee Mission (AME), 37, 48
Cherry Lake, 109

Chipley, 187
Chipley, W. D., 138
Chisolm, H. F., 119, 149
Christburgh, George C., 111, 115
Christian Herald, 17, 21
Christian Recorder, 39, 53, 59, 75, 91, 96, 106, 138, 145–46, 148–49, 152, 157
Churchill, John, 54, 110
Citra, 119
civil rights and AME policy, 56, 86
Civil Rights Act of 1873 (Fla.), 86
Civil Rights Act of 1875 (U.S.), 102–3, 140
Clark, James, 135
Clary, S. C., 135
Clay County, 69, 72, 118
Clearwater, 187
Clemmings, William, 49
clerical morality, 89, 91, 96, 103–4, 115, 136, 143, 159, 163–64, 172
Cleveland, Grover, 144
Coffee, I. D., 177
Coke, Thomas, 4, 6
Cole, William C., 60, 89, 95, 110, 126
Coleman, Oliver J., 124
Coleman, Singleton H., 89–90, 95, 119, 132, 138, 144, 156, 174, 176, 188
Collins, A. B., 135, 156, 164
Colored Farmers' Alliance, 177
Colored Methodist Episcopal (CME) Church, 50, 66–67
Columbia City, 187
Columbia County, 13, 30, 39, 71, 87, 101, 118–19, 149, 164, 171, 185, 187
Comer, Mrs. M. A., 191
Commends, William, 68
Concord AME Church: Gadsden County, 111, 187; Miccosukee, 13, 45, 48, 111, 129
Conover, Simon P., 86, 103, 116
constitutional convention: (1868), 53; (1885), 145–46
cotton belt, 2–3
Cottondale, 13, 16–17, 28
Cotton States Exposition, 196–97
Crescent City, 156, 173
Crescent City Mission, 156

Crews, Harry, 46
Crews, Joseph C., 119
The Crisis, 143
Cromartie, A. A., 119
Cromidy, Berry, 135
Crooms, Peter, 68, 109, 119, 139
Cuyler, P. L., 154

Dade City, 171
Darbyville, 105
Dash, John, 135
Daughters of Mt. Zion, 192
Davis, Anthony, 110
Davis, Isaac, 68
Davis, Miss S., 149
Davison, Anthony, 108
Day, Miss. *See* Mrs. E. C. Smith
Day, Samuel, 79
Dean, Allen, 95
DeFuniak Springs, 178
DeLand, 118, 123, 193
DeLand, Henry A., 108
Delaney, Ray S., 72
Delaney, Thomas S., 108
Delaware (state), 59, 112, 115
Denham, Tally C., 89, 108-9, 119, 128, 132, 137-38
Derrick, W. B., 198
DeSoto County, 171
DeVaughn, Herbert B., 95, 111
Disney AME Church, Satsuma, 187
Divinity High School, 137, 149-52, 162, 168-69, 172-74. *See also* East Florida Divinity High School; Edward Waters College
Dorsey, Douglas, 10
Douglass, Frederick, 32, 169-70, 196-97
Drew, George F., 116, 118
Dry Creek, 54
Du Bois, W. E. B., 23, 143, 162
Dudley, Asa B., 95, 108, 110, 129, 136
Dukes, John W., 183-84
Duval County, 13, 16, 24, 39, 84, 87, 102-3, 108-9, 118, 130, 153, 176
Dyer, Peter, 54, 60

East Florida, 2, 37, 72, 95, 99, 105, 118, 131, 178

East Florida Conference (AME): creation of, 100, 112-16; first annual session (1878), 119; second annual session (1879), 119; third annual session (1880), 119; fourth annual session (1881), 128; fifth annual session (1882), 128, 132-33; sixth annual session (1883), 136-37; seventh annual session (1884), 139; eighth annual session (1885), 144, 150-51; ninth annual session (1886), 146; eleventh annual session (1888), 157-59; twelfth annual session (1889), 167-69; thirteenth annual session (1890), 173; fifteenth annual session (1892), 182-83; South Florida Conference created from, 182-84; sixteenth annual session (1893), 186; eighteenth annual session (1895), 189, 196; mentioned, xvii, 142
East Florida Divinity High School, 136-38, 140. *See also* Florida Divinity High School
Eaton, Josiah C., 108
Eatonville, 190, 197
Eatonville Circuit, 157
Ebeneezer AME Church, Marion County, 72
economic depression. *See* Panic of 1873; Panic of 1893
education policy. *See* schools
Edwards, James, 78, 108, 119
Edwards, William, 3-4
Edward Waters College: burned in 1901, xvii, 198; engraving of, 151; created, 174, 182; financial problems of, 190, 198; ordered relocated to Eatonville, 197; mentioned, 170, 175-76, 191. *See also* East Florida Divinity High School; Divinity High School
Elby, Caesar, 54
Ellaville, 110
Ely, William, 49, 54
emancipation, 23-24
Emancipation Proclamation, 22
Embry, J. C., 197
emigrationist movements, 116
"emotionalism," 141
Enterprise, 16, 109, 138, 156

Enterprise District (AME), 138, 154, 156–57, 171, 184
episcopal residence, Jacksonville, 187, 194
Eppes, Robert, 108, 110, 119
Epton, R. *See* Robert Eppes
Erwin, Auburn H., 52, 119
Escambia County, 41, 113
Evinston, 187
Exodusters movement, 116

Fahey, David M., 106
Fairfield, 173
Federal Point, 171
Fernandina, xvii, 28, 35, 45, 49, 52, 68, 70, 72, 99, 109, 120, 123, 128, 132, 153, 164, 176
Ferrell, Andrew J., Sr., 16
Fifteenth Amendment, 73
Finley High School, Lake City, 191
Flagler, Henry M., xviii, 123, 155, 189
Florida: acquisition of, from Spain, 1; establishment of territorial capital of, 2–3; admission of, as a state, 7–8, 11; secession of, 12; Civil War's impact on, 26–27; presidential reconstruction in, 30–32, 41–42; and congressional reconstruction, 43–44, 46, 50–52, 54–58, 70, 75, 79–80, 82–84, 86–88, 92–93, 95, 98, 101–2; and the elections of 1876, 113; and the end of Republican rule, 116; increasing urbanization of, 122–25; and the elections of 1884, 142, 144; 1885 constitutional convention in, 145–46. *See also* East Florida; Middle Florida; West Florida
Florida Agricultural and Mechanical University. *See* State Normal College for Colored Students
Florida Christian Recorder, 190
Florida Conference (AME): creation and organization of, 45–49; first annual session (1867), 47–49, 64; second annual session (1868), 53–55; third annual session (1869), 59–63; fourth annual session (1869–1870), 68–71, 103; fifth annual session (1870), 75–76; sixth annual session (1871), 77–79; seventh annual session (1872–1873), 84–86; eighth annual session (1873), 93–95; ninth annual session (1874–1875), 97–98; tenth annual session (1876), 100–2, 107–12, 126; separation of East Florida Conference from, 100, 112–16; eleventh annual session (1877), 114–16; twelfth annual session (1878), 116; fourteenth annual session (1880), 116; temporary separation of Pensacola from, 117–18; fifteenth annual session (1881), 128; sixteenth annual session (1882), 134–36; seventeenth annual session (1883), 139–40; eighteenth annual session (1884), 144; twentieth annual session (1886), 147–48, 154–55; twenty-first annual session (1887), 155; twenty-second annual session (1888), 165–67; twenty-third annual session (1889), 171–72; twenty-fourth annual session (1890), 173; twenty-fifth annual session (1891), 177; twenty-sixth annual session (1893), 177, 186; thirtieth annual session (1897), 197; mentioned, xvii, 142
Florida Divinity High School. *See* Florida Normal and Divinity High School
Florida Institute, Live Oak, 125–26
Florida Normal and Divinity High School. *See* Edward Waters College
Florida Normal, Scientific, Industrial, and Divinity High School. *See* Edward Waters College
Foreman, Emory, 48
Forest City, 119
Fort, Adam, 79, 109, 119
Fort Myers, 171, 195
Fort Union AME Church, Suwannee County, 72
Fort White, 171
Fortune, Emanuel, 52, 87
Foster, David, 48
Franklin County, 57
Frazer, S. W., 135
Free African Society, Philadelphia, 19
Freedmen's Bank, 95–96
Freedmen's Bureau, 30–31, 41, 51
Freeport, 130
freezes. *See* Great Freeze of 1895

Fruit Cove, 157
Fuller, Dennis, 108, 119

Gadsden County, 2, 13–15, 26, 36–37, 39, 45, 57, 75, 130, 134, 187
Gaines, W. J., 168
Gainesville, 35, 46, 49, 54, 68, 72, 76, 94, 110, 123, 129–30, 132, 136, 150, 173
Gainesville District (AME), 110, 138, 184
Garden Circuit, 110
Garfield, 119
Gaskins, James, 68
general conferences (Florida AME), 76–77
Georgetown, 118, 157
Georgia (state), xvii, 24, 28, 34–35, 38, 48, 64, 76, 80, 86, 102, 135, 162, 168, 177, 179, 185. *See also* Bainbridge; Savannah; Valdosta
Georgia Conference (AME), 99
Gibbs, B. C., 135
Gibbs, Jonathan C., 86–87, 95, 141, 152
Gibbs, Thomas V., 141, 152–53
Gilbert, John W. H., 110, 135
Gillislee, D. W., 132, 138, 182–83
Glenn, Joshua Nichols, 1–2
Glenwood, 130
Glimp, Walter, 108, 110, 119
Godwin, Alexander, 108, 111
Goen, C. C., 6
Good Templars, International Order of, 104–6
Gould, Theodore, 192
Gowens, Primus, 78, 108, 110, 119, 125, 138, 150
Graham, Noah, 54, 75
Grant, Abram: early life and career of, xv–xvi, 185–86; as bishop of Florida, xv–xviii, 194–97; as Florida churchman, 95, 100, 108–9, 113, 115–16, 118, 132; transfer of, to Texas, 119; as assistant to Bishop Thomas M. D. Ward, 185–89, 193–94; likeness of, 186
Grant, Florida, 185–86
Grant, Isaac, 185
Grant, Mariah, 192
Grant Chapel AME Church: Cedar Keys, 72; Oviedo, 156

Grant's Chapel AME Church, Jacksonville, 193
Grant's Tabernacle AME Church, Chipley, 187
Greater Bethel AME Church, Miami, xviii, 198
Great Freeze of 1895, xvii, 195–96
Green Cove Springs, 72, 109, 123, 130
Greenville AME Church, Ashville, 130
Greenville Mission, 110
Greenwood, 49, 54
Greenwood, Martha S., 39, 41, 191
Greenwood Circuit, 138–39
Grimes, Jerry G., 119, 166–67
Groom, Alexander, 110
Groover, J. A., 189
Gum Swamp, 109, 129

Hadley, C. L., 108, 110, 119
Haiti (Saint-Domingue), 6, 128, 170
Hall, Amsley, 68
Hall, Bolden, 4
Hall, Henry, 78, 110
Hall, James D. S., 17, 22
Hamilton, Darcey, 110
Hamilton, David, 119
Hamilton, Henry, 130
Hamilton, W. C., 131, 135
Hamilton County, 2, 26, 57, 123, 171
Hammond, Aaron, 108, 111
Handy, James A., 24–25, 171–72
Hansberry, A. R., 136
Harbour Island, 110
Hargrett, Lafayette, 46, 54, 79, 111
Harper, Frances E. W., 73
Harris, J. D., 95
Harrison, Richardson, 54
Hart, Catharine, 41
Hart, Henry L., 15
Hart, Ossian B.: as Southern Loyalist leader, 41–42, 44; as Republican party founder, 51–52; and Charles H. Pearce's pardon, 80; as advocate for black education, 80–81; AME support for gubernatorial candidacy of, 83; as governor, 86–88, 93; death of, 95, 97; mentioned, 7–8, 84
Havana, 178

Hayes, Rutherford B., 113
Haynes, John D., 78, 111
Hays, Richard, 108
Henderson, G. C., 190
Hernando County, 71
Higginbotham, Thomas, 100, 108–9, 119, 138, 164
High Springs, 130
Hill, Frederick, 46, 52, 75, 83, 85, 101
Hill, G. B., 156, 173
Hill, Leonard, 78, 108
Hillsborough County, 71
Holmes Valley, 3, 49
Holmes Valley Mission, 49, 110
Hope Henry Church, Columbia County, 13, 30, 39
Hopeville, 110
Houser Chapel AME Church, Pensacola, 172–73
Houston Mission, 54, 109
Howard, Oliver O., 11, 30–31
Howard University, 123, 126–27, 152
Hughes, Sarah Ann, 192–93
Humphreys, Harris, 135

Iamonia Slough, 111
Institute for Colored Youth, Philadelphia, 126
Interlachen, 158
"invisible church," 10–11
Island District (AME), 110, 138

Jackson, "Brother," 17
Jackson, Samuel, 108–9, 119
Jackson County, 2, 13, 26, 28, 30, 36–37, 39, 45, 69, 87, 124, 131, 134, 171
Jacksonville, xvii, 16, 18, 22, 24, 26–30, 34–35, 37–38, 41, 43–48, 58–59, 72, 74, 79, 88, 95, 99–102, 104–5, 109, 113, 118, 123–25, 130, 137–39, 151, 153, 155, 158, 164, 167, 170–71, 176, 179, 182, 187–88, 190, 192–94, 198
Jacksonville District (AME), 69, 71–72, 89, 96, 109, 138, 171
James, Washington, 108
Jasper Circuit, 109
Jefferson County, 2–3, 26, 30, 45, 49, 57, 75, 82, 87, 98, 102–3, 106–7, 116, 123, 130, 173
Jenkins, N. S., 149
Jensen, 173, 196
Jerusalem, 110
Jeslam Church, Madison County, 13
Jim Crow racial segregation, 140, 176, 180. *See also* racial discrimination
Johns, M. G., 110
Johnson, Andrew, 30, 32, 43, 52, 55
Johnson, E. W., 135, 150, 176
Johnson, James H. A., 25
Johnson, James Weldon, 143
Johnson, Lewis, 119
Johnson, Major, 45, 48, 52, 54, 69, 119, 188
Johnson, P., 135
Johnson, William D., 63, 66, 68, 73, 78, 86
Johnston, Joseph E., 23
Jones, Alfred, 177
Jones, Allen, Jr., 78, 95, 110, 119–20
Jones, Allen, Sr., 13, 30, 36, 39, 45–46, 48, 89, 111, 118, 158–59
Jones, Forney, 135
Jones, Henry, 118
Jones, Josephine, 191
Jones, Walter L. G., 108–9, 114, 132, 135, 146, 148
Jones, Washington, 95, 110, 119, 130
Jones, William, 78, 110
Jones Chapel Zion AME Church, Evinston, 187
Jubilee, Day of, 23

Kendrick, 156
Kentucky (state), 140
Kershaw, Albert Julius: as Florida churchman, 108, 139, 148, 154–55, 171; likeness of, 111; early life of, 145; and the campaign against political preachers, 145–46, 177; as trustee of Edward Waters College, 174, 176; mentioned, 13
Kershaw, Joe Lang, 146
Key West, 8, 11–12, 27, 45, 49, 68, 72, 76, 89, 94, 104–5, 123, 125, 132–33, 138, 153, 165–66, 171, 176, 181–82
Key West District (AME), 184
King, Francis, 60, 78

King's Chapel AME Church, Wellborn, 119
Kirsey AME Church, Leon County, 113
Kissimmee, 123, 130, 156, 184
Knights of Labor, 146, 153, 155, 177

La Crosse, 119
La Cruse, Joseph C. *See* Crews, Joseph C.
Lake City, 13, 30, 36, 39, 45, 48, 87, 109, 118, 120, 123–24, 132, 185, 191
Lake County, 119, 130
Lake George, 69
Lake Griffin, 61
Lake Jackson, 111, 139
Lakeland, 194
Lane, C. L., 135, 167
Lavette, Francis, 108, 111, 117
LaVilla, 72, 78, 105, 109, 138
Lawtey, 179
Lee, Joseph E.: as political activist, 101–2, 106, 155, 176; and the temperance movement, 104–6, 146; as exemplar of emergence of university trained clergy, 126; and Divinity High School, 137, 149; as Florida churchman, 138, 164, 170
Lee, Robert E., 22–23
Leesburg, 110, 119, 123, 130
Leigh, C. C., 22
Leon County, 2–3, 8, 13, 26, 45, 48, 57, 62, 75, 79, 83, 113, 123, 131, 134
Levy County, 41, 71–72, 119, 171, 187
Lewey, M. M., 196
Lewis, George A., 176
Lewis, John, 77
Lewis, Robert, 157
Lewis, Serry, 135
Lewis, Timothy Willard, 28, 35
Ley, John C., 12, 27
Liberia, 116
Liberty County Mission, 111
Lightbourne, Alexander C., Sr., xviii
Lime Sink, 111
Lincoln, Abraham, 17, 22
Littlefield, Milton D., 88
Live Oak, 48, 64–66, 79–80, 86, 89, 91, 96, 100, 114, 125–26, 132, 177
Live Oak Circuit, 109

Live Oak District (AME), 79, 85–86, 89, 109–10, 134, 138, 183
Livingston, Jacob, 13, 16, 39, 45, 49, 110, 154
Livingston, Smart, 49, 54, 68
Lofton, Alexander, 60, 108, 119
Logan, Rayford, 198
Long, Charles S., xviii, 16, 28, 71, 93, 115, 128, 174, 185–86
Long, Thomas W., 53–54, 57–58, 66, 68–72, 76, 83–85, 101, 104, 106, 110, 113, 119, 122–23, 129, 132, 145, 150, 157, 171, 174, 176, 184, 188
Long Pond, 3
Long Swamp, 61, 110
Louisiana (state), 21, 140, 177. *See also* New Orleans
Lowe, Jacob I., 72, 108–9, 119–20
Lynch, James, 22
lynchings. *See* violence, racial

Macedonia AME Church: Fernandina, 72, 120, 153, 193; Fort White, 171; Oak Hill, 173
Macon, Charles Henry, Sr., xvii
Madison, 3, 13, 36, 45, 48, 58, 76, 89, 91, 119, 124, 138, 168
Madison Circuit, 109
Madison County, 2–3, 13, 26, 30, 41, 57, 69, 75, 116, 123, 165
Magnolia, 105, 110
Maine (state), 123
Maitland, 138, 156–57, 190. *See also* Eatonville
Manatee, 138
Manatee County, 187
Manatee River, 195
Mandarin, 105, 157
maps: of principal Florida towns during late nineteenth century, 5; of the early heartland of African Methodism in Florida, 29
Marianna, 3, 13, 28, 30, 36, 45, 48, 88, 97, 110, 128, 135, 138, 145–46
Marianna District (AME), 13, 48–49, 54, 69, 77, 110, 131, 134, 138–39, 145, 148, 155, 173

Marion County, 3, 13, 71–72, 113, 119, 122–23, 130, 156, 173, 187
Marshall, Silas, 108
Martin County, 173
Marvin, William, 30
Maryland (state), 14, 21, 45, 73, 84, 127–28. *See also* Baltimore
Massachusetts (state), 59, 107
Mathews, Donald G., 7
McCook, Robert J., 12
McCormick, J., 48
McCray, Amanda, 10
McDougal, J. W., 48
McGriff, Austin, 95
McInnis, Daniel M., 83–84
McKinley, William, 162
McKinney, George P., 10
McPherson, Cornelia, 93
McPherson, David, 93
Meacham, Robert: likeness of, 14, 85, 97; early life of, 15–16; as Tallahassee congregation founder, 30–31, 36; as AME churchman, 37, 40–41, 45–48, 54, 69–71, 73–74, 78, 89, 109; as political activist, 46, 50–52, 56–58, 73–74, 75–76, 82–83, 86–87, 98, 101, 103, 106, 111, 120; and conflict with Charles H. Pearce, 55, 70, 74–76, 82; as victim of temperance movement, 106–7; and conflict with Bishop Daniel A. Payne, 144; transfer of, to East Florida Conference, 144; and AMEZ ministry, 146, 154; and the yellow fever outbreak of 1888, 164; mentioned, 39, 197
Meacham, Stella, 15
Melbourne, 156
membership: 1867, 46; 1868, 52; 1869, 58; 1870, 75, 175; 1871, 77; 1872, 85; 1873, 89, 92; 1874, 98; 1875, 99; 1878, 119–20; 1882, 134; 1883–84, 140; 1886–87, 156; 1888–90, 162, 172, 175
Menard, John Willis, 64, 83–84
Methodist Episcopal Church: established in Florida, 1–3; "colored missions" of, 3–4; attitudes of, toward slavery, 4–7; division of, 7; in Florida during and after the Civil War, 27–28, 35–36, 49, 67, 72, 125
Methodist Episcopal Church, South: created, 7; proslavery attitudes of, 8; membership of slaves in, 11–13, 16; ministers of, as slaveholders and supporters of the Confederacy, 12; initiatives of, to retain black members, 27; early assistance of, to AME Church, 35, 41, 167–68; and attempts of black members to intimidate AME ministers, 50; and organization of the Colored Methodist Episcopal Church, 50
Miami, xviii, 198
Micanopy, 110, 130
Miccosukee, 13
Michigan (state), 59
Middle Florida, xvii, 2–3, 26, 28, 36, 73, 88, 91, 95, 99–100, 109, 120, 123–24, 131, 134, 138, 159, 162, 178
Midway, Duval County, 13, 16, 28, 138, 179
Midway, Gadsden County, 111, 134, 139, 187
Midway ("Mother Midway") AME Church, Duval County, 18, 28, 112, 179
Miller, A. P., 132
Miller, Mary E., 35, 39, 137, 149, 191–92
Mills, Anthony, 52
Milton, 117
Milton Circuit, 111
Mims, S. L., 111, 135
ministerial training: and standards for study adopted, 67; and college and university education, 126, 141
Mississippi (state), 80, 140, 174, 177
Mitchell, Henry L., 189
Molino, 113
Monroe County, 71
Montbrook, 72
Montgomery, William E., 192
Monticello, 30, 36, 39–41, 45–46, 49, 55, 70, 75–76, 84, 89, 103, 105, 109, 113–14, 129, 134–35, 165
Monticello District (AME), 134, 146
Monticello Mission, 54, 109
Moore, Joseph Leandria, 156, 177

Moore, Morris Marcellus: as church historian, 96, 99; as Florida churchman, 126, 135–37, 190, 193, 196; likeness of, 147; dismissed as Pensacola pastor and transferred to East Florida Conference, 148; as trustee of Divinity High School, 150; as trustee of Edward Waters College, 174, 176; as head of Enterprise District of South Florida Conference, 184; as founder of *Florida Christian Recorder*, 190; election of, as bishop, 190; death of, 190
Moorer, Thomas, 135, 138
morality of clergymen. *See* clerical morality
Morgan, Samuel, 48, 54, 138
Moses, Kelley, 110
Mosquito River, 49, 61
Mt. Bethel AME Church, Callahan, 119
Mt. Carmel AME Church, Tampa, 187
Mt. Moriah Church, Daisy, 13
Mt. Moriah AME Church: Jacksonville, 171; Tarpon Springs, 173; Welaka, 157
Mt. Nebo AME Church, Silver Springs, 156
Mt. Olive AME Church: Anthony, 130; Bushnell, 187; Clearwater, 187; Glenwood, 130; Jacksonville, 109, 112–14, 138, 171; Montbrook, 72; Orlando, 130, 132; Williston, 187
Mt. Olive Church, Jackson County, 13, 30, 129
Mt. Pisgah AME Church: Archer, 72; Federal Point, 171; Freeport, 130; Lake City, 118; Summerfield, 130; Webster, 171
Mt. Pleasant, 130
Mt. Pleasant AME Church: Adamsville, 72; Sumter County, 72; Suwannee County, 173
Mt. Sinai AME Church, Columbia City, 187
Mt. Tabor AME Church: Columbia County, 39, 45, 48, 110, 149, 164; Forest City, 119; Kendrick, 156
Mt. Zion AME Church: Arcadia, 179; Brooksville, 72; Dade City, 171; Green Cove Springs, 72; Jacksonville, 35, 38, 44, 46–47, 58–59, 69–70, 97, 101, 130,

137, 139, 149–52, 169, 171, 179, 182–83, 188, 190, 192–95, 198; Lawtey, 179; Mt. Pleasant, 130; Ocala, 178; Orange City, 130; Putnam Hall, 156, 158; Raleigh, 72, 171; Watertown, 187
Mt. Zion Mission, 110
Mount Vernon, 49. *See also* Chattahoochee
Mule Team, 52, 54
Munroe, R. H., 135
Murphy, William L., 12
Myers, Eliza, 192
Myers, Oscar A., 8, 12

Nassau, Bahamas, 110
Nassau County, 119
Nathan, Benjamin, 68
National Association for the Advancement of Colored People (NAACP), 143
Navy Yard Station (Pensacola District), 111, 116
Nazrey, Willis, 21
Neal, K. P., 135
Neal, Voss, 68, 70
New Bethel AME Church: Gadsden County, 187; Ormond Beach, 156; Port Orange, 156; White Springs, 171
New Hope AME Church: Bronson, 119; Jacksonville, 118, 179, 192
New Jersey (state), 191
New Orleans, La., 21
New Providence, 110
New St. Paul AME Church, St. Augustine, 156, 158
New Smyrna, 49, 61, 179
New York, N.Y., 20, 39, 113
New Zion AME Church, Raleigh, 171
Newberry, 187
Newnansville, 110
newspapers, church. *See Christian Herald, Christian Recorder,* and *Florida Christian Recorder*
Newtown, 119
Nickerson, Margrett, 10
North Alabama Conference (AME), 142
North Carolina (state), 14, 24, 37, 140, 193. *See also* Wilmington

Oak Hill, 49, 173
Oaklawn AME Church, Sumter County, 187
Oats, Joseph, 31–32
Oberlin College, 59, 152
Ocala, 54, 72, 105, 110, 119, 123, 125, 129, 132, 151, 156, 178, 184, 196
Ocala Circuit, 110
Ocala District (AME), 110
Ocoee AME Church, 173
Okahumpka, 156
Ohio (state), 59, 161–62
Olustee Creek, 39
Onley, Annie. *See* Annie O. Chandler
Onley, John E., 125
Orange City, 130
Orange County, 108–9, 130
Orange Creek, 110
Orangedale, 157
Orange Lake, 156
Orange Lake AME Church, 156
Orange Park, 118
Orange Springs, 173
organic union, 184–85
Orlando, 108, 123, 130, 132, 138, 156–57, 179, 183, 190
Orlando District (AME), 190
Ormond Beach, 156
Osborn, Thomas W., 30, 41, 51–52, 56–57, 62, 70, 75, 80, 82, 86
Osborn Ring, 56–57, 70, 75, 79, 82–83, 93, 102
Osceola District (AME), 130
Osgood, Alfred B., 75, 101
Oviedo, 156

Page, James, 8–10, 37, 75, 79, 83, 125
Palace AME Church (Havana), 178
Palatka, xvii, 15, 33, 45, 48, 76–77, 119, 123–24, 126, 128, 130, 132, 141, 157
Palatka Circuit, 109
Palmetto, 187
Panhandle. *See* Middle Florida
Panic of 1893, xviii, 185, 189–90
Panic of 1873, 91, 95
Parkhill, Mrs. R. C., 41

Parkhill family, 8–9
Pasco County, 171
Payne, Daniel A.: death of, xvii; early life of, 20–22, 142–43; role of, in sponsoring post-Civil War AME Florida ministry, 24–25, 32–34, 37–38, 45; attitudes of, regarding ministerial training, 67; and ministerial involvement in politics, 76, 143; as temperance advocate, 106, 143; as winter resident of Florida, 125, 130; and pride in Wilberforce University, 126; stance of, against racial discrimination, 132–34; as advocate for higher education, 136–37; as bishop of Florida, 142–60; eightieth birthday celebration for, 179; mentioned, 166–67, 170, 174, 182
Payne, London, 143
Payne, Martha, 143
Payne Chapel AME Church, West Palm Beach, 187
Payne's Chapel AME Church, Putnam County, 130
Pearce, Charles H.: death of, xvii, 154, 159; likeness of, 31; early life and career of, 32; description of, 33–34; initiation of Florida ministry of, 34–42, 167; as organizer of Florida Conference, 43–49; as political activist, 46, 50–52, 55–59, 62, 75–76, 79–80, 82–84, 90–92, 98, 102–3, 106, 113, 120, 125; as presiding elder and churchman of Florida Conference, 54–55, 59–64, 66–75, 77–81, 85–86, 90–91, 100, 107, 116; and conflict with Robert Meacham, 55, 71, 74–76, 82; criminal proceedings against, 75, 79; as agent for Brown Theological Institute, 79–81, 86–89; transfer of, to East Florida Conference, 130; as trustee of Divinity High School, 150; mentioned, 23, 143, 197
Pearce, Ellen, 41
Peeler, Anderson, 3
Pemberton Ferry, 156
Pembroke, Daniel M., 41
Pennsylvania (state), 20, 84, 94, 137. *See also* Philadelphia

240 · Index

Pensacola, 1–2, 27, 36–37, 45–46, 49, 54, 61, 68, 97–99, 105, 107, 110, 117–18, 123, 131–32, 134–35, 138, 144–45, 148, 152–53, 155, 160, 163–64, 166–67, 171–73, 182, 193
Pensacola and Georgia Railroad, 64
Pensacola District (AME), 69, 99, 110–11, 116, 166
People's Party, 177
Perry, Edward A., 144
Peters, Fagan, 135
Peterson, John H., 60, 79, 89
Pettis, S. P., 157
Phillips, D. J., 74
Philadelphia, Pa., 19–20, 22, 39, 41, 59, 113, 127, 184, 197
Philadelphia AME Conference, 127
Pinckney, Edwin, 108
Pineville, 110
Pittsburgh Conference (AME), 137
Plant, Henry B., xvi, 123–24, 155
plantation belt, 2–3. *See also* Middle Florida
Plant City, 131, 156, 173
Pleasant Grove AME Church, Georgetown, 118, 157
Pleasant View AME Church, Fairfield, 173
Plessy v. Ferguson, xvi, 197
political activism: at commencement of congressional reconstruction, 50–52, 54–58; as cause of intra-church feuds, 55, 135. *See also* African Methodist Episcopal Church; political ministers
political corruption, 71, 75, 88
political ministers, campaign against, 76–79, 89–91, 102–3, 120, 124, 135–36, 145–47, 162
Polk County, xvii, 144
Pomona, 156–57
Ponce de Leon Hotel, St. Augustine, 155
Pope, John, 54
Pope, Washington, 83, 85
Pope Chapel, 110
Port Orange, 156
Post Oak AME Church, Bascom, 171
Powell, Sidney, 95, 108
Presbyterian Church, 41, 95, 125

public schools, 57–58, 86–87, 95, 150. *See also* schools
Punta Gorda, 171
Putnam County, 109, 118, 130, 156, 171, 187
Putnam Hall, 156

Quarterman, Dernard, 117, 139, 154
Quarterman, J. A., 156–57
Quarterman, R. S., 156
Quincy, 13–15, 30, 36–37, 45–46, 48, 61, 68, 73–74, 111, 116, 139, 159, 172, 177, 186–87
Quincy Academy, 15
Quinn, Benjamin W., 45, 48
Quinn, William Paul, 21

racial discrimination, xvi, 104–5, 132–34, 140, 153, 176, 180, 197
racial violence. *See* violence, racial
Raif, Susan W., 191
railroads: impact of, on Florida development, xvi, xviii, 123–24, 138, 198; as corrupt schemes, 88; and the institution of racial discrimination policies, 132–34, 153
Raleigh, 72, 171
Randolph, A. Philip, 23, 148, 163
Randolph, James, 148, 163
Randolph, Noah, 135
Raney, Susan E. *See* Stewart, Susan R.
Raymon, R., 135
Reconstruction: presidential, 30–32, 41–42; congressional, 43–44, 46, 50–52, 54–58, 70, 75, 79–80, 82–84, 86–88, 92–93, 95, 98, 101–2
Redemption (political), 113
Reed, G., 108
Reed, Harrison, 52, 56–58, 69–71, 75, 77, 79–80, 82–83, 87, 107
Republican party, 50–52, 77, 80, 83, 86, 95, 101, 103, 113, 120, 122–23, 176–77
revivals: 71–76, 116, 172, 187
Richards, Daniel, 42, 51–52, 55–56
Richardson, Simon Peter, 2, 8, 11
Rickes, J. W., 111
Rivers, Washington, 45, 49, 69

Rixford, 130
Roberts, Benjamin W., 78, 89, 94–95, 104, 108, 110, 119, 131–32, 134–35, 138
Roberts, J. E., 135
Roberts, Scott, 108, 110
Robinson, E. R., 135, 139
Robinson, John R., 108–9, 119, 129, 138
Robinson, Moses, 108
Rock Comfort, 111
Rockefeller, John D., 123, 55
Rogers, Gordon G., 190
Roman Catholicism, 1, 35, 99
Rose, Samuel, 111
Roseman, John, 138
Ross, William P., 137, 149–52, 164
Rusk, Jacob, 49

Sabbath schools. *See* Sunday schools
St. Andrew's AME Church, Palmetto, 187
St. Augustine, xvii, 1, 35, 48, 61, 99, 123, 130, 138, 156, 158, 164, 196
St. George Methodist Church, Philadelphia, 19
St. James AME Church: Bartow, xv–xviii, 156, 195; Kissimmee, 130; Marianna, 30; Rixford, 130; Sanford, 119
St. James Chapel AME Church, Orange Park, 118
St. Johns (Pensacola District), 111
St. Johns County, 108–9
St. Johns River, 108, 137, 154, 158, 188
St. John's AME Church: Citra, 119; Concord, 187; Tavares, 130
St. John's Mission, Gadsden County, 45–46, 48, 111
St. Joseph AME Church, DeFuniak Springs, 178
St. Joseph's AME Church, Leesburg, 130
St. Lukes, Pensacola District, 111
St. Mark's AME Church, Jacksonville. *See* Grant's Chapel AME Church, Jacksonville
St. Nicholas, 105
St. Paul AME Church: Garfield, 119; LaVilla, 72, 78, 113, 174; Ocala, 119; Tampa, 72–73, 130–31, 186

St. Paul's AME Church: Apalachicola, 37–38; Apopka, 156
St. Peter's AME Church, Gadsden County, 187
St. Peter's Chapel AME Church, Jensen, 173
St. Petersburg, 187
St. Philip's AME Church, Wacissa, 173
St. Stephen's AME Church, Newtown, 119
Saint-Domingue (Haiti), 6
Sampson, Solomon, 159
Sampson, William W., 69, 77, 93, 107, 109, 119, 136–37, 150, 158, 164
Sanderson, 48, 61
Sanford, 119, 123, 132, 187
Sanford, Henry S., 108
San Mateo, 130
Santa Rosa Circuit, 117
Santa Rosa County, 41
Satsuma, 187
Saunders, William U., 51–52, 55
Savannah, Ga., 37, 39, 64
Sawyer, Joseph J., 13, 33–34, 99, 109, 119, 124, 126, 128, 149
Saxton, Rufus, 25
schools, 34–35, 39, 40–41, 52, 56–59, 68, 73, 77, 89–90, 107–8, 114–16, 126, 136–37. *See also* Brown Theological Institute; East Florida Divinity High School; Edward Waters College; Florida Divinity High School; public schools; Sunday schools
Scott, John R., Sr., likeness of, 44; as political activist, 44, 71, 75, 83–84, 86, 92, 103, 106; as AME churchman, 68, 70, 72, 77–78, 89, 99–100, 108, 119; as federal official, 102–3; as temperance advocate, 105–6; death of, 116; mentioned, xvii
Scott, John R., Jr.: as Wilberforce student, 126; and the Divinity High School, 137, 139, 149; likeness of, 139; as AME clergyman, 164; and Edward Waters College, 174, 190; as political activist, 176
Scott, Thomas D., 126
Seals, William, 59
Seminole County, 119, 156

"separate but equal" doctrine, 140, 197. See also Jim Crow racial segregation
Seville, 187
Sewell, Isaac, 3
Shells, W. W., 119
Sheppard, John, 118
Sherwood, Rev., 163–64, 166
Shiloh AME Church: Columbia County, 119; Marion County, 119; Suwannee County, 72
Shorter University, 174
Sickles, Martha D. See Greenwood, Martha S.
Sidney, R. O., 92, 96, 99, 185
Silver Springs, 156
Simkins, Caleb, 80
Simmons, Cataline B., 84
Sim's Harbor, 49, 54
Sinai AME Church, Gadsden County, 187
Singleton, George, 143
slaves: as members of white Methodist churches, 1–4; and the Baptist Church, 8–10; and the "invisible church," 10–11; enthusiasm of, about white churches generally, 11–13; African-based religious practices of, 11; as organizers of independent Methodist congregations, 13–19
Small, Adam, 54
Small, Robert, 25
Smith, Charles Spencer, 184
Smith, Edmund, 108, 110, 19
Smith, Edward Kirby, 23
Smith, John, 48
Smith, Mrs. M. E. C., 39, 191–92
South Carolina (state), 16–17, 21–25, 28, 177. See also Beaufort; Charleston
South Carolina Conference (AME), 22, 24, 37–39, 45
South Florida, 68, 71, 155–57, 159, 164–65, 183, 189, 196
South Florida Conference (AME): creation of, xvii, 182–84; first annual session (1893), 186–87; third annual session (1895), 196
South Florida Railroad, 124
Spears, Joseph H., 97, 129, 155

Spears, Peter, 49, 54, 110
Spears, Washington, 111
Speight, John, 95, 108, 111, 132, 148
Spencer, James D., 88
Spencer, Romulus, 119
Spires, Charles, 135
Spring Creek Mission, 3–4
Springfield AME Church, Jackson County, 30, 45, 49, 110, 138
Springfield Mission, Duval County, 110
Standard Oil Company, 155
Stanton Institute, Jacksonville, 125
Starke, 93, 110, 129–30
Starkes, M. A., 130, 132
Starks, Henry, 135, 139
State Normal College for Colored Students, Tallahassee, 152
Station One, 92
Stearns, Marcellus, 93, 97, 102
Sterritt, N. B., 104, 108
Stevens, Thaddeus, 56
Steward, Mack, 37, 45, 48, 50, 54, 69, 77
Stewart, Solomon D., 48, 54
Stewart, Susan R., 24
Stewart, William G.: early life of, 24; and introduction of African Methodism to Florida, 24–28, 32, 34, 36–37, 172; brief returns of, to South Carolina, 37; as AME churchman, 54, 69, 73–74, 77, 85, 103, 188; as political activist, 75, 83–84, 103, 120; and the Tallahassee post office, 91, 103; mentioned, 23, 197
Still, Mary, 59–60, 191
Stockton, King, 54, 68, 108, 119
Stokes, John N., 79, 83
Stowe, Harriet Beecher, 97
Sub-Tropical Exposition, Jacksonville, 170
Summerfield, 130
Sumter County, 71–72, 110, 156, 171, 187
Sunday schools, 34–35, 39, 41, 46, 89, 138, 193–94
Sutton, Jacob, 108, 110, 119
Suwannee County, 72, 119, 130, 173
Suwannee River, 2
Swaim, John, 28, 35
Swain, Walker, 108, 111

Sweet Canaan AME Church, Wacahoota, 72
Sweetwater, 179, 189

Tabor, James, 3
Tallahassee, xvii, 2–3, 8–9, 15–16, 30–33, 36–37, 39, 46–48, 50–51, 53, 55, 69, 76–77, 91, 95, 98, 111, 115, 118, 123–25, 134–35, 144, 150
Tallahassee District (AME), 48–49, 54, 63, 69, 73–74, 79, 89, 100, 111, 118, 134, 139, 145
Tampa, 11–12, 61, 71–73, 89, 105, 107, 110, 123, 130–31, 141, 156, 165, 183, 186–87
Tanner, B. T., 53, 192
Tarpon Springs, 173
Tavares, 130
Taylor, C. A. A., 187–88, 193
Taylor, Mary Jane, 192–93
Taylor, John, 108, 111, 116
Taylor, Levi, 48, 60
Taylor, Long, 78
temperance, 77, 91, 103–4, 106–7, 136, 143, 146, 177. *See also* Good Templars, International Order of
Tennessee (state), 16, 80
Texas (state), xvi, 94, 118–19, 140, 162
Thomas, John, 16, 18, 28, 53–54, 61, 113
Thomas AME Church, Molino, 113
Thompson, F. J., 135
Thompson, Thomas T., 60, 66, 79, 89, 109, 119, 124
Thompson Valley, 109
Thornton, John, 48
Tice, S. Timothy, 164–65
Tick Ridge. *See* Jensen
tobacco use, 77, 91, 136, 143
Trapp, Milton A., 95, 108, 129, 136, 138
Trapp, William, 87
Trappe, Edward, 45
Tucker, Thomas De Saille, 152
Turkey Scratch Circuit, 48, 78
Turner, Henry McNeal, 22, 34, 76, 102, 108, 179, 192–93
Tyler, John, 108, 119

Union Bethel AME Church, Crescent City, 157, 173

Unitarian Theological Seminary, 137
United States Congress, 54–55, 99, 121
United States Military Academy, 152
United States Supreme Court, xvi, 140
urbanization, 155–56

Valdosta, Ga., 48
Vaughn, George, 48
Vesey, Denmark, 21
violence, racial, 93–95, 102, 116, 152, 163, 176–77, 180
Virginia (state), 140
Volusia County, 109, 118–19, 130, 156, 173, 187

Wacahoota, 72
Wacissa, 172
"Waiting at Live Oak" (poem), 65–66
Wakulla County, 109, 111, 134
Walker, A. W., 105
Walker, David, 31
Walker, Thomas W., 154
Walker Mission, 111, 139
Walls, Josiah, 75, 77, 99
Walls, William J., 185
Walton County, 87, 117, 130
Ward, Thomas M. D.: death of, xvii, 193–94; as bishop of Florida, 80, 84–86–87, 89–100, 108, 113, 185–94; early life of, 84–85; mentioned, 115
Ward's Campground (Lakeland), 194
Ward's Chapel AME Church, Seville, 187
Washington, Booker T., 177, 197
Washington, D.C., 55–56, 127, 170, 196
Washington, George, 124
Washington, W., 135
Washington County, 187
Washington County Circuit, 116
Waterman, Mrs. G. G., 191–92
Waterman, Susan L. *See* Raif, Susan W.
Waters, Edward, 21
Waters, James C., 105, 109, 115, 119, 130
Watertown, 187
Watson, D., 13
Watson, J. H., 119
Watson, Nelson S., 108

Watson, Robert, 54
Waukeenah, 36, 129
Waycross station, 138
Wayman, Alexander W.: death of, xvii; and the creation of the Florida Conference, 45–46; as bishop of Florida, 47–48, 52–54, 64–65, 122, 128–143; likeness of, 49; and ministerial involvement in politics, 76; early life of, 127–28; description of, 128; mentioned, 14, 148–49, 154
Wayman Chapel AME Church, Jacksonville, 130
Weaver, Elisha, 17
Webbville, 3
Webster, 171
Weir, John R., 109
Welaka, 157
Welch, Annie L., 170
Welch, Isaiah H., 107–8, 110, 117, 126
Welch, John H., 152, 164, 168–69, 172–73, 183
Wellborn, 119
Wells, Pat, 177
Wesley, John, 5–6
Wesleyan Academy, 59
Wesley Chapel AME Church, Marion County, 113
West Florida, 2, 26, 37, 95, 116, 120, 131, 134, 138
West Florida Association (Baptist), 9
West Palm Beach, 187
White, David, 54
White, Fuller M., 45, 48, 54, 77, 87, 110, 131, 135, 139, 154
White, Joseph, 118
White Springs, 109, 171
Wiggins, Robert L., 35, 167–68
Wilberforce University, 94, 107, 126, 136, 149, 173–74
Wiley, Bulley, 130–31, 138
Williams, Benjamin, 108, 111
Williams, Edmund, 108–9
Williams, Jacob, 119
Williams, S. D., 138
Williams, Wiley P., 78, 95, 110
Williston, 187
Wilmington, N.C., 45–46, 48
Wilson, Cupid, 119
Wilson, David, 68
Winter Park, 157, 190
Witherspoon, George W.: as Florida churchman, 60, 69, 79, 109, 129; and accusation of adultery and other vices, 89, 163–64; as political activist, 98, 102–3, 120–21; as temperance advocate, 105–7; and conflict with Bishop Daniel A. Payne, 144; support by, of Democratic takeover of Pensacola town government, 145; as trustee of Divinity High School, 150; transfer of, to East Florida Conference, 166–67; death of, 181–82; mentioned, xvii, 197
women ministers, 192–93
women's involvements, 35, 39, 58–59, 190–94
Wood, Dennis, 13–14, 30, 36–37, 45, 48, 119
Wood, Warder R., 95, 119
Woodbury, Samuel, 3
Woods, Warren R., 78, 109
Woodville Mission, 49
Wyatt, John W., 52, 75, 95, 97–99, 110, 117
Wynn, G. W. T., 135, 139

yellow fever, 114, 134, 164, 181–82
Young, Brady, 177
Young, David, 39, 48, 54, 110
Young, Harry, 72
Young, William, 72
Younge's Chapel AME Church, Ocala, 156

Zion AME Church, Center Hill, 156

Larry Eugene Rivers is professor of history at Florida Agricultural and Mechanical University. He is the author of over 20 articles, including publications in the *Journal of Negro History* and *Florida Historical Quarterly*, and of *Slavery in Florida: Territorial Days to Emancipation* (UPF, 2000). Rivers is a native of Sharon Hill, Pennsylvania.

Canter Brown Jr. is a historian and lawyer. He is the author or co-author of numerous books, including *Florida's Peace River Frontier* (UPF, 1991) and *The Supreme Court of Florida and Its Predecessor Courts, 1821–1917* (UPF, 1997). Brown taught from 1993 to 1996 at Florida Agricultural and Mechanical University. He is a native of Fort Meade, Polk County, Florida.

www.ingramcontent.com/pod-product-compliance
Lightning Source LLC
Chambersburg PA
CBHW021347230426
43666CB00006B/440